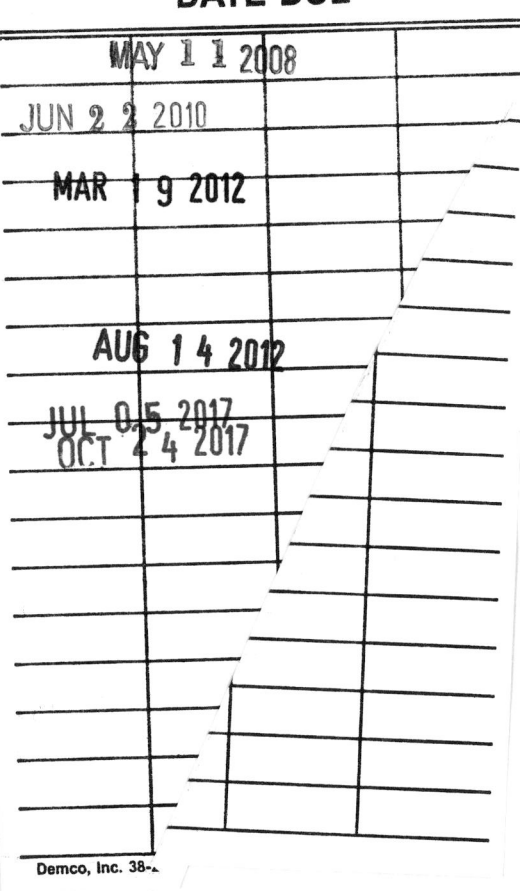

DATE DUE

The Educated Parent

THE EDUCATED PARENT

Recent Trends in Raising Children

Joseph D. Sclafani

Child Psychology and Mental Health
Hiram E. Fitzgerald and Susanne Ayres Denham, Series Editors

Westport, Connecticut
London

Library of Congress Cataloging-in-Publication Data

Sclafani, Joseph D.
    The educated parent : recent trends in raising children / Joseph D. Sclafani.
        p. cm.—(Child psychology and mental health, ISSN 1538–8883)
    Includes bibliographical references and index.
    ISBN: 0–275–98224–6
    1. Parenting. 2. Parent and child. 3. Parenting, Part-time. 4. Child development.
    5. Child psychology. I. Title. II. Series.

HQ755.8.S36 2004
649´.1—dc22   2004002507

British Library Cataloguing in Publication Data is available.

Library of Congress Catalog Card Number: 2004002507
ISBN: 0–275–98224–6
ISSN: 1538–8883

First published in 2004

Praeger Publishers, 88 Post Road West, Westport, CT 06881
An imprint of Greenwood Publishing Group, Inc.
www.praeger.com

Printed in the United States of America

∞"

The paper used in this book complies with the
Permanent Paper Standard issued by the National
Information Standards Organization (Z39.48–1984).

10 9 8 7 6 5 4 3 2 1

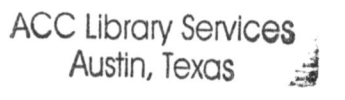

To my wife and life partner, Linda
And to our parents, who taught us so much.

CONTENTS

SERIES FOREWORD

The twentieth century closed with a decade devoted to the study of brain structure, function, and development that in parallel with studies of the human genome has revealed the extraordinary plasticity of biobehavioral organization and development. The twenty-first century opens with a decade focusing on behavior, but the linkages between brain and behavior are as dynamic as the linkages between parents and children, and children and environment.

The Child Psychology and Mental Health series is designed to capture much of this dynamic interplay by advocating for strengthening the science of child development and linking that science to issues related to mental health, child care, parenting and public policy.

The series consists of individual monographs, each dealing with a subject that advances knowledge related to the interplay between normal developmental process and developmental psychopathology. The books are intended to reflect the diverse methodologies and content areas encompassed by an age period ranging from conception to late adolescence. Topics of contemporary interest include studies of socioemotional development, behavioral undercontrol, aggression, attachment disorders and substance abuse.

Investigators involved with prospective longitudinal studies, large epidemiologic cross-sectional samples, intensely followed clinical cases or those wishing to report a systematic sequence of connected experiments are invited to submit manuscripts. Investigators from all fields in social

and behavioral sciences, neurobiological sciences, medical and clinical
sciences and education are invited to submit manuscripts with implications for child and adolescent mental health.

Hiram E. Fitzgerald
Susanne Ayres Denham
Series Editors

PREFACE

Writing a book is always a cooperative effort. I am grateful to The University of Tampa, and President Ronald L. Vaughn, for awarding my sabbatical leave in 2002. That time off allowed me the chance to integrate and focus all of my ideas, thoughts, and research into the book you read today.

Special thanks go to Elizabeth A. Potenza, my Assistant Editor at Praeger Publishers/Greenwood. She served well as my contact and connection, answering my many questions and offering helpful suggestions as I labored to present a readable overview of the literature on parenting. She also helped to guide me through the production process, teaching me that you're not finished even though you wrote your last word. I especially wish to thank Brenda Scott and the Impressions team, and copyeditor Lyn Rosen, for helping me make this book a professionally polished work.

The Praeger Series Editor and Reviewer, Dr. Hiram E. Fitzgerald, University Distinguished Professor of Psychology and Assistant Provost for University Outreach at Michigan State University provided excellent feedback and ideas for me to include across the entire manuscript. My book is more accurate and on-target thanks to his comments.

I also gratefully acknowledge the detailed feedback from two early manuscript readers, Col. Deidre Dixon and Lynnae Wocken. They boldly went where few would go, commenting on rough drafts. Others, including real parents, also read and commented on chapters or parts of chapters. You know who you are, and I owe you one.

Finally, this project would never have happened without the loving and complete support of my wife, Linda. She too read and proofed my writing, offering constructive criticism as needed. She also kept the cats away and the house quiet when I needed to concentrate, and she kept me fed and watered when I fell into my writer's groove.

As parenting information is constantly changing, I also want to alert the educated parent to visit the Web site that accompanies this book, *TheEducatedParent.com*. This site is updated monthly to include the latest information on a variety of parenting resources and information.

INTRODUCTION

The joys of parents are secret, and so are their griefs and fears.
—Sir Francis Bacon

Just about everyone has an opinion on parenting, and most are willing to share theirs freely. First-time parents come prepared with their own views and philosophies when it is their turn. Some new parents are prepared by the parenting they received as a child—either as an endorsement to repeat the good work or as a rejection via a pledge to not repeat the mistakes of their own parents.

It is also the case that experts have opinions on parenting. Like me, they are willing to share their thoughts with you—to the tune of thousands of books that you can read on the topic. I have come to understand that the vast amount of information available has gone from helpful to overwhelming. Instead of speaking with one voice, the parenting books provide often contradictory or mixed messages that muddle rather than clarify.

And for many new parents, there is a feeling that I call the imposter syndrome. It is as if someone made a mistake in allowing you to have, and be responsible for, a newborn. Feelings of uncertainty, ignorance, and fear quickly kick in. You begin to pepper yourself with self-doubt as to your ability to pull this off.

Rest assured that just about every new parent has some degree of this response when considering the seemingly overwhelming task of safely raising another human being to become a healthy, well-adjusted, productive member of society. Especially when you are still trying to figure out your own life plan and can't control all the important aspects of your own life, just how are you going to be responsible for another, though small, person? Whoa. Stop.

Although a big-picture perspective is a good and necessary thing, parenting allows you to get by in stages. When you come home from the hospital you don't need to worry about strategies to complete first-grade homework or enforcing car curfews just yet. All you have to do is stay one stage ahead of your baby and you'll be okay through adolescence and into adulthood. I can also promise you that the more you do things right in the first few years, the easier it will be for you in the teen years.

Please allow me the privilege of providing you a background of information that will help you to make good choices about your parenting behavior. As a child psychologist and family therapist since 1984, I have read much and studied hard in an effort to learn all about good parenting. For 10 years of private practice after 3 years of work in a community mental health center, I saw hundreds of families in disarray and distress because they were overwhelmed by child behavior issues. As a family therapist, I rarely worked with children alone, believing that child problems were almost always family problems. For many families, working on improving parenting (from direct education to improving the quality of the marital relationship) made a significant difference for everyone.

RATIONALE FOR THIS BOOK

There are so many books on parenting that you might ask, "What is so special about this one?" Well, I have tried to do something I have not seen elsewhere—write a book that is grounded in the research bases of the social sciences, primarily psychology. I hope to inform readers of the truly important aspects of child outcome research, many of which are repeated in various books available in your bookstore and library. When the opinions in popular books clash or when parents try to learn but become confused, there is a problem. I hope to help reduce the confusion.

It is my desire to offer you a blend of the gist of social science research on parenting, and my perspectives and experiences as a mental health professional. This book is written in a friendly, conversational style to make its reading a little easier and more enjoyable. But the book covers serious material and brings to the everyday parent a summary and an explanation of some of the most important research in the area of parenting. Some of the chapters may seem a little technical and some of the material may seem tangential at first reading. My task is to present the applicable research, most of which is interesting, and also help you to see the importance and the relevance of these studies to your parenting practices.

Where can one go to learn about being a parent? It's been said that having children makes one no more a parent than having a piano makes one a pianist. They don't give instruction manuals at the hospital. I want to provide information that you can use to become an expert parent. By providing you with the rationale for certain behaviors or approaches, I hope to make you more able to make intelligent choices in how you parent.

With this book I share a variety of information that I'm confident you will find interesting, relevant, and useable. My sources are varied and many are on-line, as, for example, Marc Bornstein's Web-based essay *Refocusing on Parenting,* which looks at parenthood and parenting from a big-picture perspective.

Whether you are a first-time parent struggling with lots of different advice, or a seasoned parent of six, the information in this book should give you a grounding to style your parenting to your child's needs. Every parent can be more effective through enhanced knowledge, and parenting is a job where new challenges arise every week. The more you know, the better your decisions will be.

It is my hope that every parent will not only read this book, but will go out and buy 10 others. The range of specific book topics allows parents to learn about any aspect of parenting they desire to know. Parenting education is a good thing, and I hope you will join the ranks of educated mothers and fathers.

In my mind, no role or responsibility is greater than that of being a good parent. Parents are the first role models for children. They are the child's first love and attachment object. The parental influence is one of the primary shapers of who we become, how we approach the world, and how we think of ourselves. Parents are our first socializers, the first shapers of our self-esteem and consciences. Bad parenting has serious long-term negative consequences that are overcome only with years of hard work by other corrective influences.

Some have challenged the long-term importance of parenting, stating that peer influence and other factors become dominant in later childhood and adolescence. These peer influences are said to wipe out the early years' effects of parenting behavior. The data I am aware of challenge this assertion. The research does suggest that parental authority and control wane as an influence as children become teenagers, but even teens remain closely, emotionally connected to their parents and family. Want proof?

In August 2003, the Horatio Alger Association published its State of Our Nation's Youth Survey. Among the findings from its 1,055 high school–age respondents were these gems: (1) 50 percent (the highest-ranked response) said they would spend more time with their parents and family if they could; (2) 27 percent reported getting along with their parents extremely well; (3) 47 percent reported getting along with their parents very well; and (4) these teens ranked family members ahead of entertainers and athletes as role models.

The fact that peer influence becomes a powerful force in adolescence does not negate the work that parents put into the first 11 to 12 years of a child's life. In fact, I believe that good parenting in the first dozen years sets the stage for all later behavior and choices that people make into adulthood. That is another reason why parenting is such an important topic for me.

MY ASSUMPTIONS AND BIASES

Allow me to begin by telling you of my assumptions and biases as a child-development expert, as well as to point out some of the themes that you will see repeated as we review the research base. These assumptions are my starting point, and no matter what content I will discuss, these will serve as an ever-present backdrop.

Biopsychosocial Development in Children

First among these assumptions is that all child development is a *biopsychosocial* phenomenon. By this I mean that a child's development is the sum total of the influences of biology and heredity (the *bio*-logical), of language, of personality and cognitive processes (the *psycho*-logical), and of many family and other social and environmental experiences (the *social*). Parenting behavior shapes the psycho and the social aspects of your child's growth, and the parental genetic heritage is a major factor in the bio area. This book will address the parents' role in promoting the most healthy psychological development through creation of an adaptive, positive environment for their children. It will also point out certain biological factors that must be addressed, as these will interact with your efforts in guiding and directing your child's life.

Parenting Is Done Best by Two People

A second assumption is that the best parenting is a two-person job. With the exception of the by-product of conflict or disagreement, parenting is best practiced and accomplished by two adult participants. By this I mean that having two loving and concerned adults makes for the best parenting situation. When those adults introduce and engage in conflict behavior (constant disagreements, fighting, arguing), then the quality is diminished. This is why it is correctly said that "staying together for the sake of the children" is not always the best alternative.

The research is fairly clear in support of the notion that children's well-being is harmed by such conflict exposure. For example, in one study I reviewed, the grand result was that "parental conflict was associated with lower cognitive and social competence, GPA, and behavioral functioning in young adolescents." In English, parents' fighting at home was found to be related to poorer schoolwork and general life quality for teens.

Having two parents allows each the opportunity for a break when needed, and for mutual support, which is always needed. I like to make the analogy of tag-team wrestling when discussing the importance of a parents-as-team approach. If you know this pseudo-sport, you know that in tag teams, one person at a time from the team is in the ring. When that person tires or is in a losing position, he is allowed to tag his partner. The partner then can enter the ring and pick up where the first partner left off. In this manner, the new person in the ring can enter with new vigor and a new attitude and become successful in dealing with the opponent. In some ways, parenting can feel like being in a wrestling match. To have the security of your "tag partner" always gives hope that even if you are not successful in a particular situation, your partner will be. If your parenting team is on the same page and has discussed its strategy, you will be more likely to be successful in the long run.

Having said the above, it is also a reality that child rearing is practiced by many single parents and an ever-growing number of grandparents. Much of the information in this book applies to any caring adult who has direct responsibility for children. My point is not to be judgmental, but to state the obvious. It is easier to raise children when two people work together than when one person does it alone.

Parenting Is One of Many Influences on Children

A third assumption I must share is that despite all of your best efforts, children may turn out in ways that you did not promote or intend. It would be less than truthful to assert that parenting effects alone are anywhere near 100 percent responsible for a child's outcome. Put another way, you can't take all of the credit if your child becomes a wonderful adult or all of the blame if he or she has failed to live up to your expectations. While I believe that parenting is the single most important variable in determining child outcome, it does not account for every influence that shapes and determines a child's "final ending" as an adult.

Further, the parenting influence may be diluted in cases of divorce, especially if the parents have very different values and expectations. This leads to confusion in the child. Extra-family influences are another major source of impact. These include certain life-changing environmental experiences such as abuse or poverty. Genetic or hereditary traits that may emerge in an unwanted direction in spite of your best parenting intentions also can affect child outcomes.

On a positive note, other extra-family influences may be affirmative for children. Good teachers and coaches may have long-lasting and profound effects that carry across the lifespan. A good neighborhood and concerned neighbors can serve in the same way. Parents play a role in determining what environment children will be raised in. Remember, child development is multi-determined and all of these influences combined will contribute to the "final product."

And before we explore themes in the research, allow me to express what I consider to be my primary bias—parents have to be responsible for and in charge of their children. This means if you don't think you have the time and energy to make sacrifices and place your needs second for 18-plus years, then don't have, adopt, or become responsible for a child. It may seem strange to find this sentence in a parenting book, but I would be remiss if I did not share this belief. It also means that once you have a child, you have to take on the obligations of providing guidance and discipline, as well as nurturance and being responsive to your child. These are full-time, no-vacation duties—24/7 tasks, if you will. Good parenting is hard work, filled with years of sacrifices and commitments and, if you're fortunate, rewards in the form of your child's love, and satisfaction in a job well done.

(When should parents be *excluded* from a child's life? Such situations would include those involving drug and alcohol abuse, violence and aggression problems, certain personality disorders, and severe, untreated mental illness. This book is focused on parents who have the capacity to love, nurture, and guide their children. Active drug- and alcohol-abusing parents, or any persons who lack the psychological abilities we will explore, have no grounds to be allowed an active role in their children's lives. They are takers and destroyers. Until and unless they are "clean" or changed they should be removed from proximity and direct care responsibilities.)

Over the past 40 years, it seems to me that parents have abrogated many of their responsibilities, often turning them over to an overburdened and over-obligated school system. Basic health care, nutrition needs, sex education, child care, and general supervision duties—previously all done by parents or extended family as recently as the 1950s—are now expected from schools.

Parents have also seen some rights diminished with the emergence of power in often understaffed and overworked state-run child-welfare systems. Parental fears of being "turned in" by someone (perhaps even their own child) for alleged abuse have caused some parents to become "gun-shy." This is an oft-stated rationale for some parents who do not discipline their children. This is bogus. Parental authority is still generally recognized, and although abuses by state welfare agencies do occur, these mistakes are corrected.

I am not saying that children are chattel to be used and abused by their parents as is their "right." No child should be subjected to any sort of abuse, and child abusers need to be punished as well as helped. Children do have rights—rights to be raised in a home with loving, caring, and committed parents who do their best to provide for their welfare. Some well-intentioned but misguided people have sought to extend children's rights to supersede parental rights. This is wrong.

By the way, the issue of corporal punishment is addressed in some detail in chapter 4. For the record, I am *not* a literal "spare the rod, spoil the child" proponent. Although I do believe that parents who fail to discipline their children properly and consistently are the leading cause of bad behavior, I also believe that there are many ways to provide proper discipline that do not involve striking a child, as I will show.

CHILD-DEVELOPMENT THEMES

Parenting Is Individualized

In addition to these assumptions and my parents-in-charge viewpoint are a set of themes that will emerge and become readily apparent as you read on. The first is that parenting is a very individualized set of behaviors and attitudes. That is one reason why I did not (or will not) write a book that tells you specifically how to parent your children. Each family has its own set of values and beliefs about the role of fathers and mothers and the impact they can make on their children. After reading this book, I hope you can successfully blend your values and attitudes with what we know from years of research to create a parenting style that is both effective and educated, and good for your children.

Parent–Child Relations Are Reciprocal

A second theme I hope to highlight is that parenting, as all social relationships, is a reciprocal process. Over the course of your child's life, you will say and do things that will influence your child, and he or she will say and do things that will influence you. As you will see, this interaction starts in infancy with attachment, and continues on into childhood and adolescence as the needs of the parent and the child evolve and develop over time. Parents affect their children and children affect their parents. Both grow and create new opportunities as the years pass. The quality of the parent–child interaction also changes over time, with your infant being much more controlled by your actions than your teen will be. We will explore this in more detail in chapter 1.

Families Consist of Interrelated Subsystems

A third theme, related to the reciprocity theme, is that of the family as a set of interconnected systems. In my family therapy training and experience, I have come to learn that everyone is shaped by the people with whom they associate, and that they shape those people in return. In family systems, the parenting, or executive, subsystem plays a large role in the development of a child. We will explore this fully in chapter 4.

The marital/co-parenting relationship is the foundation for other outcomes. If there is a healthy, functional executive subsystem (a relatively happy, supportive wife-and-husband team), children are properly attended to and parents work together as a unit. The functional parenting team is better equipped to handle the challenges and surprises that arise over time. If the marital/co-parenting team is in stress and conflict, then this negative effect will be seen in less efficient parenting. Children are negatively affected directly and indirectly from parents who are a source of instability and unpredictability.

The other major family subsystem is that of siblings. Variables such as the number of siblings, their age spacing, gender, and birth order all interact to also influence child outcome. Being the last-born girl in a family of four boys, or being the fifth-born girl of a family will have very different results, from very different sibling interactions and play materials to availability of hand-me-down clothing. Sibling subsystems can be a source of comfort and support when there are problems in the parenting subsystem. They can also be a source of bitter rivalry and competition for parental attention and family resources.

The topics covered in this book reflect my view of which topics are of the most importance for the educated parent. There may be some information you are looking for that I did not cover. If it is important for you, it is important. You will need to look further for a resource to help you. There may also be some information that on first review may not seem applicable to you. I suggest you read through it anyway. You never know when you or a friend may need the ideas or data presented.

Chapter 1 covers some basic information, relevant to all good parenting. Chapters 2 and 3 cover the three fundamental, foundational areas necessary for healthy child development. Chapter 4 discusses family structure and discipline. Chapter 5 explores the parenting role in education, including information about homeschooling. Chapter 6 examines divorce and remarriage effects on children. Day care placement and its effects are reviewed in chapter 7. Chapter 8 presents information about stress, including cultural factors that impact children. Chapter 9 reviews the special role and place of fathers in children's lives. And I end with a discussion of what I call special-topics issues—adoption issues, the effects of chronic illness on families, and death and loss.

Whether you choose to believe in a more dominant or less dominant role in your child's life as a parent, it is always important to know that your impact is permanent. It is also the case, as we shall see, that your life will be forever changed dramatically as a result of this usually wonderful, sometimes exasperating, often joyful, and never boring adventure in child rearing. Please read on, so that you may become an educated parent.

Chapter 1

PARENTING—THE BASICS

> If a community values its children, it must cherish their parents.
> —John Bowlby

Parenting is one of the few jobs where experience doesn't necessarily make things easier the second (or third) time around. If you have the opportunity to raise more than one child, you will often find yourself marveling at how different and unique each child is. The upside is that you can enjoy each child for his or her own special array of strengths and weaknesses, and talents and limitations. The downside is that once you have gone through a period of growth and challenge with one child, what you learned from that experience may not always apply neatly to the next child.

FOUNDATIONAL PARENTING SKILLS

Having said that, let me also add this clarification: *The foundational parenting skills of consistent discipline, meeting the child's needs for love and nurturance, and the control and guidance functions of parenting always apply.* It is in the fine details that previous experience may fail you. For example, one child may be easily controlled by a nasty parental stare, whereas a second child may shrug that off and need to be physically confronted in order to change a behavior. Yet both child types need your follow-through, and need to know you mean what you say.

Fortunately, being a parent does not mean you have to always be perfect, 100 percent consistent, or all-wise in order to raise a healthy, functional child. The phrase "good enough parenting" has been coined to refer to the fact that a parent simply must be that—good enough, but not perfect. This revelation is a great guilt-reducer. Many parents have a number of specific things they have done or said that they would like to take back. Or there are things never done that they wished they had made time for. The good news is that children are generally forgiving and that you usually have to go out of your way to create permanent harm or interfere with normal development. The previous sentence is so important it's worth repeating.

The good news is that children are generally forgiving and that you usually have to go out of your way to create permanent harm or interfere with normal development. This means that short of abuse or neglect, you have a lot of leeway in the choices you make in how to raise a healthy child. If it weren't this way, even more people would be more maladjusted than actually are. Again, I am not saying that you do not have to be consistent. I am saying that in trying to be so, you will be unable to be 100 percent consistent all of the time. When you slip, assuming a quick recovery, your child will still be alright.

"GOOD ENOUGH" PARENTING

Good enough parenting means that you are trying your best, but that you have limitations of your own that keep you from being patient, caring, understanding, nurturing, firm, and consistent all the time. What human being could ever be all these things at all times? Again, it is important to value and strive for these important parenting traits. But don't beat yourself up when you fall short.

Good enough parenting means that you are as consistent, fair, and firm as you can be. The more consistent you are, the easier it will be for your child to learn what is expected and how to behave properly. To be a consistent, fair, and firm parent requires planning and effort. You have to know when you are at your best and when you are not, and then plan the challenging aspects of the daily routine around your strengths and limitations.

Parents who are too inconsistent set up an interesting dynamic for their children. Basically, the children are turned into gamblers. In essence, a child now has to guess when the parent "really means it" or when the parent is just talking. For example, your child is playing with his glass of milk at the table. You say, "Stop playing with your milk or you'll spill it, and I'll send you to your room." What does your child do?

If the last few times you said this you failed to follow through with consequences after your child continued to play with his glass, he is likely to ignore your warning. He is ready to gamble (from past experience) on the chance that you do not mean it this time. If however, you previously followed up with: (a) taking the glass away and saying, "I told you to stop, now you don't get any more milk"; (b) "I told you to stop playing with your glass—one more time and your milk is gone, Buster"; or (c) "If you don't stop playing with that glass by the time I count to three, no TV tonight" then your child is more likely to see you are serious and mean what you say. Of course, you must deliver on whatever consequence/ choice you gave. To act as in "b" or "c" and then not take the milk or cut off TV for the night, creates a more gifted gambler who has more variables to consider the next time.

Inconsistency from the past is a leading cause for children to ask, "Why did you do X?" after you have disciplined them after one or no warnings. They are simply not prepared for your consequence since, from past experience, its delivery is hit and miss. This pattern eventually leads to a loss of respect toward the parent, so it is important to mean what you say and follow up. The sooner you establish this respect, the better. *Once a child reaches adolescence, you can practically give up on trying to earn new respect if you never had it earlier.* You may be successful in trying to regain lost respect, but that will depend on a lot of different variables.

All of this by now probably sounds like hard work. If I may borrow from the old U.S. Navy commercials, parenting is "the toughest job you'll ever love." Too many parents today seem to believe that kids will somehow raise themselves, or that they need little parenting soon after they start school. This is a poor attitude and wrongful thinking. In fact, parents are "lifers." When you have or adopt a child, they will be with you, in some way, until death. In other words, you have a life sentence of connectedness and some level of responsibility and concern.

Further, many parents raise their children in a way that makes sure those children will "be their friend" or have to "like them." I hate to sound like an old curmudgeon, but this is also wrong and a formula for disaster. I cannot "prove" the origin of this shift in parental expectation, but I do believe that it is a leftover, misguided result of parenting information presented in the 1960s and 1970s. I do not mean to single out a single person or school of thought for criticism, as many are deserving of my disapproval. However, the work of Dorothy Briggs and her popular 1970s book, *Your Child's Self Esteem,* professed ideas that I consider plain wrong and potentially harmful to anyone who followed the advice.

In this book, Briggs called for parents to share power within the family, allowing children a greater say, and even "an equal part," in setting limits and family rules. In one especially gravely mistaken section, it was argued that "democracy has little meaning to a child unless he feels the daily benefits of it at home." She completely ignored the basic fact that children are incapable of making sound, mature, well thought out decisions and cannot possibly be asked to share equally or democratically in the responsibility of running a family. How a child's self-esteem could be developed in an atmosphere of insecurity and false empowerment owing to parental abrogation of their leadership and guidance roles is beyond me.

In my opinion, other books like these of the time asked parents to be more understanding and sensitive and to spend more quality time with their children. These are all worthy goals. However, these very goals were somehow distorted and translated into a directive to be more chummy and friendlike with your child. This is a bad idea because the parent must always be in charge, and friends are not in charge of each other. It is also scary to a child if he or she does not believe that a capable, older, and wiser parent is in charge.

Children do not have to like (or love) their parents or their guidance. And parents don't have to like their children's behavior. When a child decides to engage in "conditional positive regard" behavior, that means that the message to the parent is, "I'll love you if...." The blank is a stated or unstated message that the parent do or say a certain thing or the child will withhold his or her love. This is clearly a case of emotional blackmail and should be ignored at the least, and not tolerated or given any serious weight. As soon as a parent begins to cave in to these arguments, then the child has become the person in charge. This violates the natural and mentally healthy hierarchy that a family should have and operate under.

If parents truly believe that their child's love is so flimsy that it can be taken away because of a denied favor or added to through giving in, then there is actually a parental self-esteem issue to be dealt with. Because I have repeatedly seen this in my therapy office, let me tell you that another root issue is often parental guilt. Where does this guilt originate? It can be from a parent's regret over a divorce. It can be guilt from the parent's own high standards that cannot be met. And it can be from within the marital relationship, a guilt felt or perceived from the parenting partner's disapproval or criticism.

If guilt interferes with your ability to set limits and parent properly, then you must eliminate or reduce your guilt as soon as possible. This might mean individual, family, or group therapy. Parent support groups are actually great places to unburden yourself in front of people who know exactly what you are going through. They can also be sources of ideas to help you parent better and more effectively.

Children, to be secure and feel safe in a big, unknown world, need to respect their parents and their parental authority. By establishing authority at home, your children will be more cooperative and successful when they start school and have to mind the teacher. Your children will be appreciative that you, the adult, are in charge and will safely guide them through their lives. This does not mean that I advocate raising a child who blindly follows authority without thinking. It does mean that children need to experience benevolent authority at home as a starting point to live in society as it is now organized.

In 1997, Charles Schaefer surveyed mental health professionals about the topic of verbal abuse toward children. Ten categories of verbally abusive parental behavior were identified as "never acceptable." From a chart taken from a textbook written by E. Mavis Hetherington and Ross Parke based upon Schaefer's work, these are the 10 verbal don'ts:

Verbal Abuse Category	**Example**
Rejection/withdrawal of love	"Nobody could love you."
Verbal put-downs	"You dummy."
Demands for perfection	"How come you came in second?"
Negative predictions	"You'll never amount to anything."
Negative comparison	"Why can't you be more like your sister?"
Scapegoating	"You're the reason we're getting a divorce."
Shaming	"Look, everybody, at what a baby Johnny is."
Cursing or swearing	"Go to hell."
Threats	"I'm going to kill you!"
Guilt induction	"How could you do that after all I've done for you?"

Adapted from: E. Hetherington and R. Parke, *Child Psychology.* Published by McGraw-Hill Education, New York, NY. Copyright © 2003. Reprinted by permission of the publisher.

SUPPORTING AND PROTECTING CHILDREN

As is readily apparent, these hurtful comments can easily be taken directly to heart and will diminish any child's self-esteem. For children, they will first and foremost consider the source—a parent! Once the words come out of a parent's mouth, they really can't be taken back no matter how hard you try. Apologies have a limited return, and are better than not trying to undo the damage. *But the time to prevent any abusive results is before you say something negative.* Saying any of these comments once is not likely to cause permanent damage, but every parent should note these categories and practice serious self-editing before talking with any child. If a parent repeats such comments in any of the categories over time, the child will be hurt in ways that can be seen and ways that cannot.

When a verbal punishment or reprimand is needed, the parent must nail the behavior and not the child. It is never okay to say, "You're bad," but important to specifically point out that "Your behavior (and specify it) is bad, wrong, and/or unacceptable." The subtle difference allows the child to maintain some self-esteem and sense of value but also communicates that the inappropriate behavior will not be allowed or tolerated. If you consistently tell a child that he is bad, he will live down to your declarations and prove you right.

The topics of abuse and punishment always remind me of an obvious, fundamental feature of parenting that also must be addressed—protection of children from harm. Good parents are very careful about the environment their child is placed in. Protection of children starts in the home. Parents must not verbally, sexually, or physically abuse. They must also child-proof a home where small children are at play. As the child grows older, other accident prevention measures must be taken—putting up fences around pools, locking away dangerous medications and cleaning agents, or securing any firearms in the house, to name a few.

Parents must be protective of their children outside the home as well. Knowing where your child is, who is supervising him, and what he is doing is important at all times. Young children should not be left alone or with peers. Until and unless you know that your teen is responsible and levelheaded, the rule applies here as well. The educated parent is aware of his or her child's immediate situation and only allows the child's continued presence when satisfied the situation is as safe and supervised as can be expected. Never assume your child is safe—go and check it out with your own eyes. *You can never be too careful, although you have to strike a balance between allowable risk and overprotection.* This is an ongoing parenting dynamic, which changes as your child becomes more able to protect himself. When your children are young, only you can protect them with your physical proximity and supervision.

Should your child be sexually abused, the educated parent needs to know how to respond in a way that is supportive and protective. Teresa and John Rudisill, Irma Johnston, and Mark Eddy have produced a guide for responding to sexual abuse disclosures. Briefly, in the event of this traumatic situation, a parent needs to stay calm and stay in control. If your child has the courage to tell you, you must assume that he or she is truthful about the abuse. One also must listen carefully to the child and let the child know that it was right to come forward. You must then notify law enforcement and get a medical/physical exam. Finally, you must reassure your child and take steps to prevent future abuse.

Once the abuse charge is "in the system" the next best thing to do as a parent is to be available and listen to your child. Allow your child to come to you when the child is ready; otherwise, respect the child's privacy or desire to not talk about the event. Avoid any child blaming and do all you can to help your child begin to recover his or her self-image and sense of security. Children can feel damaged or bad or blame themselves for what happened. Finally, do not expect that your child will heal or get by without professional help. Use the full force of the legal and mental health systems to get justice and help your child and your family begin the process of healing and recovery.

This section on protection probably has the most "must statements" of any part of this book. It has to. As a parent, your children are dependent upon you to get them off to a safe start in the world. You have to do all you can. The alternative is unthinkable.

Another technique I wish to present to the educated parent is that of the notion of *scaffolding*. Scaffolding is the term given to the emotional and environmental framework that parents create in which their children can experiment, grow, and blossom. Scaffolding refers to parenting behaviors that support and better enable children to develop skills and abilities than they would have been if left on their own. Children respond well and flourish when they have parental encouragement in words and actions. Like the support apparatus erected around a building to allow the structure to be built, added to, or enhanced, parental scaffolding has similar results. Allow me to use an analogy of a fenced yard.

When your child is young and immature, say two years old, if you allowed him to play in the yard, you would be there to monitor his every behavior. Even though the fenced area might be 2,500 square feet, you would be there within a few steps to be sure that your child could safely play and explore. You might bring toys or other play equipment to your child or your child to the equipment. At this age, you are supporting appropriate developmental opportunities and you are close by to see that all goes well. You are also allowing your child to become more skillful and to benefit from the resources and support you have provided.

When this child is seven years old, he may be allowed the entire yard to play in. The necessity to closely monitor and supervise is lessened as your child has more skills and abilities. However, you have still provided a safe yard area with appropriate play equipment and toys. In this bounded area, again your child is free, with your support, to explore and grow, perhaps to be a better climber or a better soccer dribbler.

As this child becomes a teen, he is now allowed past the yard into the world, but again with your support. Depending on the resources you have now provided (like some transportation), your teen can now acquire more skills and achieve even more owing to the underlying direct and indirect support from your parenting. Other supports would include having modeled and reinforced proper behavior so your teen has a basis to make good judgments.

Scaffolding is a concept that all parents should know and establish to the largest extent possible. In providing your children with the support and resources needed, you enable them to use their individual talents and traits to achieve at levels beyond what could be attained without your facilitation and encouragement. This goes beyond buying the right toys for infants to providing for school, sports, and other endeavors that your child and teen will pursue.

RECIPROCAL PARENT–CHILD INFLUENCES

As mentioned earlier, parents not only play a profound role in influencing their children, but children influence and affect their parents. As you begin your parenting journey, you will be shaped and changed by the children whom you will shape and guide through their young lives. Children affect their parents in multiple ways. Some parents will become stronger and better human beings as a result of their experiences. Other parents will be torn down and made weaker by the stresses and demands that their children bring to the family.

Anne-Marie Ambert has researched and written an interesting book that highlights "the effect of children on parents." Allow me to present some of her most telling findings. In an early chapter in her book, Ambert reviews the literature on child characteristics shown to affect parents, the types of parents who are most likely to be influenced by their children, and the social situations that enhance or limit child effects on parents. Let's take a look.

What is it about a child that can cause such profound changes in a parent? Specific child attributes include age, gender, and birth order and the place in the sibling group (if any). So-called "personal characteristics" include the child's health status, intelligence level, personality traits and attachment quality, school performance, general emotional and behavioral quality, and quality of relationships with others. It is in these personal characteristics where one finds data suggesting that certain children have a greater impact on their parents. The more a child deviates negatively from what would be expected normal ranges of these personal characteristics, the more a child's effect on the parents will be negative.

When the behavioral deviation from the norms is "child-driven," the more the impact on the parents will be negative or unwanted. Examples of child-driven characteristics would be regular oppositional behavior by a child or drug use and juvenile delinquency in a teen. These conditions are different from a child whose health status is poor, a factor out of the child's control by virtue of having an "external" origin.

Ambert hypothesizes and finds data in support of the fact that the child who differs from the norms violates parental expectations. In other words, parents have a set of ideas and images of what raising their child will be like, what their role and actions will be, and how that child will be. To the extent that a child does not develop or act as was expected, a parent is disappointed or disillusioned or frustrated. The greater the discrepancy between the parental expectation or vision, the more that "different" child affects the parents and their feelings of identity as parents. Such parents have to change their ideas (and possibly their dreams) of what their and their child's roles would and will be. This is a major identity shift, not easily swallowed. The result is a more negative view of the parental self and/or your child.

On a much more upbeat note, the opposite, positive effect is also the case. The more a child deviates "positively" from these norms, the more the parental effect will be positive. Having a gifted child or a socially competent "all around great kid" can change and shape parents and their identities in a positive and desirable fashion. Of course, these same "positive deviations" can also be experienced as negative by another parent, depending on the circumstances and situations. The same intellectually gifted child desired in one household may prove to be more of a challenge and trial in another. This discrepancy ties into the concept of *goodness of fit.* The better the match between a child's qualities and attributes with those of the parents, the better the situation for both the parents and the child.

What parental characteristics have been seen in the research to determine that a parent is more susceptible to being affected or changed by his or her child than usual? Again, Ambert's review has a summary of demographic and personal characteristics. Demographic attributes include age of parent (at the child's birth and at the time of review in a study), gender, marital status, ethnicity, variables related to any other children, and whether the parent is biological or adoptive.

It is generally true that children affect and influence their mothers far greater than their fathers, primarily because of the different amounts of time committed to the parent–child relationships. In general, the research reveals (this is no shock here) that children are in more conflict with their mothers, and are also more emotionally close to their mothers than with their fathers. Single parenting is another variable that plays an important role. Lack of support from a co-parent and the usual poorer economic conditions of single parenting play key roles here. Younger parents are more shaped by their children than older parents. This is due to socioeconomic factors as well as personal maturity and patience levels. The number of children and their spacing also plays a role. Having "four under five" was once more common (my mother did this 40-plus years ago and she still doesn't drink to excess!), but imagine the personal stress levels in having to keep up with multiple infants and toddlers 24/7. Finally, a topic we will explore in greater detail in chapter 10, adoptive or biological status, plays an important role in the reciprocity of parent–child relations.

The personal characteristic variables for parents include abilities and competencies, personality type, personal history of parenting as a child, parental skills and expectations, personal health, quality of marital relationship, and relationship quality with others. Again, I find no surprises here in this list. In fact, if I had asked you ahead of time to guess this set of variables, I bet you would have come up with all of these on your own. But why were you able to guess these factors? Because of their obvious importance and relevance to being able, as an adult, to deal with the stresses and challenges associated with raising a child or a group of children.

The final variable researched by Ambert was the "characteristics of the societal response." Societal response is defined as the extra-family resources made available to parents to help them raise their children. Take a moment to pause here and think about what external variables would impact (positively if desirable and negatively if undesirable) your ability to raise your child. What resources, pressures, and expectations from our society and culture help to support or interfere with good parenting?

Ambert's list begins with adequate housing, quality and availability of day care (preschools and after-school care) and schools, and health resources (insurance coverage and clinics). She then lists availability of parenting education, neighborhood safety, and appropriate and available recreational facilities (parks and playgrounds). Finally, the grander cultural and societal factors of acknowledgment of parents' contributions and workloads, the acceptance of more equal co-parenting and domestic work sharing, and the tolerance of family diversity of differing people, attitudes, and beliefs.

The grander cultural and societal factors say much for how we, as a people, encourage and respect or ignore and fail to appreciate parents and "family values." How does America really promote the pro-family, pro-child agenda? I too often see far more talk and way less action in this regard. In the absence of extended family supports (which for many are unavailable), it falls to the village to help raise its children. I am not arguing for every adult to raise everyone else's child. I am simply saying that policies and programs (often governmental, but some in business) need to be in association or cooperation with parental supports, and not just another source of stress and grief.

(For a more thorough and thought provoking view on this topic, I urge the educated parent to read the essay by James Garbarino, cited as an online reference in the bibliography. Garbarino explores social policies and how they have evolved over time.)

Another very important thing that all parents need to learn is what to expect and when to expect certain behaviors, abilities, or skills from their growing and ever-changing child. Depending upon how much time you have spent with children, through having a number of siblings or being responsible for and working with children (e.g., babysitting or team coaching experiences), you will come to know what children in particular age groups can be expected to do. To the extent that your child exposure time is limited, it will be more difficult to know what's going on or what's coming.

Not knowing these developmental norms can cause problems for the parent and the child. I once worked with a well-educated mother who came to me to complain that her 17-month-old was still not potty trained. Further, he was probably wetting himself to spite her, she reported, since she was often busy and he knew that she did not like to change diapers. If you know boys, then you know that it is best to wait until 24–27 months of age to start toilet training if you want to be successful and avoid frustration and failure. Similarly, the idea that an infant would act in a spiteful, purposeful way toward his mother is unlikely given the child's level of mental development. I was able to educate this mother on proper expectations and norms, and she was able to see her child in a more appropriate and positive light.

This book will not present these developmental norms, but they are available in a number of places. Most infant parenting books have explicit information on all aspects of the various developmental milestones occurring in physical, mental, language, and social development in the first two years. Any child or developmental psychology book and/or class will have this information as well as expectations for older children's competencies. In fact, I heartily recommend that at least one member of the parenting team (preferably both) take a course on child development. These courses are offered for hardly any cost through local community mental health centers, some school districts, or a community college. Then keep your notes and your textbook/course materials on hand for ready reference.

Finally, if you ever have a question or a doubt about your child and his or her abilities, ask. Ask your pediatrician, ask your mother, ask other more experienced mothers in your neighborhood. All will either help you or send you to someone who can. The question of when or whether a child should be expected to do something is termed *developmental readiness*. Often this term is used specifically in determining if a child is prepared physically, mentally, and emotionally for school. We will visit this topic again in chapter 5. For now, we will consider readiness in a more general way.

Allow me here to add a complementary note on comparing children. A simple developmental fact of life is that children grow at their own rates. That is why we use *normative range data*. Normative range data are basically windows of time in which 90 percent of normal children develop a certain ability or skill. For example, the ability to walk alone will happen in most children between 11 months, 1 week of age through 14 months, 1 week of age, with an average age of about 12 months. This means that you should not expect your child to be walking at 9 months, and that you should not be too worried if your child hasn't started to walk at 13 months. Just because other children with the same birth date are walking first does not mean your child has a major problem. And if your child is walking early, don't rush off to pay the gifted school tuition payment just yet.

Biologically based development occurs at a rate determined by maturation of the nervous and other related systems (a nature factor) *and* the amount of experience and opportunity a child has to display a certain skill or behavior (a nurture factor). Much research has been conducted to show that you can't hurry or accelerate these processes. This same body of research has found that these two key developmental processes—maturation and experience—are interdependent. So, once again, no aspect of child growth is *solely* biological, although in certain areas like motor development, biology may be the more limiting factor.

If you want your child to walk alone as soon as possible, all you can really do is feed him a healthy diet and let him get on the floor to crawl and climb up on furniture and exercise his musculo-skeletal system. Special exercises or specific muscle training is not likely to add any more than a day or two to when your child will start to walk, so just allow nature to take its course. Providing a stimulating environment can add motivation to walk, which will cause the child to grow optimally, but not necessarily any faster than he or she would have according to the genetic plan.

We also know that children tend to grow in spurts. So what a child could not do on Sunday, he may be able to do two Sundays later with even more new skills and abilities. Any developmental testing always has to account for this, so a bad performance on one test date is never enough to lead to a diagnosis of a problem.

One final developmental expectation I wish to include that is related to parenting is the issue of *co-regulation.* Co-regulation is defined as the sharing of control in the gradual process of shifting behavioral regulation from parent to child. Knowing that your primary authority occurs early on and that your direct influence will wane is another important developmental factor to keep in mind. But it is just as important to note and remember that you will remain the parent and you should maintain and reinforce your expectations for appropriate and proper behavior and choices even with your 18-year-old. The difference at age 18 is that your teen will make the final decisions.

When your child is an infant, you as the parent will have practically complete control over his or her behavior and options. As your infant grows into a child, efforts at autonomy will appear (the terrible twos and the frequent use of the word "no"), much to your dismay. From around two to three years of age through adolescence, with each passing year, your child's increased competencies will allow for more self-determined behavior and the need for less supervision and direct guidance from you. As your child becomes a teen, even less direct control will be possible, in part because your teen will spend so much time physically away from you, whether at school, at work, or with peers. By this time, you must hope that you have taught your child well, so that he or she has the ability and will to make proper decisions. Ultimately, your job as a parent will near its formal end as your teen becomes an independent young adult in the world.

Keys to co-regulation are related to the notion of scaffolding. By providing appropriate supports and resources, you will allow your child the space to learn to make decisions that are healthy and self-directed. By intervening when necessary, or by simply being available, your guidance and strength will be accessible when your child needs it.

WELLNESS FOR PARENTS AND CHILDREN

When one considers what an educated parent should try to accomplish in raising a child, the idea of helping to shape and mold a well-rounded healthy person makes sense. Another name used for such an overall positive outcome is wellness. If one looks at wellness models for adults, it is easy to translate this approach to an interesting blueprint or recipe for themes in child development.

An exciting new development within the field of U.S. psychology has been a turn to what is called *positive psychology*. Positive psychology looks specifically at human strengths and focuses research on ways that we can use what we know about people to improve their situations. There is no reason why healthy, functional parenting should not include behaviors and information on playing to the strengths and adaptive abilities of children from the earliest times. Educated parents can apply this information to their own and their children's lives.

Wellness refers to a balanced lifestyle that promotes health in all aspects of a person's life. Some people use the imagery of a *wellness wheel*. This analogy is a good one in that for a wheel to operate, all of its spokes must be functional. The wellness wheel is designed as follows. It has a hub at its center. The hub is what ties the spokes together and keeps the wheel functional. The spokes are comprised of five aspects of a balanced life—the physical, the intellectual, the mental/emotional, the social, and the spiritual. Let us consider these elements one at a time.

At the hub of the wellness wheel is the self. Specifically, what keeps a person balanced and feeling positive about themselves are concepts like self-esteem, self-concept, self-efficacy, and body image. *Self-esteem* refers to how a child feels about him- or herself. It is a self-judgment about whether one is good. Self-esteem is an emotional concept, tied to feelings of self-worth. Children with strong, developed self-esteem feel good about who they are. One could argue that this single concept is at the core of a person's well-being.

Self-concept is about how a child defines his or her identity. Self-concept would be found in the answer to the question of who you are. Some children may identify themselves as a son or daughter, brother or sister. They may go with where they are in school or if they are a Girl Scout or an animal lover. A good self-concept is tied in with self-esteem. Generally a child with a positive self-concept likes who he is and what he is doing, and has positive self-esteem as well.

Self-efficacy is related to the above. Self-efficacy is a belief in oneself that you can be successful and able to do what you need to in the world. A child with self-efficacy takes responsibility for his or her actions. Self-efficacy allows a child the belief that he can achieve and be successful based upon his effort. Self-efficacy is the basis for motivation and persistence, especially when placed in a challenging situation.

Finally, *body image* refers to a person's view of his or her physical self. The first three hub aspects are about psychological dimensions; body image is about one's physical features. Often body image is tied back to self-esteem—if you like your appearance, you will like at least that part of yourself. Body image is shaped by culture and ethnicity. In the United States, girls are faced with more concerns about body image because of cultural/media messages about what is acceptable or desirable. Within a family, parental attitudes and messages to both genders will be a strong determinant of how a child grows to perceive his or her body.

It is these four aspects of the hub that are at the core of a person's sense of well-being. They are the foundation of a healthy, well-adjusted adult member of society. Let us now review the spokes.

The *physical* spoke is about keeping healthy and fit. In the United States, there are real problems with the amount of exercise children engage in. We have developed a sedentary world—we sit for TV, for movies, in school, while being transported. Healthy physical development requires exercise on a daily basis. Walking, swimming, running, jumping—just about any large-muscle activity is good. This establishes an exercise mentality and is good in preventing later heart disease and other health problems like Type II diabetes.

The physical spoke is also about teaching children hygiene and self-care. Bathing, brushing teeth, and grooming skills are all part of teaching children to be responsible for their own health and body. Also, safety habits like always using seat belts, helmets and knee pads, and proper bicycle behavior are necessary for good physical health and accident prevention. In this same vein, getting a good night's sleep or taking naps when under five years of age is another self-care habit to be established. Finally, good nutrition is a must. Parents need to carefully monitor their child's eating habits. Too many children are sugar-guzzling soda addicts or fast-food aficionados. While okay in moderation, a constant diet of this food will lead to obesity and poor nutrition. Picky eaters can be changed, but you have to work at it.

The second spoke is the *intellectual* one. Children need exposure to enrichment activities and general cognitive stimulation. Starting with a colorful crib mobile and toys in infancy, and moving to reading to children regularly will lay a foundation for your child's becoming a lifelong learner. The more one structures the home environment to being learning friendly, the more school will be a positive experience. Children should not be left to rot in front of TV sets. Games that require thinking and planning, like Stratego or Clue, and then more sophisticated mental and creative challenges should be encouraged.

An equally important dimension in the intellectual spoke is allowing for creative expression. Coloring, finger paints, blocks and Legos are all fun ways for children to exercise their developing brains. Other creative outlets like cooking and baking, gardening, crafts, and whatever you like should also be made available. These exercises are enjoyable, teach important skills, and can provide a wonderful parent–child interaction event.

We next explore the *mental/emotional* spoke. Mental/emotional activities are about teaching children how to stay in control of themselves. It is about teaching coping skills and ways to react to situations that are both positive and negative. Children must be shown how to modulate extreme emotional responses. It starts with babies, who learn to soothe themselves at eight weeks when they are crying in their cribs, and carries on to learning how to deal with friends who are mean.

Parents can assist their children in this spoke dimension by encouraging and rewarding positive attitudes and ignoring negative ones. Not allowing whining or not tolerating excessive sulking and negativity are important for developing interpersonal-related skills. Children can be taught to better handle frustration or delay gratification by how their parents treat them, and in what the parents allow or tolerate. Much recent data on emotional factors, the so-called "EQ," suggest that this is a far more important dimension than has been previously recognized.

The fourth spoke is the *social* one. We are a social species, which requires us to interact with others. Learning how to treat others with respect is an essential lesson. Children should be involved along with their parents in service activities for others. Whether it is a visit to a nursing home, helping out at a religious-related or community facility, or learning to donate to others in need, children need regular exposure to these pro-social habits.

Their parents' strong loving marriage provides a template for children's later expectations and behavior in adult intimate relationships. Parents who are respectful of one another and their children are modeling excellent behaviors. Finally, having humor in a household makes everything go better. The old cliché is true—smiling and laughter are nature's relationship builders. It is great to learn to laugh at oneself and to find humor in all sorts of situations. Certain family "inside jokes" are a great way of establishing lifelong bonds and memories.

The final spoke of the wellness wheel is the *spiritual* one. Of all the dimensions so far covered I would guess that this is the least discussed by a great number of parents. The spiritual dimension is not just about organized religion, although that is the primary way most children in U.S. society are introduced to spirituality. In the wellness model, spirituality is also about having a sense of purpose, meaning, and direction in your life. All too often, a criticism of the current young generation (16–24-year-olds) is a lack of direction or life motivation. Many are apparently in search for this meaning, often looking in places where it is unlikely to be found—in drug use, promiscuity, and risk taking.

The spiritual dimension is an important aspect for any person to be whole and complete. Parents who can model a spiritual side make it easier for children to acquire their own. Again, this is not just about religion or faith, it is about self-actualizing and becoming the best person you can be. This self-actualized person is in touch with his or her strengths and weaknesses, striving to become as close as possible to an idealized model of a good, complete person.

All of these comments about the wellness wheel apply to both parents and children. Parents on their way to achieving balance and wellness will be natural role models for their children. A parent who practices these five regimens will be in a better, healthier position to raise children who can also reach an overall state of health and well-being.

SPIRITUALITY

Allow me to add a few comments about religion and development of a religious philosophy. David Elkind has written about children's acquisition of knowledge about religions and their participation. He has linked his interpretation of this developmental process to the growing cognitive abilities of children, especially from ages 5 to 12. Basically, a child's religiosity is related to his ability to understand and appreciate more and more abstract qualities about religion and faith. By adolescence, the teen can fully appreciate, on an adultlike basis, what religion is and what it means in a person's life.

Elkind also specifically looked at prayer and how children understand this behavior. He asked standardized questions to his subjects. Among the questions: "Do you pray?" "Does your family pray?" "What is a prayer?" "Can you pray for more than one thing?" and "Where do prayers go?" Based upon analysis of responses in individual interviews, Elkind discovered that children seem to pass through three stages. These stages are directly related to cognitive ability.

Children's understanding of prayer follows three themes. The first is that children learn what prayer is. They then create their own individual meaning, some of which is learned from instruction and some from a "spontaneous" source. The second theme is that over time, a child's prayers will become more adultlike in content and intention. Basically, a child is continuously rethinking and reshaping what prayer is and its role. Finally, the child's concept of prayer will reflect a combination of the child's experiences and instruction and his or her level of mental ability. As Elkind summarized, "...the child's conception of prayer represents the creative product of thought interacting with experience."

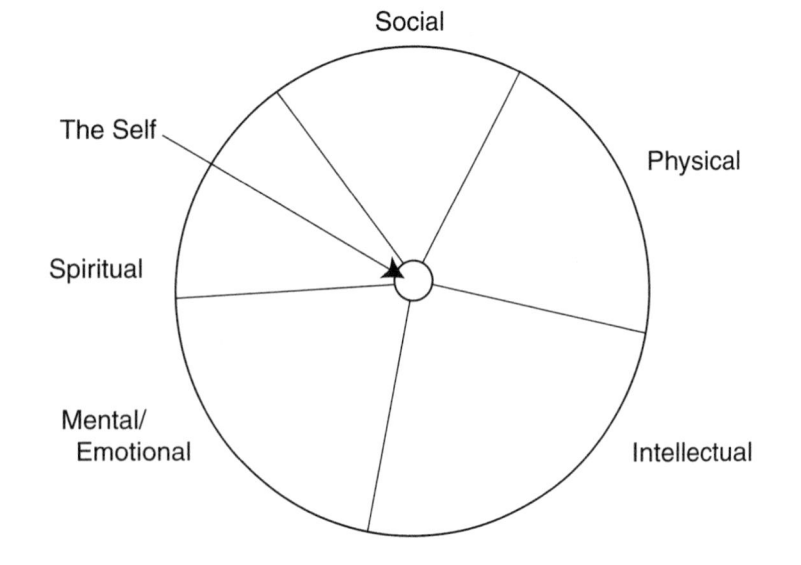

Figure 1.1 The Wellness Wheel

In this opening chapter, I have laid out what I consider to be important, basic aspects and products related to good parenting. Educated parents will consider the above and apply what makes sense to their approach to successfully raising their child.

In this chapter we have reviewed the need for consistency and the establishment of parental authority. We have discussed the dangers of abuse and the need for parents to protect their children from harm. We examined some important techniques that parents can use to support their children and the need to know about your child's developmental levels. Finally, we discussed wellness as a model for raising responsible and healthy children, including the spiritual dimension of children.

Chapter 2

THE DEVELOPMENTAL TRIAD (PART ONE): FOUNDATIONS OF CHILD OUTCOME

When you are a mother, you are never really alone in your thoughts. You are connected to your child and to all those who touch your lives. A mother always has to think twice, once for herself and once for her child.

—Sophia Loren

In this chapter we will begin a review of the three primary developmental components that are responsible for determining how your child will turn out, or, as it is known in the psychology field, his or her developmental outcome. As mentioned previously, there are actually hundreds or thousands of variables that come together to fully explain how and why a child becomes the adult he becomes. However, many of those variables are a subset of the three we will now present. Again, how any adult is shaped over time from infancy and childhood is a complex process, and there are never simple answers to complex questions. The triad of developmental variables we next look at are among the major influences identified over years of research. Thousands of research studies have been conducted in these areas. I hope to present the essential findings for your consideration and review as an educated parent.

Ultimately, it is the interplay of three global factors that seem to ordain much of the final product in child development, a grouping I call the child developmental triad. These are: the child's temperament, his attachment quality, and the style of parenting he receives. We will explore these phenomena in turn in this chapter and the next, and then discuss their interaction.

DEFINITION AND EXPLANATION OF TEMPERAMENT

For psychologists, temperament has an explicit definition. It is a rich concept that includes one's reaction to the environment, or one's "constitution," and it serves as a foundation for one's personality. Temperament is a psychological construct, a person-designed invention created to organize theory and information to help understand and explain why people generally respond as they do. Most child psychologists agree that the temperament construct has four features:

- it is objectively definable,
- it has a biological basis,
- it is measurable in infancy, and
- it remains relatively stable across development.

Your temperament is your inborn predisposition to how you will react and interact with other people, situations in your life, and events. For a parent, your child's temperament will be the "default setting" that your new son or daughter will enter the world with. As a parent, you will need to respect this and modify your parenting behavior and your expectations around what your child brings to your family situation. Trying to change these "initial settings" is not easy, though not impossible either. More on this aspect will be presented later.

TEMPERAMENT THEORIES AND MODELS

Temperament has been investigated in different ways. Among the most researched and respected models for temperament is the New York Longitudinal Study (NYLS). We will also consider the more recent work of the behavioral geneticist Robert Plomin and his associates.

The NYLS was one of the first systematic research attempts to define and study temperament over the life of individuals. This long-term, or longitudinal, type of research is especially important when looking at development because it allows for comparisons of any one person as he or she grows and changes. This research method is also important because it allows a chance to see the dynamic changes over time that no other method can reveal.

More than 125 subjects were measured over 20-plus years at predetermined intervals from infancy into early adulthood. From these measurements, the NYLS group derived three overall temperament classifications (easy, difficult, and slow-to-warm) based upon assessment in nine categories. See the chart for details.

Components of Temperament in the NYLS

Rhythmicity	What was the regularity of biological processes like eating, sleeping, and elimination patterns? Were they predictable or unexpected?
Activity level	What was the general energy or activity level of the child, including how much motor movement was displayed? Was the child passive and hypoactive or energetic and hyperactive?
Approach/withdrawal	When presented with a new stimulus, how did the child respond? Did he move toward the new object or situation or move away?
Adaptability	How well did the child adapt to changes in schedule or to usual routine—in an accepting way or with difficulty or fussiness?
Sensory threshold	How sensitive was the child to outer stimuli like noise or light? Does he tolerate environmental events or react strongly?
Predominant mood quality	Was the child usually in a happy (positive) or unhappy (negative) mood? Was the child most often smiling and content or fussy and unable to be soothed?
Mood intensity	When the child responded, did he do so in a manner appropriate to the situation: that is, did the child overreact wildly when the stimulus did not seem to warrant such a reaction?
Distractibility	While a child is engaged, how easily does a new stimulus take away his attention?
Persistency/attention span	How long does the child stay engaged and focused on a particular activity?

A consistent set of observations and measures were made, and adjustments were made as the children grew older. Surprisingly, the children's ratings stayed pretty much the same over time, giving rise to the ability to classify them by their score sets. (After more years of measurement, these ratings were also found to be relatively stable into adulthood.)

On the basis of how the child was scored (e.g., high on rhythmicity, low on activity, tendency to approach, etc.), three overall classifications were derived as follows:

Easy babies are those whose temperament makes them ready to manage, and children who seem to quickly adapt to their parents and caregivers. These babies easily handle new experiences and quickly develop eating, sleeping, and elimination schedules, which make them predictable. Such a child is predominantly positive in mood and has mild to moderate mood intensity levels. Their frustration tolerance is age appropriate. Roughly 40 percent of the children followed were classified as easy. As I like to say, a mother and father who are blessed with an easy child are ready to have a dozen more, as this is as good as it gets.

Difficult babies have a style that makes raising them more difficult and challenging for their parents. These babies may resist cuddling, may be fussy (negative mood), may not tolerate any deviations from their daily schedules, and are more difficult to predict. These children exhibit behaviors that can make parents feel inadequate and unprepared since the parents' perception is that they cannot soothe or take care of their baby properly. These children have high activity levels (they're "squirmy"), adjust slowly and with difficulty to change, and are likely to throw tantrums when frustrated. About 10 percent of children are identified as difficult. If you have a difficult baby first, it may be the case that you will strongly consider the "only child" family model.

Slow-to-warm babies are a bit in the middle. They have some traits of the easy child and some of the difficult. In general, they are described as having low activity level, mildly negative reactions to new stimuli, display a low intensity of mood, and will eventually like and accept new situations only after repeated opportunities and on their own timetable. Most parents would call their slow-to-warm child "shy." Of the NYLS children, 15 percent were classified as slow-to-warm.

If you have done the math, you know that only about 65 percent of infants were cleanly typed. The other 35 percent had qualities that did not allow them to be placed in one category as first defined by the researchers. There was nothing wrong with these babies; if there was a problem it was with the inexact system of labeling. (A later set of criteria allowed for almost total categorization—60% were typed as easy, 15% as difficult, and 23% as slow-to-warm.)

The NYLS group was also one of the first to demonstrate that temperament was a *trait variable;* that is, a relatively permanent feature that tends to persist over time and different environmental situations. Many other studies have confirmed this significant finding. This is important to know because it allows you as a parent to begin to make some decisions about how to raise your child and what parenting techniques will work best or which will lead to difficulties. It also allows you to predict possible trouble spots, which you can then attempt to modify to make your child's life a bit easier.

The NYLS group also discovered the importance of matching parenting behavior to the child's temperament, and revealed that parenting may be one of the few jobs where previous experience may not count for much if you are raising two children who differ in temperament. Simply put, what worked for child #1 may not apply to child #2.

The concept of *goodness of fit* is one that psychologists use to describe the level of match between the child's temperament and their social context, primarily the style of parenting in the early years. (This term was first used by the NYLS team.) A harmonious fit, where the parenting techniques and expectations match up with the child's temperament characteristics leads to the best outcome. To accomplish this, the parents have to be aware of and sensitive to what the child brings to the family and then coordinate their behavior to take advantage of the best way to shape the child as he or she grows.

For another view, we turn to Robert Plomin. Plomin's work is called *the EAS model,* where E is for emotionality, A is for activity level, and S is for sociability. These variables overlap with the NYLS findings. The *emotionality* variable is a measure of the intensity of emotional reactions, much like the NYLS reaction-intensity variable. This can be rated from the low end of little display of emotion (a kind of stoicism) to very intense, overblown reactions far out of measure to what the situation calls for.

Activity level refers to the child's natural level of physical exertion. There is a distribution of preferred activity level in people ranging from the extremes of hyperactivity to hypoactivity. Five activity components were assessed by Plomin, including one called the reaction to "enforced idleness." This last factor looked at children's response when forced to sit or be still—how did they handle their restlessness and built up energy? As you know, some children just simply cannot be expected to stay still. Plomin's work helps to show that expecting that from certain children is unreasonable.

Finally, *sociability* refers to whether a child is outgoing and people friendly or more shy and reserved. It has its roots in the personality traits of extraversion and introversion. This refers to whether a person prefers to be with people or to operate alone. Plomin also looked at choice (prefer-ence to play alone or with others), direction (moves toward or away from others), and restriction (what did the child do when isolated?) in social settings.

Based upon his work, Plomin developed a way to type children on their levels of three factors: emotional responsiveness, activity level, and sociability. His work, in part, relied on twin and adoption study data, the main tools of the behavioral genetics researcher. These research methods allow for conclusions about the influence of genetic or inherited influences in the attainment of traits. These are actually very difficult questions to investigate. How can one ever isolate genetic influences from behavior? The best way would be if one could use genetically identical people and then vary their environment. Genetically identical people are available— they're called identical (or monozygotic) twins. Ethically, we cannot raise one twin one way and another a second or separate way by design. We can however, rely on life circumstances that lead to some twins being reared apart, often with adoption histories. When this happens, although other variables enter in so that we never get a clean comparison, we can make some statistical corrections and go from there.

Like the NYLS, Buss and Plomin "emphasizes matches and mismatches between the child and its environment, especially between the child and its parents" (Buss & Plomin, 1984, p. 156). Buss and Plomin's work stands apart in its emphasis on the genetic foundations of temperament, while also inviting investigation of how environmental factors then impact these inborn predispositions. His influence and perspective as a behavioral geneticist has added an important dimension to this area of research. And his findings have supported the work done by social scientists. Let us now see how this work applies to parenting.

IMPORTANCE OF TEMPERAMENT AS A CHILD CHARACTERISTIC

As an example of how and why temperament is an important aspect to know about a child, a study by Avshalom Caspi and associates followed 800-plus children and measured them at ages 3, 5, 7, 9, 11, and then 15. (They later followed up again at age 21.) This study, as have others of this type, found that aspects of temperament identified when the children were three years old were predictive of specific behavioral outcomes as they grew older. For example, certain teen problems were seen as "predictable" on the basis of how the child's temperament was years before the problems emerged.

Children identified early on as having difficulties with self-control and self-focus behaviors (the undercontrollable type) were the ones that got into trouble for not being able to control or mind themselves as teens. Their troubles were related to impulsive behavior, aggression, and many interpersonal difficulties that lasted into early adulthood. "Externalized behaviors" such as delinquency and acting out at 13 and 15 years of age were also strongly related to observations and measures of irritability and distractibility at the 3- and 5-year-old period.

This means that how your child behaves in younger years can be a clue as to what you need to teach him in order to overcome inborn tendencies that could cause him later trouble. In this specific case, an undercontrollable child needs increased structure and consistent behavioral consequences in order to help him to internalize controls he otherwise does not possess.

Inhibited-type children in their study grew up (at age 21) to become overcontrolled, cautious, and nonassertive adults. Also, the children with easy-type temperament qualities (termed well-adjusted or confident types) continued to express these positive and adaptive traits as they entered adolescence, making their lives a bit easier and a lot more trouble free. The inhibited-type child could probably benefit from parenting that encourages spontaneity and flexibility, while minimizing a child's tendencies toward passivity.

Another study, by McCrae, asked parents from different parts of the world to describe their children. He and his group found significant overlap. This means that the variables they identified are important to the adults of any group, and emerge independent of culture or parenting style or child rearing practices. All of this ties back into the notion that temperament is biologically based (within the human species). As such, parents need to be aware that their contribution to this aspect of their child was made at conception and is not likely to be easily changed once they get their shot at raising their new child.

How exactly is temperament, with all of its social implications, biologically determined? This is another complex question for which I do not have a simple answer. The best, though limited, explanation that science has is related to the child's nervous system (especially the brain). Each brain is wired in such a way as to have tendencies to respond to both internal and external stimuli in a certain manner. Different brain wirings lead to people who are more or less sensitive to events.

Let's consider some examples. For one child who is an overresponder, any time something happens he or she will likely have a high emotional response. This could be overjoy at the positive or despair at the negative. Another child may have a high activity response—hyperactivity and great energy in reaction to an event. This child is "wired" to be this way, through a combination of genetic and other biological factors. Certain environmental training can be given to help such a child to gain more control and be more measured in his responses. However, the child's *tendency* will always be toward an exaggerated response.

These types of tendencies were investigated by Nancy Bayley as they relate to intelligence and mental development. Bayley found that aspects of temperament like levels of arousal and activity can influence cognitive development. It was found that so-called low intensity infants are more advanced in factors such as speech and manipulative skills. A low-intensity infant is one who is less distractible and less bothered by external stimuli. So even in infancy and early development, a child's mental status is affected by reactivity.

Temperament's far-reaching implications across a child's life include school. For example, Mary Rothbart and Laura Jones have proposed the use of child temperament data as an aid for teachers who can then tailor their approaches to a specific child based upon that child's likely responsivity. Rothbart and Jones specifically focused on temperament dimensions related to activity level, "attentional persistence," and irritability/frustration tolerance. They applied knowledge from the temperament database to specific ways that teachers might approach a student based upon their measured levels of the above. We will return to this in chapter 5.

Will a person always be a certain way based upon temperament? Yes, in terms of predisposition and natural inclination. However, such a child is not doomed to a predetermined fate or unable to be changed. But to change, this child (and eventual adult) will need to work hard at trying to fight his or her nature, so to speak. So an overresponder can learn to modulate his response so that he can "stay in the middle" more and not be all over the place emotionally or in activity level. But this will take effort and there will be slips. Your parenting and your modeling of behavior are two variables that will help shape your child's eventual manner.

How did you contribute to this at conception? Your and your co-parent's genes combined to produce this new and unique genetic combination. Again, as a complex variable, this trait is not passed on like eye color or even height. This is important to note as it explains how two easy-temperamented parents can produce a difficult-temperamented child without invoking any "mailman scenarios." Temperament most likely involves combining a number of genetic inputs to make the ultimate outcome. (This process is hardly understood or explainable at current levels of knowledge, so you have to take my word for it.) This complexity also explains why in a three-child family with the same parents, each child can be so different in temperament type. Further, the genetics provide only the template; life experiences shape each child in different ways as well for the final outcome.

Having previously made my case for the stability of these temperament characteristics and their measurement over time, I must add the following. Some studies have shown that NYLS categories such as rhythmicity and mood quality may be more variable than others such as adaptability or activity level. Similarly, a variable like attention span may be found to be high in infancy and then clearly observed again when the then eight-year-old is sitting still doing homework after a long day in third grade. However, at 14, during a time of great hormone surges and other developmental change, the same on-task child has now become a distractible, unable-to-concentrate teenager.

So the point is that some conditions or changes in development can alter the otherwise stable temperament. Ultimately, temperament features will interact with environmental constraints and opportunities to result in how your child will turn out. The resultant expression of temperament will become more determined and influenced by environmental factors over time.

The truth is that people are so open to so many inputs that can alter behavior that all of what I have and will present in this book can only be noted as "usually" or "for the most part" or "in all likelihood" but never as a done deal. Having said that, do not toss this book aside just yet. There is enough good information to go on that you can be a better parent armed with this knowledge. Just remember it is always subject to some exception or difference when you are dealing with your child in your home.

IMPLICATIONS OF TEMPERAMENT FOR PARENTING

So what does this have to do with parenting? The psychologists Ann Sanson and Mary Rothbart suggest that at least three important messages for parents have emerged from the body of temperament studies. First, they believe that each child must have attention and respect paid to his or her individuality. Parents must try their best to be sensitive and flexible in their approach to their child. Being sensitive means that the parent be a good observer of the signs and signals that the child presents through his behavior. As previously mentioned, having parented one child well may not prepare you for the best way to rear the second or third child, even in the same family with the same two parents.

We already know that parents will respond differently to a child based upon a number of variables. For example, infant boys are more likely to be played with in a rougher way than infant girls. (It is also true that a child *thought* to be a boy will be treated as a boy even if she is a girl, and vice versa.) Toddler boys will be allowed more hyperactive behavior than a toddler girl. Boys are expected to and allowed to be more rambunctious. Parents of both genders allow and support this difference.

In different cultures, infant behavior will elicit a different parenting response. For example, Japanese parents react more quickly to soothe a crying infant than their American counterparts. In the United States, parents may have been counseled to let their baby learn to not get too dependent on having a parent immediately respond when "summoned." Similarly, most American parents value an active exploring child, while parents in China, for example, prefer more passivity in their infants. So the infant born with a high level of activity (as measured by the research described earlier) is better off born to American parents in this case scenario. The active child might experience some negative parental response if born to Chinese parents.

As another example, a crying fussy baby is set up to have less interaction with a parent over time owing to the irritability behavior. Crying babies inadvertently create a negative experience for future parental approach behaviors. This lessened parental contact may cause further "negative" behavior by the infant who is desiring contact and expressing it through crying. The extra crying leads to an even further reduction in parenting contact time.

All of this goes on without being noticed by the people in the middle of it. This is not a criticism of the parent or the infant. I raise the point to illustrate one of the many subtle ways an infant's temperament has a direct effect on parenting behavior and how the altered parental behavior then influences the child in return. These reciprocal effects then affect other aspects of behavior and development.

A second conclusion reached by Sanson and Rothbart is that parents need to carefully think about how they will structure the child's environment and regulate the events of the child's life as these factors relate to the child's temperament style. A difficult child who is more agitated and bothered by noise and light owing to an inborn oversensitivity to stimuli needs a quieter, less busy space than a child of easy temperament. Putting a child in an environment that is overstimulating stresses the child and leads to behavior and responses that you may not want to develop.

A slow-to-warm, shy-type child may need more time and reassurance when exposed to a new situation like placement into day care. For example, such a child may need to have a parent with him for decreasing amounts of time over several days before being left alone or left for a half or full day of day care supervision. To make that child's new experience less stressful and more manageable, a transition in increments reflects the educated parents' sensitivity to their child's needs.

As a final point, it was suggested that parents have much to gain if informed about how temperament shapes their child's behavior and how understanding that behavior can make raising the child easier or harder. Books and parenting programs designed to help parents identify their child's type and then tailor their child rearing behavior to maximize a good fit are available in most cities. Most are centered on the challenges of raising difficult-temperamented children. This is a good thing, as some research has also shown that these children face a higher chance of being abused. However, if you want to learn more about a slow-to-warm or easy child, ask around or search your bookstore or library.

Having said all this, I must also be sure that no reader walks away with the conclusion that difficult-temperamented children are bad or unworthy or not worth the effort. Nothing could be further from the truth. In fact, any child can be a handful if not raised properly. And even properly raised children don't always turn out as hoped for.

So be careful about the dangers of labeling a child. The foremost worry I have is that a labeled child then has his or her destiny etched in stone, for better or worse. Such a self-fulfilling hypothesis of troubles and dangers ahead is unwarranted and constitutes its own form of parental abuse. The research does not support such a conclusion and neither does common sense. If you have a difficult-temperamented child, you can be quite successful as a parent and your child can become a well-adjusted, competent, functioning adult. Knowing what to expect and how to deal with any temperament makes the educated parent more successful and the child better off.

My point is that a parent armed with this information should (and will) take comfort in knowing that successful parenting strategies exist for every child. It is no poor reflection on a parent to acknowledge that raising some children is more of a challenge than raising others. It is a reality.

My final point is the reminder that parenting involves a complex set of reciprocal behaviors between caregiver and infant/child/teen. There are no "bad" children to get stuck with; whatever problems emerge are never the child's alone. We will tie all of this information together as we go on.

(As a sidebar, some children can handle stress or pressure better than others. This is another temperament-based ability, but one that is readily aided by proper environmentally taught techniques for stress reduction or outright protection or removal from the stressors. The parents' ability to identify what the stressors are in their child's life and the child's capacity to adequately cope is a related necessary parenting skill. So too is the ability of the parent to structure a child's life as to minimize undue levels of stress. We'll discuss this further in chapter 8.)

DEFINITION AND EXPLANATION OF ATTACHMENT

The second leg of our triad is the developmental construct of *attachment*. Attachment is defined as the strong affectional ties that bond people together. This is according to the man who was among the first to bring the significance of this phenomenon to center stage, John Bowlby. Among his findings: people, especially young children, take comfort in being with another person (the caregiver) in times of stress, uncertainty, or difficulty. In lay terms, the word "bonding" comes closest to capturing the essence of what Bowlby described. Another major figure in this area of research, Mary Ainsworth, further discussed ways and levels of patterns of attachment and devised a technique to measure these. We will review their contributions and those of others who followed their work at length next.

In the early 1960s, Rudolph Schaffer and Peggy Emerson followed the development of attachment behavior in infants through their first 18 months. Their work remains a source of reference today, as they were able to show that infants progress through four steps, or stages, as they develop their initial emotional bonds with their primary caregivers.

Schaffer and Emerson found that in the first six weeks, infants are primarily asocial. They are very limited in their ability to discriminate or respond to social versus nonsocial stimuli. Then, from about six weeks though seven months or so (all of these time frames are inexact and individually determined), infants will smile at most anyone or thing with a face that approaches them. This could include a loving mother, a Raggedy Ann doll, or a stranger. They will then protest when they are put down or attention is shifted away from them.

Then between seven months and nine months, a specific attachment or set of specific attachments form. Now the child becomes rather picky in whom he or she chooses to be social with and accepting of. It is usually the mother who is the first attachment object, but can also be the day care worker whom the child knows and trusts. This child will now exhibit a behavior known as *stranger anxiety,* or *stranger wariness,* in the presence of unfamiliar faces. (FYI, it was once thought that every baby would show stranger anxiety or wariness. For some infants this anxiety/wariness period is so brief as to be unobservable.)

These are the first genuine attachments and form the foundation for later attachment patterns. After this first specific attachment is formed, the child will begin over time to form multiple attachments with other regularly interacting people such as the father, siblings, or a frequently employed baby-sitter. (Some research has suggested that older infants may even form an attachment to the family dog.) This development indicates that human infants are born to be social. They need and want to be connected to others in their lives. It is important that parents be there to make these attachments real.

It was the work of Schaffer and Emerson that demonstrated that the two early precursors (and foundation behaviors) of attachment were the level of maternal responsivity, and the total amount of stimulation provided by the mother. A mom who was predictable in her response to the infant's call for attention and interaction, and the mom who was there to play and sing and cuddle with, was the mom who had the closest level of attachment behavior. (We also know that this can happen with fathers if they are the primary caregiver. When this research was conducted, most fathers had less of a role with infants or simply weren't studied. As a result, most of this literature is mother dominated.)

Of more interest (at least to me) are the ethological theories and accounts of what attachment is and its importance as a survival mechanism for infants. Bowlby, initially a Freudian-trained psychoanalyst, made the case that attachment makes sense as a way for nature to ensure that mothers (this can be true for fathers as well) and infants both get their needs met. For the infant, the needs are obvious—feeding, care, and protection. For the mother, the needs are less physical, but include a psychological well-being in feeling needed and wanted, as well as a proposed stimulus feature of the infant that is irresistible to mothers.

Bowlby, and others such as Konrad Lorenz (of the famous imprinting studies with ducklings), further believed that human adults had built-in (this means instinctual) perceptions of all immature organisms. These perceptions elicit automatic responses of caring and positive approach behaviors. Known by some as the "Kewpie doll effect," it has been shown that adults favorably respond to infantlike features.

This is certainly true about a big-eyed, loveable baby, whose head size is one-fourth of its total length, as opposed to the final outcome as an adult when the proportion becomes one-sixth. It is equally true when we see a puppy or kitten. Puppies and kittens, in their immature physical states, also have a larger head-to-total-body-length ratio (not to mention big ears and eyes, and fluffy, soft fur). As a result, puppies and kittens also elicit positive approach caregiving responses. This feature invites protection from harm and is useful to any immature animal to have adults predisposed to care for it. This is the survival benefit.

Additionally, babies come into the world with "cuteness." Their reflexive smiling behavior, their cooing and gurgling, their sucking and grasping reflexes—all of these give the infant an endearing quality. The perception in the mother is that the baby is happy to be with her and loves her. I don't mean to sound so clinical (or cynical), but I want to cover these important theoretical points as we go on. Still, such an analysis pokes a big hole in the Norman Rockwell–ish fantasy view of motherhood, which is an entirely different topic I will not get into here. (It is also impossible to verify whether a small, prelinguistic infant loves anybody or anything, or what love might mean to a baby.)

Other ethologists have also pointed to features and characteristics that help with the attachment process. Babies are born with a reflexive smile that occurs when the baby looks at other people. These other people, especially mothers, believe the behavior is purposeful and directed at them. Again, there is no way to know when a newborn's smile is on purpose. But we know that early smiles are reflexes that occur in response to the right stimulus. In any event, the smile captures the mother and the baby is more likely to be taken care of.

When babies breast-feed, their faces are about nine inches or so from their mother's faces. Ethologists like to declare that it is no coincidence that a baby's undeveloped visual system is most functional when trying to view visual stimuli that are about 8–10 inches away. So, do you think an evolutional plan emerged to enable babies to immediately begin to focus in and begin to make face recognition memories (and perhaps imprint) on their mother? If so, then you are an ethologist too. In any event, this early visual ability sets up a process of interactions that leads to attachment patterns over the next months.

To tie this together, it was Bowlby's premise that both infant and mother were biologically (again, read instinctually) prepared to join in a reflexive interactive dance. Their behaviors are reciprocal, each signaling the other to elicit more behavior to bring them closer together. The cute baby elicits nurturing behaviors and feelings of warmth in the mother. The mother's nurturing behavior in turn signals the baby to smile and coo, which leads to more intense mothering. This is followed by more cute baby responses.

In this way, the mom is now hooked—she will not only take good care of this baby, she will lay down her life for him. The baby has been practically guaranteed a shot at growing safely into adulthood, and ultimately to sexually reproduce. Ensuring that the family genes can move on to their next generation is the true goal of evolutional-directed behavior. A kind of genetic immortality (or at least the chance to go on for one more generational cycle) is the objective.

Bowlby's view also emphasized that the infant plays an active role in the attachment process. That the infant has a key role in the interactions that develop and promote creation of attachment bonds suggests that attachment is very important to establish. If one believes that certain behaviors are determined for survival this all makes sense.

One final point about ethological views of attachment is in order. Ethologists talk about *critical periods*. These are certain windows of opportunity when the biology of the organism is primed to acquire or develop a specific ability. The concept has been updated and is now called a *sensitive period*. The sensitive period is like a critical period but with more leeway. It had been initially believed that attachment had a critical period within the first three or so years of life. After that it was too late.

If you missed this window, a secure attachment would not be possible after that time. With the sensitive period hypothesis, we know that the first three to four years are of prime importance, but there are still opportunities (although more limited as time goes on) for a secure attachment to develop after that. Over time, the cues and responses involved in attachment diminish. The early years are essential for a secure attachment.

When you were feeling those warm, fuzzy, love emotions with your infant, you probably weren't thinking at all along these biological lines. That's the beauty of this—it just happens. No (or, more accurately, very little) thinking is required in this natural process. However, all of this has its purpose, which is to set the stage for further infant-caregiver interactions that lead to healthy growth in the child with the protection and supervision of the adult and parenting behavior.

ATTACHMENT THEORIES AND MODELS

How does one measure how much attachment exists between infant and caregiver or between child/teen and parent? Can this be quantified? What would such a thing mean? In fact, there is a method in which attachment can be typed—this is a qualitative and not a quantitative method. Further, one can only speculate as to the degree of attachment; there are no numbers assigned. Even with this existing state of affairs, there is controversy about whether the currently accepted format is valid, and the more central issue of what it means for future development to be attached.

The standard for assessing attachment in infancy was developed by Mary Ainsworth in the 1960s. She was a contemporary and friend of John Bowlby and her work complemented his in many respects. Ainsworth's original work was with mother-infant pairs in Uganda in equatorial Africa. She later elaborated on her work in other cultural settings. Ainsworth created what is now called the Strange situation as a formal systematic protocol to assess type of attachment style in mother-infant dyad pairs.

Briefly, the Strange situation works like this: In consecutive three-minute-long "episodes" a mother-child dyad is first left in a playroom (the controlled lab setting designed for this interaction observation). The mother sits while the child is free to explore the space. Then the Experimenter (the stranger) enters and talks with the mother. The mother then leaves the room, leaving the baby (usually between 18 and 26 months old) with the stranger. Next, the parent returns to the room and the stranger leaves. The parent then leaves the young child alone. The stranger then returns alone, and finally the mother returns. At each interval, key behaviors are observed and recorded. Upon the mother's returns, the essential behavior of note is how the young child interacts with the mother. Does the child approach or ignore the mother? Does the child seek the mother for comfort? Does the child interact with the stranger, and in what manner?

From these observations of separation and reunion responses, four types of attachment patterns can be determined (originally there were three). They are called secure, resistant, avoidant, and disorganized. The most desirable pattern is the secure attachment. Roughly two out of three North American children studied fall in this category. Secure-attached children have the best outcome in our culture.

These *securely attached* children are at ease and contented when the mother is present, even approaching and interacting with the stranger in the comforting knowledge that Mom is there if anything goes wrong. The mother is said to provide a secure base from which the child is able to explore the environment. When the mother returns, the child is happy to see her and seeks comfort and physical contact.

Ten percent of children are categorized as having a *resistant attachment*. In a resistant attachment (one of three so-called insecure patterns), the child stays close to the mother and does not engage in the desirable exploration behavior. The child is quite visibly distressed when left by the mother and upon the reunion seems ambivalent about her. It is as if the child is angered at the leaving and cannot decide whether to go to the mother for comfort or stay away and resist maternal efforts to comfort or console the child.

Twenty percent of young children are typed as the insecure-attachment pattern termed avoidant. *Avoidant-attached* children are not distressed when left by their mothers. They choose to avoid or turn away from their mother in the reunion episodes, even when the mother actively solicits the child's attention.

The final 5–10 percent of young children are classified as disorganized. In the *disorganized-attachment* pattern, these children show the most distress and confusion. These are the least secure of all attachment types. To some observers, the disorganized-pattern child is a cross between the resistant and avoidant. The child seemingly acts like a proverbial deer in the headlights. In essence, at the reunion, the child freezes or acts in the approach-avoid behavior of the resistant-type child.

For children older than two years or so, a more refined psychological instrument called the Attachment Q-set, or AQS, is used. The AQS has a parent or other adult who has spent time with the child sort a series of behavior descriptions to get a classification. At present, it is believed that the AQS yields ratings that correlate well with the Strange situation scenario.

By now, you know more than you may have wanted about the assessment of attachment. I wanted to give you the details so that when you read about how certain studies were conducted, you can have a feel for whether the methods (and the findings) make sense. As mentioned earlier, there are challenges to the validity and uses of this method. What kind of studies use these methods? Well, of most interest to parents are studies that measure the effects of day care participation on children. One of the primary reasons to label day care "bad for children" is the argument that attachment is disrupted.

Is this true, and so what?

As you might imagine, that is a loaded question. You have also probably guessed that there cannot possibly be a definitive answer. You are correct. We will explore this area of research more fully in chapter 7, so don't forget this section.

IMPORTANCE OF ATTACHMENT AS A PARENT–CHILD CHARACTERISTIC

The secure attachment pattern is the preferred style in North American culture. Other cultures have different expectations and so other outcomes are more acceptable. For example, German parents value and promote more independent behavior, and so their children are more likely to be assessed as avoidant on the basis of their reunion behavior in the Strange situation. In most Western cultures, the desired secure attachment occurs when the child feels free to explore his or her environment (while looking over a shoulder to see that Mom is still there) and is allowed to act in an autonomous self-directed manner. The key is that the child exhibits a sense of security and feels safe in his environment as a result of the knowledge that a parent is there for protection and comfort if needed.

It was Ainsworth's contention that attachment quality was based upon the amount and kind of attention received from the parent. Termed the *caregiving hypothesis,* Ainsworth believed that securely attached children are made (not born) as a result of sensitive, aware, and responsive parenting involvement. A 1997 publication that reviewed 60-plus attachment studies determined that six separate but correlated parental behaviors most often yielded the secure attachment outcome. In this review, Marianne DeWolff and Marinus van IJzendoorn reported the following behavior characteristics:

Sensitivity—the prompt response level of the parent to the child's signals/needs

Positive attitude—expressions of positive emotion and affection toward the child

Synchrony—the structuring of reciprocal interactions with the child, matching parental behavior to the child's mood and activity level

Mutuality—the coordination of mother and infant to the same activity or event

Support—watching for the child's signals to provide emotional support for the child's activities and behavior

Stimulation—the active direction of behaviors and stimuli to the infant

These six behaviors are considered "the how-to" for making a secure attachment with your child. If as a parent you can tailor your interactions with your infant to include the above, you greatly increase your chances for a secure attachment. You cannot guarantee a secure attachment on the merits of parental behavior alone—remember, this is a reciprocal and interactive process that requires input from your infant as well.

(As a side note, you may have also heard about a movement called *attachment parenting*. Designed by William Sears, a pediatrician, attachment parenting is a program of certain key behaviors such as extended breast-feeding that promote formation of secure attachments in infants and children.)

How are the insecure attachments formed? In a phrase, inconsistent parenting responses toward the infant. When a parent's behavior is unpredictable and/or unresponsive, the infant is not receiving the needed stimulation to keep the attachment dance going. There is a breakdown in the stimulus-response-stimulus cycle that leads to the infant at first increasing his attempts to get maternal involvement. If these efforts are not successful, the infant apparently gets frustrated and gives up. This is how Ainsworth believed that resistant-attached relationships were formed. (I say *apparently* because it's hard to know exactly how an infant between 7 and 16 months is internalizing these events.)

Avoidant-attached babies seem to emerge as a result of impatient caregiving responses and an ignoring of the baby's signals. This behavior has been interpreted by Ainsworth to indicate that the mothers are, at some level, rejecting their babies. It has also been reported that avoidant-attached babies may be the result of overzealous parenting where the baby is overstimulated and must retreat (by avoiding the overwhelming input) to protect himself.

The disorganized-attached infant seems to result from unpredictable caregiving that may also involve neglect or abusive behavior. Most abused infants are assessed as having the disorganized type of attachment relationship. Additionally, very depressed mothers who provide inconsistent care as a result of their psychiatric disability have been found to alternate some level of care with periods of neglect, also leading to the disorganized-attachment type.

Why would any parent not engage in the six behavior characteristics listed above as being needed for the production of a secure attachment? There are many reasons. The one just discussed—clinical depression—is a good example. For some mothers, a postpartum depressive episode (or depression for other reasons) limits their capacity to be responsive and fully engaged. In other cases, a caregiver who was abused or neglected as a child may lack the necessary sensitivity and/or feel rejected themselves when their baby is fussy or cries often. Similarly, a substance abusing parent cannot be sensitive and responsive. This leads to a cycle of withdrawal and further neglect and leads to an insecure form of attachment.

Finally, any person who was not ready for, or outright did not want a baby at the time is a candidate for parenting in a way that will lead to an insecure attachment. This would include many single-mother situations (this is not a condemnation of all single mothers) as well as parents in high levels of marital dysfunction. Having a baby, with all of the attendant responsibilities, is something a parent must want and be prepared for.

Jay Belsky has reported that emotional difficulties in children can often be traced back to couples with serious marital discord. It is as if the child cannot receive the needed attention and care when parents are fighting. This parental fighting limits their availability for the child. This makes sense as does the opposite finding regarding happily married couples. These couples are found to help and support each other in the duties of parenting, resulting in a securely attached and well-adjusted child. Family therapy theory also supports the finding that a dysfunctional system disrupts the psychologically healthy function of all of its members. This will be reviewed fully in chapter 4.

IMPLICATIONS OF ATTACHMENT STYLE FOR PARENTING

So why have I spent so much time on this topic? Well one of Ainsworth's original goals was to find out whether these attachment patterns were predictive of later developmental phenomena; that is, outcome measures. She wanted to find a system of classification that could help sort out parent–child relationships so that certain types could be changed for the child's betterment.

For parents, a secure-attached infant grows into a secure-attached child and then teen. Secure-attached children (one to two year olds in the original study) are noted for their level of cooperation with parental requests and are much more easily socialized. This leads to a greater likelihood of social competence, which in turn allows for many successful and positive life situations. The apparent internal sense of security is also a foundation for future positive outcomes in self-esteem and self-concept, and another important variable termed self-efficacy. Self-efficacy is an internal belief system that one is competent and able to learn new things and to be responsible for one's actions. These are quite desirable traits for any child to have in our culture.

Resistant-attached children, as a result of generally more crying time, come to lack the same level of security as the securely attached ones. This leads to less exploratory behavior and less opportunities for learning about the world. One consequence for these children is that they generally do more poorly on tests of cognitive ability.

The avoidant-attached child is at risk for difficulties in future relationships with others. Because of these early negative experiences, they are seemingly avoidant of, and more hesitant in, making close relationships with others. A sad consequence for these children is that they are more likely to have trouble in making and maintaining peer friendships.

Disorganized-attached children are much like the avoidant children in terms of long-term consequences. They too seem to have difficulty in forming close relationships with others. They are also more likely to have difficulty in school.

Here is a good point to again remind ourselves that less desirable parenting practices alone may lead to insecure attachments. But recall that establishing attachment is a relationship process that also has input from the infant. As you might have guessed, a major factor brought to the table by the infant is his or her temperament. In addition, parenting style is a third dimension with a large influence. We will explore these at length in the next chapter when we see how the triad factors interact.

A few final notes are important. Alan Sroufe has warned of the need to be careful about overinterpreting the importance of attachment status. Sroufe argues that attachment has only a limited connection with later cognitive development, and that there are no established causal links between attachment and later psychiatric difficulties. Many of the associations we have reviewed thus far are statistically significant, but their meaning in the real world remains open to discussion and debate. I agree that one should not overinterpret research findings. However, much data have been collected to support the negative long-term consequences of disrupted- or insecure-attachment relationships in our culture.

It is also the case that we be careful to not assume that only secure attachments are normal or desirable. Since 60 percent of children measured form secure attachments, that means 40 percent do not. As a biological and ethological consideration, there is no way that a 40 percent outcome could be construed as abnormal. A range of attachment statuses and their differences are apparently what nature had in mind. It is up to researchers to discover their meaning.

Chapter 3

THE DEVELOPMENTAL TRIAD (PART TWO): PARENTING STYLES AND TRIAD INTERACTIONS

Parents are often so busy with the physical rearing of children that they miss the glory of parenthood, just as the grandeur of the trees is lost when raking leaves.

—Marcelene Cox

As discussed in the first chapter, the issue of parenting styles is open to many opinions, and many people have definite feelings about what parenting philosophy is best. I can assure you that few, if any, child psychologists believe that there is one, true parenting approach to fit everyone's situation. Recall the notion of goodness of fit; it is most important for the educated parent to match his or her child rearing behaviors to the child's temperament for the best outcome. Here again is why I believe that this book is unlike other parenting books. I cannot promote any particular regimen because I don't know your family. Rather, I will provide you a basis upon which you can determine what works best in your family.

DEFINITION AND EXPLANATION OF PARENTING STYLES

Much has been published and presented about parenting. After you read this book, see what perspective or routine fits with your views. Then look again to see how the ideas you have adopted fit with what you now know about the research findings. You too can be an informed and knowledgeable consumer of parenting philosophies and become a more effective, educated parent.

Having said this, let us now review one of the most influential and well-studied theories of parenting behavior—the work of Diana Baumrind. It was Baumrind who first identified three styles of parenting. She termed them *authoritative, authoritarian,* and *permissive.* She determined these not by observing parents, but by first observing children and the extent to which they exhibited something she called *instrumental competence.*

Instrumental competence was the term she used to describe a child who was functional and competent in social settings, and able to relate properly to peers and adults. These children could regulate their emotions and their behaviors. They had good frustration tolerance and could delay gratification. They were leaders in their peer group and responsible in their actions. Being instrumentally competent meant that a child was self-directed and self-modulated in his or her behavior and was pretty much a together kid.

After first categorizing the children on the basis of level of instrumental competence, she then went to their parents and had them give her information about how they parented their children. She and her team interviewed and observed how the parents interacted with their children. From this, the three original parenting styles were derived.

In 1971, Baumrind turned her attention to direct parental observation in the home. She wanted to determine if her initial results were valid, and she added a piece on gender differences—how boys and girls are affected by these parenting styles and whether there are better methods of child rearing for one gender over the other.

Observing 60 girls and 74 boys of above average intelligence at an average age of about four years at their day care placement, she and her assistants tracked the behaviors of each child on seven key behaviors. These included achievement orientation (e.g., the child likes to learn new things versus quits easily when frustrated), dominance-submissiveness (e.g., the child acts as a peer leader versus being a follower), and purposiveness (the child acts confidently and is self-directing versus appearing disoriented and being a spectator).

For the parents' behavior, Baumrind and her team went into the homes to observe the parents from just before dinnertime until the child was put to bed for the night. This time of day was chosen because it is a high-stress time and people are usually tired and not able to act anything but naturally. Imagine having strangers in your home after a hard day at work, and knowing they were watching you.

Baumrind was then able to comprise a list of the most important parenting behaviors for fathers and mothers. For both fathers and mothers the list included behaviors like firm rule-enforcement, encouraging of independence and individuality, and acceptance of the child. Joint parenting behaviors were things like expectations that the child would help with chores, parents acting in a directive (teaching) manner, the discouraging of emotional dependency or infantile/regressive behavior, and the provision of an enriched environment.

Baumrind was able to confirm her original parenting style categories and was also able to link style with child outcome. Let us first describe the parenting styles and then see what worked best. Let me add here that since the 1971 study, Baumrind has continually updated and refined her data, and many others have worked in this area as well. As a result, four parenting styles are now recognized, with the fourth one being a refinement of one of the original three categories.

PARENTING STYLE THEORIES AND MODELS

In tabular form, we get these four parenting types:

Parenting Behavior Styles

	Accepting, Responsive	Rejecting, unresponsive
Demanding, controlling	AUTHORITATIVE	AUTHORITARIAN
Undemanding, uncontrolling	PERMISSIVE-INDULGENT	PERMISSIVE-NEGLECTFUL

The table has acceptance and nurturing levels in the vertical columns and expectations, controls, and demands in the horizontal rows. An authoritative parent rates high on both, acting in ways that are accepting and nurturing, and demanding and controlled at the same time. Authoritarian parents are low on the acceptance/nurturance dimension, but high on expectations, controls, and demands. Permissive-indulgent parents are high on acceptance and nurturing behaviors, but low on expectations, controls, and demands. And the permissive-neglectful parent is low on the acceptance/nurturance dimension, and low on expectations, controls, and demands.

IMPLICATIONS OF PARENTING STYLE ON CHILD OUTCOME

So how do the different parenting styles affect children? Let us look at each of the four styles and the typical child characteristics found in the offspring of parents using each approach. The authoritative parents, by virtue of their warm, involved, and responsive behavior make for a pleasant home environment. These parents create a situation where alternatives and choices are presented to children. The children have input and all appropriate wishes are considered. These parents set standards and limits and communicate these clearly and firmly. They will confront all bad behavior and will not play the never-ending "lawyer games" of negotiating with children who are never their equals in terms of power and control. Authoritative parents expect and demand independent behavior that is age-appropriate. No infantilizing or babying is allowed. These parents are responsive to their children in every way, and are family-centered in their daily lives.

Children of authoritative parents are well-behaved and self-assured. They have achievement-oriented behavior and their daily activities are goal-oriented. They are good self-managers and know how to cope with stress and handle problems in calm and purposive ways. They are excellent playmates and great peer companions. They are often high energy, but in a directed, non-hyperactive way. Finally, they have and show respect for adults and authority figures, acting in cooperative and compliant ways rather than in a disobedient or challenging manner.

As an example, a child of an authoritative parent may want to stay up past bedtime to watch a special show. This child would be allowed to ask for the exception, and the parent would likely respond with the reasons why the bedtime is what it is. The authoritative parent would further relate that to stay up late might mean less sleep and a grumpy tomorrow morning. The child would, with parental approval, need to agree that he would be fine the next morning and stick with it. The parent might also remind the child that this was an exception and to not expect to stay up late again any time soon. It should be noted that in a follow-up study, Baumrind found this parenting style to be associated with the fewest number of drug issues and problems when the children reached adolescence.

The authoritarian parent is known best for rule enforcement and order. The rules are there but not necessarily explained in a clear fashion. These parents do not interact in positive ways with their children. They are seen as aloof and detached. They can be emotional when it comes to negative affect, easily showing anger and displeasure. When pushed, they are punitive and harsh in reply. They tend to see their, and all, children as little hellions in need of discipline and control. They do not allow questioning of their rules or authority, and do not care to hear the opinions of their children because, since they're just kids, they can't know anything important.

Children of authoritarian parents are often fearful and anxiety-ridden. They appear as moody and unhappy. They can be deceitful and secretive. They are hostile, but rarely display their hostility in open and direct ways. They can be unpredictable, alternating between aggressive outbursts and pouty, sullen passivity. Because of their anxiety and lack of coping, they are quite vulnerable to stress, making matters worse.

If there were a motto for authoritarian parents, it would be, "Because I am the parent, that's why." Using the previous example, the child of an authoritarian parent quickly learns not to bother to ask about staying up late in violation of the bedtime rule. Such a child would look for a way to sneak in front of a TV if possible or just sulk and become resentful.

Permissive-indulgent parents are often quite warm and accepting. They view children as free spirits who need lots of room to grow and flower. They are pleased to see, and encourage, free thinking and unconventional behavior. They are reluctant to set rules or limits for fear of disturbing the natural desires of their offspring. When discipline is applied it is inconsistent. The rules may change as the circumstances do, so children are not sure of what rules may be in place. These parents will "cave in" to whining and emotional blackmail in an effort to keep the peace and limit conflict and confrontation. For this reason, they also let much unacceptable behavior go without challenge.

Children of permissive-indulgent parents lack any self-control since none was expected. They are quite impulsive and lack self-confidence or self-efficacy. They are generally aimless, living lives with no or unclear directions. They can be unpleasant, alternately acting aggressively or angrily, followed by a sharp reversal into apparent cheerfulness. They are domineering and stubborn and will try most anything to get their way, other than work and effort.

Permissive-neglectful parents barely qualify for the title. They are equally neglectful and self-absorbed. Their narcissism will win out over their children's welfare. They are nonresponsive to their children and find ways to avoid interaction, contact, or responsibility. They are often unaware of their child's whereabouts or activities. These parents are psychologically fragile and are somewhat childlike in their interpersonal behavior. These individuals have poor marriages and are likely to be divorced, often multiple times.

The children of permissive-neglectful parents have low self-esteem and are insecure-attached. This alienation permeates their lives. They have little self-image or self-confidence. They are aimless and irresponsible. They are often moody, impulsive, and cannot follow rules or answer to authority. As teens they are conduct-disordered, getting involved in truancy, substance abuse, promiscuity, and juvenile delinquency. Having no family support, they are mostly high school dropouts and have few of the skills, aptitudes, and attitudes needed for any kind of conventional success.

Any other book you may read on parenting will be some variation of the above, even if the terminology or "game plan" offered doesn't use the vocabulary used here. In a way, it's a simple philosophy. To raise a socially and instrumentally competent child, the educated parent must be loving, accepting, and responsive to his or her child's needs and signals. A good, effective parent must also not be afraid to control and direct the younger child's life using common sense, enforced discipline, and high expectations. Now the "walk" is a lot more difficult than the "talk," but the plan is relatively straightforward.

Can parents be expected to act exclusively as authoritative or authoritarian? Probably not. At times even authoritative parents may be having an off day. Based upon a lack of patience or because of stress, it may be that the authoritative parent may respond to a child in an authoritarian or permissive-indulgent way. But in general, a parent's style is what suits them, and they are more likely to respond to their child in that fashion. No parent is 100 percent consistent. That's okay as long as your style is generally predictable and your child sees your overall behavior as a pattern of caring.

THE INTERACTION OF PARENTING STYLE, ATTACHMENT, AND TEMPERAMENT

We turn now to a consideration of how the three factors of temperament, attachment, and parenting style interact, with a special focus on implications for your parenting. Let's explore more fully what they mean for parenting. Throughout the rest of this chapter, I will highlight various features of each of the parts of the triad and give a sense of how they interact, and their influence upon how your child will turn out. Let's begin with a consideration of how temperament, parenting, and attachment quality come together in child aggression.

Parenting behavior is directly related to a child/teen's development of aggression and aggressive behavior, as noted by Timothy Cavell. Parenting factors shown to be important include: effectiveness as a disciplinarian; tendencies to act in authoritarian ways (overly punitive and emotionally rejecting); lack of warmth and positive involvement; and lack of organization and family structure.

Regarding underorganization and poor family structure, the child's problems emerge as a result of inconsistency and lack of order and predictability in his world. A house of chaos with unclear boundaries and rules is a formula for disaster. Parents themselves undermine their ability to be effective or play a positive role by their disorganized home life situation.

It is believed that social learning theory (explained in chapter 4) best accounts for the processes that lead to aggressive child and teen outcomes. J. Snyder and Gerald Patterson have concluded that parents inadvertently train their children by mismanagement of early problem behaviors. *Through inefficient and inconsistent parenting responses, and lack of adequate follow-through and monitoring, children become trained to be antisocial.*

Snyder and Patterson's findings may be summed up this way: A parent's failure to control a child early on, coupled with harsh and "explosive" discipline, leads to very negative outcomes. It is believed that children in these circumstances are taught through processes of negative reinforcement and a pattern of responding called "escape conditioning." These will be fully explained in the discipline section of chapter 4.

As you may have surmised, attachment and temperament play roles as well in the development of aggression. Temperament may be either a risk factor related to having a greater tendency toward aggression or as a protective factor to shield or buffer a child from environmental jeopardy. As described above, attachment is affected through parental style. The parenting behavior described above leads to insecure attachment—a definite risk factor for aggressive, antisocial, and conduct-disordered behavior. (Conduct-disordered behavior is the psychological equivalent of the legal term juvenile delinquency.) Aggression and conduct disorders are good examples of how all three factors of the triad interact and influence child outcome.

Temperament obviously comes into play when one considers the baby's role in the establishment of attachment. Jerome Kagan is one of those people critical about interpretation of the Strange situation results described in chapter 2. He has argued that, rather than being a measure of attachment, the Strange situation attachment assessment results are actually a marker for individual differences in temperament type. He has pointed out that the average numbers of one-year-old babies classified as securely-, resistant-, and avoidant-attached (65, 10, and 20 %, respectively) are strikingly similar to the NYLS numbers of easy, difficult, and slow-to-warm children (60, 15, and 23 %, respectively).

A child with difficult temperament can easily be imagined to respond to the mother's behavior in the Strange situation by acting in a way to earn a resistant label in quality of attachment. Similarly, shy, slow-to-warm babies are likely to act distant or detached in the short period of observation. Thus they are typed as avoidant-attached. And, of course, the easy-temperament child is flexible and accommodating and so would respond with behaviors typing him as securely attached.

Taking Kagan literally, he would seem to be saying that the infant's temperament type is the primary factor in establishing type of attachment. The caregiver's behavior becomes a secondary consideration, allowing parents some relief from bearing the entire burden of attachment outcome.

Can this be? Probably not as cleanly as my presentation implies. There are several immediate problems that Kagan's viewpoint cannot explain. For example, an individual child may form a secure attachment to one adult and an insecure attachment to another. If temperament were *the* driving force this would not be the case. In this example, it would seem that the adult's behavior is primarily responsible for attachment outcome.

Again, we do know that temperament and attachment interact. But they are not the only two variables in the mix. Many other factors will mediate attachment outcome. Difficult-temperament infants are not predetermined to a life of problems. One study found that a difficult temperament led to an insecure attachment when the parenting style was highly controlling. So the temperament alone did not determine attachment; it was mediated (or modified) by parental behavior. Similarly, stressed-out parents who received support were found to then be more likely to promote a secure attachment with their infants. As Alan Sroufe has pointed out, temperament and attachment are linked, but are also part of a larger social context for emotional development.

There is also the good news that parents of difficult-temperament children ultimately form secure attachments when trained in specific ways to deal with their baby's behavior patterns. Although this takes committed, understanding, and patient parenting, not all difficult children form insecure attachments. Let's look at some parent-training efforts designed to maximize the likelihood of a secure attachment pattern.

Lisa Sheeber and Sean McDevitt describe parent-training programs based upon the child's temperament type. Purposes of such training are to "reduce stress in the parent–child" interactions and to have "parental comfort and adjustment" as a specific objective. In other words, they aim to create a goodness of fit. Another outcome is a better-established attachment relationship.

Temperament is a value-neutral entity. A certain temperament type does not make a child positive or negative, or good or bad. For parents, a child's temperament sets the stage for what can be expected to work or not work as you go about rearing him or her. Some characteristics of a temperament type may be risk factors for future problem behaviors or disorders. Other temperament characteristics may help to protect the child from a problem. We'll discuss this more in chapter 8.

Failure to match parenting style and child temperament has been linked to development of behavioral or emotional problems in some children. In part, the experience of stress associated with a "bad fit" between parenting and the child may set the stage for the development of a behavior disorder. If a parent wants to use "plan A" and the child is a "plan B" type, problems will be more likely to transpire.

For example, E. Mavis Hetherington has found that difficult-temperament children are more likely to be targets of parental aggression when the parents are stressed. Similarly, stressed mothers in particular have been shown to be more irritable and withhold affection from difficult-temperament boys. The obvious next conclusion is that a parent under stress with a difficult-temperament child will more likely produce an insecure attachment relationship. Further, such a child is set up for additional behavioral and developmental problems.

Most temperament-focused parent-training programs have two components—an education piece and an intervention plan. Based upon the NYLS goodness-of-fit example, parents are taught to match their child rearing behaviors to fit with their child's temperament characteristics.

Sean McDevitt has reported four types of temperament-based interventions for parents. We will present them in turn, with brief explanations.

1. *Parent education.* A solid introduction to temperament and what it is. These programs are psycho-educational and are extensions of the kinds of information I am presenting here.

2. *Child assessment.* Professional assessment of the child, including observations and concerns that parents may have. This leads to feedback about the child's behavior and tendencies. In these programs, the child's behavior is observed and assessed. The parents can then get a specific report about their child's temperament. This is extended to include likely parenting strategies that will be effective or ineffective.

3. *Environmental intervention.* This segment teaches parents to modify the places where the child actually lives. Such changes can remedy sleep problems, and allow for less stress and schedule changes to match the

child's activity levels. In this intervention, the parent will be asked to make environmental differences shown to be linked to temperament-based problem behaviors.

4. *Parent support groups.* This provides a forum to share trials and tribulations as well as to trade ideas and further everyone's understanding of the three parts above. As stated before, and again throughout this book, support groups are excellent places for help and assistance.

Much research has examined the parenting style–attachment quality link. We know that the majority of insecurely attached children were mistreated or abused, or raised by impaired (often depressed) parents. Parental responsivity and sensitivity remain the best predictors of a secure attachment style.

What if the parent–child fit isn't right? What can be done to help a parent–child attachment that is not secure? Many people have worked to see if attachment quality can be changed from an insecure quality to a secure one.

Phyllis Booth and Terrence Koller have written about one approach that can be employed to restore a secure attachment relationship between parent and child. Using a technique/approach called Theraplay, these authors describe an at-home intervention that relies on the parents' naturally occurring 24/7 involvement in their child's life. Being with their children allows parents to "correct" original patterns of interaction that led to the failed or insecure attachment. This level of intervention would likely be used in the most serious of situations, primarily for children with a reactive attachment disorder.

It is also true that the parent can build up a great deal of negativity. This negativity is expressed in both self-directed and child-directed ways. This is more likely to occur in a situation where a parent has exhausted all efforts and has still "failed." Or it can arise when a child has been damaged, as in the case of reactive attachment disorder. Theraplay, and other intensive interventions of this kind, can serve to reduce the negativity and allow for a restoration of positive interactions. Theraplay is described as "playful, physical, and fun" and is designed "to empower parents...(to continue) the health-promoting interactions" they learn from models in their own homes.

Other work linking parenting and attachment has been done by Nina Koren-Karie in Israel. In a series of reports, Koren-Karie has reviewed the link between parents' memories of attachment issues, as assessed by the Adult Attachment Interview (AAI), and infant attachment measured by the Strange situation. A recent meta-analysis of 18 studies conducted by

Marinus van IJzendoorn found an 80 percent level of agreement between infant classifications of attachment and the attachment classifications of their parents. (A meta-analysis study looks at existing findings from already conducted and reported research and collapses the findings to see what results continue to stand out. In any individual study, one may find any number of effects or influences. In a meta-analysis, one hones in on the conspicuous and truly replicable outcomes.)

Findings of such links between parents' attachment status and infant attachment types have caused researchers to consider how parents might transmit their own internal representations of attachment to their children. In one view, reports Koren-Karie, the thinking of secure parents regarding their own attachment relationships "facilitates their perception and responsiveness towards the attachment needs of their child" (Koren-Karie, 2000). On the other hand, insecure parents may have problems in figuring out their infant's signals of anxiety and distress, "because dealing directly with these feelings is not typical of these parents' behavior" (Koren-Karie, 2000, p. 184).

How are adults' "attachment representations" translated into parental behavior that affects infants? One mechanism involves *reflective functioning*. Reflective functioning is how one uses his personal wishes, beliefs, and value systems in order to make sense of others' behaviors. Koren-Karie believes that these reflective parents are better able to see their children's experiences from the children's point of view.

A new way to assess this parental capacity, having mothers view three videotaped segments of themselves interacting with their children, was used. The mothers were then asked about their children and their own thoughts and feelings. Results showed significant associations between the degree of reflective views of children and the security of their children's attachment. Mothers who displayed a high degree of reflective ability had more securely attached children. Alternatively, mothers who did not had children who displayed more insecure/ambivalent attachment patterns. Let's look at this by adult attachment type.

Parents with *avoidant attachment* patterns can't respond appropriately to negative feelings expressed by their infant. When the infant is in distress, such a parent cannot deal with the child's demand for closeness and comfort. This is because the parent is self-protecting by employing defense mechanisms of withdrawal and devaluation. Therefore, distorting the infant's negativity is needed for the sake of the parent's own emotional well-being. The outcome is that these parents may ignore the infant's signals and distance themselves from the child.

The parent's disregarding of the infant's signals, or refusal to deal with a child's attempts to obtain physical contact and closeness, is distressing for the child. Over time, the child learns to protect himself by avoiding the parent in times of distress. Thus a negative cycle develops between the parent's inability to relate to the entire range of emotion in the infant, and the child's hiding of emotions known to evoke parental rejection.

Parents with *preoccupied attachment* patterns are characterized by preoccupation with their own unresolved childhood conflicts. This causes problems in dealing with the dependency needs of the infant, since these are linked with intense anger and ambivalence. The parent cannot objectively understand the child's needs, as is required to be a sensitive and responsive parent. In addition, this parent may constantly need confirmation that he or she is adequate and needed by the infant. As a result, the parent may consciously or unconsciously seek continual proof that his presence is "indispensable to the infant." This leads to creation of dependent behavior by the infant. The infant learns that to gain his parent's attention he must show how much the parent is needed. At the same time, the infant responds with frustration and anger at the lack of appropriate parental response to his emotional needs. So, in stressful situations, the child's attachment behaviors are accompanied by resistance and anger.

The so-called *autonomous parent* is characterized by emotional balance and full availability to express a range of emotions. These parents are able to "be there" for the infant in a way well-suited to the child's real needs, and not their own. This parent "understands the infant's need to explore the environment and will not interpret these behaviors as rejection on the part of the child."

This parent can also provide the child with appropriate emotional support and nurturance, leading to a secure attachment. Autonomous parents are not perfect, however. Such secure parents are not necessarily warm and affectionate all the time. But their attitude provides the emotional foundation needed for secure attachment.

In the AAI, the individual's style and ability to recount his history are the links and clues one can follow to assess a parent's capacity for sensitive and responsive parenting. Koren-Karie says that findings connecting parental types of caregiving and their reporting of attachment issues are both important.

In Israel, differences were found in the attachment patterns of infants raised by parents in communal versus familial living arrangements even when parental attachment type was constant. A higher percentage of infants raised in communal sleeping arrangements displayed insecure attachment with their mothers. So although mothers in both groups were similar in terms of their level and type of attachment, the home environment affected mother abilities "to fully express" their capacity for sensitive and responsive parenting. It can be concluded that certain environmental circumstances play important roles in attachment outcomes.

Koren-Karie also argues that changes in parents' emotional organization concerning attachment issues can occur through individual therapy. Therapy "can serve as a corrective experience. In such a relationship, the client gains the feelings of security he needs to work through his difficult childhood experiences." Different research findings have supported this view.

In one study 35 of 35 patients were classified as insecure at the outset of therapy, yet 40 percent were rated to be secure upon discharge. Another study described "cases in which a change in mothers' internal representations of the past produced a change in the way they respond to their child." Like the Theraplay model presented earlier, this method of intervention works as well. Targeted at changing the parents' views of their own attachments may allow for a more sensitive, responsive, and appropriate parenting style. This can then allow for providing an appropriate emotional environment for the infant.

What do we know about temperament's role in other child behaviors or characteristics? Well, most researchers agree that various temperament characteristics cause children to be "differentially susceptible" to the way they experience events in their life. From this starting point, it is also generally agreed that problem behaviors in children and teens develop as a result of interactions between temperament and key family variables. These family variables would include parenting style, consistency of discipline, and family stress levels.

In a classic study by Emmy Werner and Ruth Smith, they found that certain at-risk children, offspring of alcoholic parents, made a good adjustment as measured in young adulthood. Another group with the same risk factors did not do as well. What was the difference? Infant temperament as assessed at one year of age! In their study, 58 percent of the infants rated as cuddly and affectionate (easy temperament) made a good adult adjustment years later. Only 14 percent of the other children, with other temperament types, had as good an outcome. This outcome is explained in terms of a variable called *resilience*. Resilience will be discussed more fully in chapter 8.

A recent article by Thomas Wills, James Sandy, Alison Yaeger, and Ori Shinar adds detail to the discussion about family factors and teen substance use as they are shaped by temperament. They examined the role of parent–child conflict levels, family life events, and parental substance use as they impact a preteen or teen's use of alcohol, marijuana, and tobacco products. Temperament of the teen was assessed as a moderator for the above variables. They used two temperament instruments, including one based on Plomin's EAS typology (discussed in chapter 2). So in this study the interaction of parenting variables and temperament was explored.

The Wills group found that temperament is an important influence in a teen's use of illicit substances. Temperament was found to be related to substance use in different ways. As they stated, "...moderation effects (of temperament) may occur through either decreasing or increasing the impact of a risk factor." It was found that temperament did "directly alter the effect of family factors" on early teen substance use. This means that the teen's temperament type was related to and interacted with parental variables (described above) to determine whether a teen used illicit substances. Their analysis, a very complex statistical model, goes on to reveal several findings of note.

First, "positive emotionality" (basically an easy-temperament style) was linked to the "dampening" of adverse reactions by the teen to family conflict levels. As a result, the teen was less likely to begin substance use because his temperament reduced the "risk-prone associations" as a result of being able to modify the otherwise negative consequences associated with family conflict.

Another example of a temperament-parent variable link was also reported. Difficult-temperament teens were found to be more likely to use substances when raised by substance using parents. For both parents who drank and smoked, teens were more likely to follow this example when their temperament was typed as difficult. This was explained as a result of those teens' greater susceptibility to modeling and/or some "exacerbation" of a biological tendency to engage in such behavior. It may be that some difficult-temperament children are more likely to seek alternatives like substance use as a result of how they react to being in a family that itself may have natural "leanings" toward substance effects.

The Wills group goes on to say that only "transactional models" seem to be useful in our understanding of the interplay of all of these variables. Simple, one-dimensional and one-directional models cannot account for the complexities involved. Research that can examine the intricate, dynamic interactions between parental characteristics and teen variables will be the only way to fully grasp what goes on. Along these lines, they raised the question as to what mechanisms might account for the observed effects.

One possibility is that internal child characteristics modify and alter the impact of the parental and family variables. So a child, based upon temperament features, can make his reaction to family stresses and parental behavior better or worse. A second possible explanation is that parental variables may actually alter the teen's temperament and any attendant changes. So it may be the case that parental discipline styles could impact a child's tendencies based upon the fit or lack of fit between parenting and child responsivity.

What else do we know about temperament and its possible moderation effects? Infants with difficult temperaments have been shown to have "more extreme cognitive reactions" to different stressors. Stressors such as noise level, being in crowded situations, or being in a family that did not fit with their temperament led to those infants having more problem responses. Other infant-based research has shown that difficult-temperament babies displayed more extreme behavioral reactions to family stressors. Depending upon the parental response, this can be the start of more and more negativity in the child and the parent–child interaction.

Three-year-olds with "inflexible temperaments" have also been shown to display more behavioral problems when faced with family stressors than those with easier temperaments. A lack of flexibility may be taken to mean a "non-easy" temperament type. Finally, difficult-temperament 7-year-olds who also had parents who were inconsistent with discipline and style developed into teens with greater amounts of psychiatric disorders when assessed at ages 12 and 16.

The interaction between temperament and parenting has been studied in other ways as well. Families that had problems disciplining children of certain temperament characteristics led to the promotion of "externalizing" problems in the children. Externalizing problems are acting-out behaviors. These can include impulsivity, frustration-tolerance problems, and oppositional and defiant behavior.

Parenting variables such as level of support and control behavior have been shown to predict teen antisocial behavior among those subjects with "negative affectivity." Negative affectivity is a pattern consisting of anxiety, anger, irritation, and stress. In these studies, lower levels of support and inconsistent parental discipline interacted with children's temperament to produce this less healthy outcome.

Finally, yet another study found that children with easy temperaments were more likely to show resilient responses in the face of elevated family stress. As one might imagine, the easy-temperament child has the flexibility and adaptability to be in control of his or her emotions. This leads to better coping and an overall more positive adjustment to life's stress.

What can we make of all of these studies? For one, there is a great, complex interaction among the many variables one can measure when looking at child outcome. Although the studies just reviewed have come to the conclusions presented, it is difficult to truly know what other variables were at play as well. My conclusion is this—we have plenty of data to show that temperament interacts with parenting style. It is the importance of this finding that I want you, as an educated parent, to be aware of.

For the educated parent, knowledge of the intricate interplay of your behavior with what your child brings to your family is essential. Beginning with the template of temperament and your parenting approach, the stage will be set for the type of attachment relationship to be formed. It is the association of all three factors of the developmental triad that will play the most important role in how the early years of your child's development will result.

Now let us examine another implication of attachment as presented in recent research—a look at its possible genetic origins. Thomas O'Connor and Carla Croft studied 110 preschool-age pairs of twins. Using the Strange situation protocol, the twins' attachment level type was assessed. Looking just at the secure-insecure dimension, they found a concordance rate of 67 percent. This means that with two out of three twin pairs, knowing one of the twin's attachment security status allowed you to predict the other's. This was found in both identical (monozygotic) and fraternal (dizygotic) pairs. As with many behavioral genetics studies, the O'Connor study was able to determine that although a genetic basis for attachment exists, there are many environmental factors that also influence the outcome.

The idea that any complex phenomenon like attachment could be *solely* genetically or environmentally caused is, of course, ridiculous. In fact many of the differences one finds between siblings are due not only to a slightly different genetic makeup but to differences in how they are raised. Even in the same household, parents treat children differently. This is due to many factors, including the fact that subsequent children are treated in a different way because of greater parental experience. Features of the children involved are also a factor. Parents treat boys differently from girls, oldest children differently from younger, and so on. These differences are called *non-shared influences.*

Non-shared influences are believed to be primarily the result of differences in parenting behavior as described above. However, even in the same house, with the same furniture, the same food, the same everything, individual children will experience these shared features differently. Again these differences are based upon differences in child perceptions and interpretations. These are based upon genetic differences, some of which are temperament related. Other differences are then the result of diverse experiences and activities as lived by the child.

Barry Schneider, Leslie Atkinson, and Christine Tardif have examined the connection between attachment quality and peer relations. Conducting a meta-analysis, the Schneider group assessed attachment quality by the Strange situation and the Attachment Q-set, as reviewed in chapter 2. They measured peer relations by several standard methods including direct observation and parental and teacher behavior ratings. They also looked for any differences that may have been present based upon primary attachment to mothers versus fathers, and the age at which attachment quality was assessed.

It was their conclusion that there is little more to be gained from the past research based on simple correlations of variables. Instead, it is time to move forward to conduct more comprehensive research. Specifically, they proposed that future research focus on both maternal and paternal parenting variables. Examining these variables in relation to the developing child's social capacities will yield important information.

In their study, they found that "child–parent attachment is correlated with peer relations." Better- (securely) attached children have stronger and more complex peer interactions. This translates into better social skills and pro-social behavior. In other words, these children make excellent play partners and friends.

There were not enough data to determine if father versus mother attachments meant different outcomes in peer relation skills. Very few studies measure or even look at children's relationships with their fathers. This is unfortunate, but reflects the mother-based parenting culture we have in the United States. This topic will be explored more in chapter 9.

Further, the attachment quality is likely related to help with peer relations as a result of other products from the securely attached relationship. These would include more reciprocity in play and greater cooperative behavior. Additionally, secure attachments are associated with authoritative parenting styles. The child may benefit from this most adaptive child rearing style, and his greater mental health may lead to better peer relations. Attachment quality was also found to correlate with "nonverbal indicators" of social competence such as sharing and other pro-social behavior.

The phenomenon of scaffolding (as described in chapter 1) applies when discussing the proper match of child temperament and parenting style. For example a slow-to-warm child may require more parental encouragement and perhaps more behind-the-scenes support. By providing this, the parents promote specific social behaviors and efforts to explore more. With slow-to-warm children, parents have to be a little more responsive and sensitive to the child's needs. For some slow-to-warm children, their behavior at home or in very familiar settings will be misleading. In those known situations, they act far more outgoing and confident. However, when placed in the new and unfamiliar, their shy and almost fearful nature quickly surfaces.

An educated parent will be aware of these differences and take steps to assist his or her child's acclimation. There is a fine line to be drawn here as well. Parents must constantly use feedback from others and their own observations to know when to "let go." The risks in not letting go at the right time are twofold. On the one hand, if not properly supported and scaffolded, the slow-to-warm child may become more anxious and learn to act more withdrawn and fearful. Enough of these experiences will inadvertently train a child to be socially delayed.

On the other hand, too much parental influence, a kind of "over-scaffolding," can lead to an overprotected child scenario. Overprotected children become dependent and unable to act autonomously or independently. Dependency thwarts normal psychological growth. Given a bad choice situation, I would advise parents to err on the side of allowing for more independence as in the first situation. One can always work with the child afterward to teach him how to handle a similar situation the next time.

PUTTING THE DEVELOPMENTAL TRIAD TO WORK

So what has the educated parent learned from these two chapters? It is my hope that you are now well aware of the importance of temperament and attachment as child variables that directly impact your parenting behavior. You now also know what the research indicates about parenting styles and how they affect child outcome. I have tried to offer some solid examples of how these three variables interact.

I have also tried to impress upon you the fact that all three legs of the triad are in constant interaction with one another. Temperament affects attachment quality and parenting style. Parenting style impacts upon attachment quality and the fit with child temperament. Attachment quality affects the parent–child interactions and can moderate temperament issues.

Knowing this information can give you an important advantage in planning and carrying out your parenting strategies. Identifying your child's temperament type and working to achieve a secure attachment relationship are the first steps. Establishing a goodness of fit with your parenting behavior is the next piece.

Temperament type will be a stable characteristic of your child. Your attachment quality can interact with your child's temperament to form a solid base for your child's emotional security and responsivity to your parenting. Then the parenting team can overlay a parenting style to maximize the psychological well-being of the child, and ultimately the family. How you discipline, the success of your discipline, what you can expect from your child, and the ease with which he establishes social relations will all derive from the interaction of the triad variables.

Each of your children will present a new mystery to be discovered and learned. Each will have a unique temperament. Each will have a different attachment quality. And each will require a special knowledge of which parenting behaviors fit best. And now it is time to apply this information to your family situation. Please be sure that both parents are aware of your particular child's assets and needs. Parents must work as a team.

We now turn to a discussion of family structure and discipline in the next chapter.

Chapter 4

FAMILY STRUCTURE AND DISCIPLINE

Call them rules or call them limits...they are an expression of loving concern.

—Mister Rogers

One of the most important roles and duties for all parents is that of setting limits and structuring their child's life through a system of incentives, rewards, and punishments. At a higher, more abstract level, this means establishing a home with certain philosophies, attitudes, and values. As was pointed out in the parenting-styles section previously, establishing consistent expectations and delivering sure and certain consequences—both positive and negative—for behavior will lead to desirable behaviors in children and minimize the undesirable ones. Providing external controls and rules in the young child's life allows this child to develop a future internalized set of controls and rules. *In other words, external discipline leads to internal self-control and self-management skills.*

Similarly, in order to establish a structured and consistent home life, a family must be organized in ways to promote this harmony and function. This organization, with certain roles to be filled and carried out, is the basis of what I will term *family structure*. A chaotic, disorganized family structure will lead to all sorts of behavioral problems and general misery for all who live in the home. Good parenting involves the setting up and carrying out of an organized, managed home base. This is the place where your children can feel safe and cared for.

In this chapter, we turn our attention to the topics of family structure, discipline, and punishment. Family structure refers to the parent-authored order and management of the home. Discipline styles are an offshoot of the structure. Punishment is actually a subset of discipline, and we will examine such matters as whether corporal punishment is ever acceptable and the need for a consistent schedule of consequences for behavior. The consistency of consequences leads to predictability and a worldview that is orderly. This in turn provides a sense of stability for your child. In a real world where predictability and order are in decreasing supply, a child with this exposure is better equipped to handle life's uncertainties when he or she becomes a self-determining adult.

FAMILY STRUCTURE DEFINED AND EXPLAINED

Family structure is a prime example of a topic most parenting books will want to cover. However, promoting a single or best view is impossible because the individual needs and circumstances of families are too different for any one-size-fits-all approach. In this section, I will present some concepts known to be effective in leading to a well-managed household, which has the best chance at producing healthy, functional children. These concepts need to be thought about, discussed, and agreed to by both parents. You can then adapt or tailor them to your family situation and gain improvements from which both parents and children will benefit.

I begin with a brief primer on family systems theory (FST). Much of what I will present is related to the work of Salvador Minuchin, a pioneer in FST and founder of a school of therapy called the Structural model. I will go beyond the work of Minuchin, and some of what I will cover is not properly an idea or concept from the Structural model, but from other schools within FST.

Allow me to begin with a review of what systems theories have in common. First, any living system is both complex and organized. With their individual, changing beings, families are very complex in their operation and daily interactions. Each person affects, and is in turn affected by, every other member of a family. These reciprocal influences help to increase the complexity of trying to understand and determine why any one member does what he does. This in part can help a parent comprehend that not everything is easily explained in a linear fashion. That is, one event does not always lead to the next, which in turn leads to the next. Sometimes one event leads to multiple events and each of these plays some role in the behavior you are trying to figure out. In many cases, the actual causal path is circular and/or cyclical. As a result, certain events become both a cause and effect of certain other behaviors. It is this complexity that makes working with families both interesting and exasperating.

As Harry Aponte, a Structural school proponent, has said, "The ability of a family to function well depends upon the degree to which the family structure is well-defined, elaborated, flexible and cohesive" (Aponte & VanDeusen, 1981, p. 315). The strength of families lies in having the capacity to grow and change to meet new challenges and face adversity. When a family structure is no longer effective, it can and should be replaced. If no structure exists to resolve an issue, a new one can be created. Let us now explore some of the characteristics of families from a systems perspective.

FAMILY SYSTEMS THEORY AND CONCEPTS

Some concepts used by systems people are obvious, others are more subtle in their meaning and applicability. First, every family has its own *identity*. A family unit is defined by who its members are and their past and current roles. These roles can be father/husband or wife/mother as well as oldest son/academic star or youngest daughter/best athlete. It is also defined by the histories and ethnicity of the parents, who bring in the pasts of their families of origin. Intergenerational identities are often very strong. Family traditions and rituals are very much part of an identity.

A *family of origin* is defined as the people who raised you, and incorporates your family's past history. For some people, it is their biological extended family; for others it may be a collection of people without biological ties such as in adoption or being raised in a group home. Often families of origin have their own stories and heroes. Your family may have tales of immigrant struggles or of great past hardships that were overcome. These themes are part of the fabric of your family and help to define you and your children.

Families have a degree of *stability* in how they operate. They tend to grow and function in predictable ways with known "rules" that every member follows. Roles become established, and functions and tasks needed to operate the family are filled and performed. This stability is desirable, to the point that families will actively try to avoid change from both inside and outside forces, a process known as *homeostasis*. The downside is that families will resist change even when their behavior patterns are hurtful or dysfunctional. This is why an "outsider" can recognize and offer solutions to a problematic pattern that goes on within someone else's family. That very problematic pattern is often continuing rather than resolving a concern or issue.

At the same time, families must evolve and change, a process termed *morphogenesis*. As we'll see shortly, families have life cycles. As members grow and develop, the needs and tasks of a family change. Members must change to accommodate these new challenges and roles. For instance, a young man first leaves his family of origin, having one set of life goals and needs. When that man marries, his needs and goals are changed to accommodate his new wife, her goals and needs, and now the needs of his new family unit. When a child is born, the man is forced to change again, now to be in the role of father with all of those new responsibilities. For mothers and children, their roles change as well as new siblings are born and as the children develop various skills and abilities over time.

Family members have an *interdependency*. As with reciprocity, family members operate individually and in concert with each other, depending on one another for certain needs. This is a quality that makes a family strong. From this connection we get phrases like "blood is thicker than water." Interdependent family members trust and rely on one another to be there for support.

Another way to look at interdependency is that the within-family qualities of interaction can influence all its systems. So when the marital/parenting couple is doing well, their happiness and love are there for the rest of the family to embrace. Such a couple is more likely to produce a sibling group that is more cooperative, friendly, and functional. However, if the couple is in distress, their problems permeate the family system. These parents may now act more impatiently or harshly with their children. In turn, these children may interact negatively with each other and in other settings like school.

Families have *hierarchies* and *structure*. A hierarchy refers to the established pattern of authority, power, and responsibility. Ideally, parents should be in charge. At times, psychologically, a child may take charge. This violates the natural hierarchy and leads to problems. When would a child be "in charge"? It happens for different reasons, but usually it is when a parent is psychologically unavailable or incapable. So during or after a divorce we may get a scenario in which the child takes on a parental role. There are also times when a chronically ill child is given too much say (and power) as a way for parents to overcompensate for their guilt. These hierarchy issues are also boundary violations as described below.

In terms of structure, *subsystems* exist as a way of further organizing families. The *executive subsystem* is the marital couple/parents who operate and manage the home and its children. Their roles are to establish rules, to be at the top of the hierarchy, and to carry out the functions needed for life—parent their children, work for money, clean, cook, and so on. The *sibling subsystem* represents all of the children. They are below the parents in terms of power and authority. Within the sibling subsystem there can be dominance and a mini-hierarchy based upon birth order, gender, or some special child status.

Boundaries play an important role in families. As Minuchin has said, boundaries "are the rules defining who participates, and how" in a family. There are boundaries within families, and families have boundaries with the outside world. An example of a boundary issue might be the roles regarding sex education. Within the family, the father may teach his sons about sex, while the mother interacts with the daughters. Or it may be decided that both parents will work with each child individually as the children reach a certain point in their development. At the same time, a family has to decide the extent to which school personnel will participate in this task, and also monitor how the culture presents models and information about sexuality. Some families may work hard to monitor their children's exposure to cultural messages by restricting music, TV, and movie access.

Boundary issues are partly about how subsystems and members interact. In some families, boundaries may be too close or overlapping, so that where one person ends and the next begins is uncertain. When two or more members of a family do not have clear and separate boundaries, the result is *enmeshment.* When there is enmeshment, the blurred boundaries prevent individual activity and this leads to a loss of autonomy. The classic enmeshment problem is when a mother gets cold and tells her children to put on a sweater. Over time, such children will not know how to act without their mother, nor will she let them act without her direct permission. This is unhealthy, as children need to explore and master their worlds as individuals. After all, mother can't be everywhere all the time.

The opposite of enmeshment is *disengagement.* Disengagement is a psychological distancing. This pattern flies in the face of interdependency needs. In this scenario, family members have become so independent that they no longer need or rely on each other. An example might be a workaholic parent who is away for 60 hours a week or travels often. The lack of proximity and interaction can evolve into a separate existence, distanced from family life. Disengagement can also lead to family underorganization, especially when it occurs in socially disadvantaged families. Underorganization means that the family lacks an appropriate operating structure or hierarchy, and is functioning individually and not interdependently. Because of the minimal external supports and problems related to financial issues, this underorganization limits a family's ability to cope and respond to family problems.

Day to day and month to month, family subsystems will form *alliances* and *coalitions.* As in real-world politics, these social forces allow members to join together in order to get their way. These are natural social groupings; there is nothing sinister or nefarious about people helping each other. So, all of the girls in a sibling subsystem may come together in order to meet some goal or need, much to the chagrin of the boys. Parents may enter these alliances and coalitions as well, sometimes as a way to settle conflict between themselves. For example, a mother and firstborn son may team together in order to force a father to make some changes.

Alliances and coalitions shift as the needs of the family member change. Structural therapists call these *alignments.* It is not unusual for one person to be aligned on "one side" for one issue and on the "other side" for another. Within families, members work together or in opposition around the many activities and desires they deal with day to day.

For parents, the goal is to stay together and aligned as much as possible. Ideally, the executive subsystem should always be in charge, and the parents should be in constant alliance to achieve what is best for the family and their children. When parents are nonaligned, children and others can exploit their differences. Regular communication between parents can facilitate this executive alignment. This results in clear expectations and rules for the children, who can now follow these guidelines more cooperatively.

Families also engage in other processes and experiences. *Complementarity* refers to the fact that two members of a family often complete each other's strengths and weaknesses. For example, when a more disciplinarian parent marries a more permissive one (as often happens) they can learn from each other to be better and more complete in their individual parental role. A disciplinarian who does not take time to nurture or listen is too one-dimensional to be effective. Similarly, a permissive parent who refuses to make or follow rules will create problems. In the ideal situation, when these two people join together, their individual characteristics will complement each other. Over time, the disciplinarian will act more nurturing and the permissive parent will be more able to discipline. These natural shifts from the extremes to the middle can be a cause of initial conflict, but when worked out lead to a better overall situation.

THE FAMILY LIFE CYCLE

Betty Carter and Monica McGoldrick have described the changes that families make as they grow and evolve—the *family life cycle*. It is a good example and explanation of the morphogenesis concept. Their work has led them to several conclusions. For example, families face their greatest stress levels as they transition from one phase into another. Certainly the homeostasis process would predict this. There are six stages in their model, although others have proposed as few as four or as many as eight. The Carter-McGoldrick stages and developmental tasks are as follows:

Life Cycle Stage	Primary Developmental Tasks
I. Leaving home as a single young adult	1. Differentiate and individuate from your family of origin. 2. Develop intimate peer relationships. 3. Establish financial independence and career path.
II. The new couple: joining two families as a new couple	1. Form a new marital/family system. 2. Realign relationships with extended family and friends to now include the new spouse.
III. Families with young children	1. System adjustments to accommodate children. 2. Alter interactions to now share childrearing, money, and household tasks. 3. Realign relationships with extended family to include new roles: parenting and grandparenting.
IV. Families with adolescents	1. Change/adjust parent–child relationships to allow the teen to move in and out of the family system. 2. Parents focus on mid-life marital and career issues. 3. Begin shift to care for the older generation.
V. Launching children	1. Renegotiate marital system back to a dyad. 2. Develop adult–adult parent–child relationships. 3. Realign relationships to include new in-laws and grandchildren. 4. Deal with losses and death of parents' parents and/or grandparents.

VI. Later life   1. Maintain personal and marital functioning as
                               health declines.
                            2. Support for a more central role of middle
                               generation.
                            3. Support of older generation without overfunction-
                               ing for them.
                            4. Deal with loss of spouse, siblings, and peers. Life
                               review and preparation for death.

Adapted from: Betty Carter & Monica McGoldrick (Eds.). *The Changing Family Life Cycle: A Framework for Family Therapy 2e.* Published by Allyn and Bacon, Boston, MA. Copyright © 1989 by Pearson Education. Reprinted by permission of the publisher.

I believe these stages and their issues are self-explanatory. As can be seen, Carter and McGoldrick have highlighted the major tasks typically faced by most families, usually in a somewhat predictable and orderly progression. For most parents, it is best if stages I and II are completed before the first child arrives. For the purposes of this book, stages III and IV apply.

Stage III has as its first task *system adjustments to accommodate children.* After a child is born, the couple moves from their roles as husband and wife to those of husband/father and wife/mother. These add-on roles lead to a need to be able to alter interactions to now share childrearing, money, and household tasks. This can be quite stressful for many couples that were used to spontaneous getaways or less responsible spending habits. Now the couple has to consider their own needs *and* the needs of the baby. Going off now takes an extra 30 minutes to pack a baby bag with diapers, food, clothes, a stroller, and all of the other gear needed. How money is spent (and earned) is another issue for negotiation. Finally, who will be taking the child for doctor visits or taking time off when the baby is sick?

The final major task to be achieved is the realignment of relationships with extended family. Now *you* are parenting and your parents are grandparenting. Are you open to their advice? Do critical comments cause problems? Is one side of the family becoming too intrusive? Is one set of grandparents off on a major spoiling streak, showering their grandchild with outrageous gifts? Is there a competition between extended families? These and many other new issues are there for the new couple to resolve.

It is essential that you reach agreement on how you will handle these matters, and be there to back up and support each other. Parental pressure on a young parent is a strong force, and many new parents feel insecure in challenging or standing up to their parents. Marital stress is high when a child enters the picture. Individual concerns about being up to the parenting role and its responsibilities are added to the couple's role-adjustment issues. Sometimes, a new parent will embrace the new parental role to the point of forgetting the coexisting role as spouse. This source of marital conflict must be addressed and resolved as a priority.

In stage IV, you face an additional role shift as your child enters adolescence. Your teen will begin to move away from family life and into the world of peers. Middle and high school pressures are tough for teens to cope with. If you have done your job well for the first 12 years, you will reap the rewards with a less stressful teen time. Your teen will be wanting more autonomy, and you need to complete the co-regulation process discussed earlier in chapter 1.

ISSUES RELATED TO TEENAGERS

Trusting their teen to make good decisions may be hard on parents whose first instinct is to continue to protect and shield their now six-foot-tall "baby." Allowing mistakes to happen is also difficult. If you know your teen is about to embark on a wrong course (as long as it is *not* a major life-changing one, like sexual activity/pregnancy or drug use), you have to let him learn by doing. I sometimes refer to this as the "train wreck scenario." You can see it coming, and you have to let it happen anyway so your teen can learn from experience.

The letting go process is usually more difficult on one parent than another. You again have to be strong for each other. You must also let your teen know you are available to talk and help him when he is ready. I am not advocating abandonment here. Recall the comments in the introduction about teen connectivity.

An equally difficult challenge is knowing when to intrude in your teen's life. Especially when you believe that your teen is considering drug or alcohol use, or feeling pressure to engage in sexual activity, parents have every right and obligation to have a good, serious one-on-one talk. This cannot simply be another "don't do it" talk. You need to assert yourself as a parent at this point. Tell your child/teen that your role is to ensure his well-being, and that you will not let him do something known to be harmful.

Try to get your teen to reveal the many pressures he is facing, and his decision process in finding a solution. Talking all about his qualms and concerns will help to relieve some stress. Offering additional options may be very helpful to a teen who may feel that he or she is in a black-and-white situation or simply lacks the life experience to know all of the possibilities.

When having such a discussion, be prepared to answer tough questions. Did *you* smoke marijuana? Why was that okay for you but not for me? Did *you* have sex as a high school student? Did *you* ever skip school and go off to drink beer with friends? In these talks, your behavior is not the issue. Helping your teen make a sound decision is your goal. You can choose to self-disclose whatever information you are comfortable with. Outright lying is not a good course of action. Don't share something you don't want your teen to know, but don't lie. Don't make the discussion about you; make it about your teen and his dilemma.

If you are asked a confronting question, one immediate response might be, "What if I did? How will that information help you in your situation?" If the teen wants to know because of how your response turned out for you, then again you have to decide how much to self-disclose. However, even in that scenario, a discussion based upon consequences is a better direction for that conversation. "So what do you think will happen if you do "A"? What will happen if you do "B"? What will happen if you don't do anything?" Considering all of the possibilities and thinking ahead to likely outcomes teaches your child directly about how to handle the current and other future problem situations.

One final comment for your consideration is this. *No matter what you actually did or did not do as a teen, you can choose to not disclose by telling your teen that your life situation is not open to discussion at this time.* If you must, self-disclose and follow up with your regrets if your behavior was not one you want your child to repeat. Be specific. Tell your child the pressures that led to your choice. Explain fully why you now believe it was a bad choice and why it would be bad for your teen. Then you have to let your teen decide, and let him know that you expect him to do the safe, healthy, proper thing.

Again, if the choice is about sexual behavior, alcohol or drug use, or any other behavior with likely serious life-changing consequences, you need to clearly state to your teen that you do not want him to engage in the behavior. Re-state all of the many reasons why it is a dangerous or wrong alternative, and have your teen repeat it back so you know he "got it." Then your teen will make his or her choice.

Many parents today are either unaware of their teen's needs or unable to engage their teen. This is made more difficult when divorce and remarriage issues are also at play. Teenagers still require strong, solid parenting. It is a very different set of behaviors, but they are just as important as those required for younger children. Somewhere in the U.S. culture, the message to parents has been to let your teen go. Many parents stop their parenting years too soon. I urge you to finish what you started, even if your teen says he or she doesn't need or want your involvement.

Assuming you have lived through your 18 years with most of these issues resolved, you pass into stage V, launching your child into the world, and eventually getting the last child off as well. Dealing with your children as adults is the final transition for parents. It is a rewarding experience.

We next turn to topics that will have made the teen years easier or harder—your discipline and punishment strategies. Remember, discipline is not only important because it creates and maintains order. It is also important as the primary way your child will internalize structure and order into his or her life. The educated parent will discipline effectively because it's good for the child.

DISCIPLINE AND PUNISHMENT

We now turn to a discussion of discipline and punishment. For our purposes, discipline refers to all of the many parental controls and consequences that children must obey and respond to. Discipline refers to your punishment regimen (e.g., time-out or grounding) and your rules, as well as your level of consistent response to both positive and negative behaviors. Punishment is used in two ways. First, it represents a set of negative consequences to inappropriate or undesirable behavior by your child. Second, it is a specific behavioral technique as explained later in this chapter.

Most of the theoretical overview we will discuss here can be found in greater detail in any psychology textbook at the introductory level. It is often found in a chapter that deals with learning. We will make the assumption that most child behaviors (more than 95 %) are learned behaviors. As such they were learned in a certain way, and can be unlearned and/or shaped into ways that are more acceptable or desirable to you as a parent.

BEHAVIOR AND LEARNING THEORIES

Knowledge of basic learning principles are another foundation related to parenting behavior and your child's response. When applied to your child, this application of learning theory is called behavior modification—your establishment of the rewards and punishments in your child's world will significantly shape or modify his or her behavior.

If you are interested in learning more details, please pursue additional reading or take a psychology class at a local community college or university. Trust me that there is so much to know in the details of this body of work that I cannot possibly begin to present it in a single chapter on parenting-related issues.

When most people think about learning, they may recall the terms classical conditioning, operant conditioning, or modeling/social learning. These are the labels for the three major theoretical explanations for all behavior according to the *Behavioral school.* Most American psychology has been influenced by these approaches to understanding behavior.

Allow me to highlight a sample of terms you may have heard about, and apply them to your parenting behavior. Let us begin with a discussion of negative reinforcement and punishment.

If a child has to emit or perform a certain behavior to *remove or avoid* a noxious event, that is called negative reinforcement. An example would be a mom who nags her son to pick up his socks. The behavior the mom seeks to increase is sock picking up. The negative reinforcement is the nagging behavior. It is noxious or negative to the son. To terminate the nagging, he has to pick up his socks. By nagging (presenting a noxious stimulus), the mom is training her son to pick up his socks (an increase in desired behavior) in order to terminate the nagging or to avoid it in the future.

Please note that both positive and negative reinforcement *increase behavior.* Many people confuse negative reinforcement with punishment; all reinforcements increase behavior while punishment is used to decrease behavior.

Just because an adult perceives a consequence to be negative does not always mean that a child will too. Take the proverbial child in need of adult attention. *After trying a number of behaviors, some acceptable and some unacceptable, the child might learn that a surefire way to get that attention is to engage in undesirable activities.* The adult attention through lecturing and other seemingly noxious (to be avoided) behavior is actually a *wanted* outcome for the child. So the child's negative behavior is actually *increased* to get the adult attention, even if it is seemingly negative or noxious! Similarly, candy and money aren't always a positive or desirable consequence for some children when using a positive reinforcement strategy.

Punishment is a consequence to a behavior that *decreases* the activity. If a child is playing with a dangerous object and you hit his hand, the child associates the playing with the object and an aversive, pain-causing response from you. Over time, the child will learn that playing with that object leads to a painful and undesirable consequence—a slap to the hand, perhaps more. Note how and why consistency is crucial here. If the punishment comes too late, the child will not know which behavior he is being punished for. Note also that if you punish sometimes and not others, the child will be confused or uncertain about whether playing with the dangerous object is a good or bad thing for him (and his hand).

Effective versus Ineffective Punishment Strategies

It is also important to note that punishment alone leaves the child in a behavioral vacuum. If his behavior has been punished he learns what *not to do,* but doesn't necessarily know what *to do.* So for punishment to be effective, it must be delivered very close in time to the activity you want to decrease, it must be done consistently, and you need to present an alternative acceptable behavior, which can then be positively reinforced. This paragraph is the simplest summary of punishment I could write. If you completely understand this information, you now have a powerful tool you can use for all 18 years of your child rearing.

How much punishment is required to decrease or eliminate a behavior? This is a good question. The adage "let the punishment fit the crime" can sometimes work here. Some people also call this approach the use of *natural consequences.* If a child decides to hit and punch a dog (undesirable behavior to be decreased or eliminated), the dog may bark loudly or snap, scaring the child into ceasing and desisting the aggression. Assuming the dog always acts this way in response to being hit, the dog used an effective, natural punishment that was delivered in a timely way and was consistent. The only thing the dog didn't do was to *explicitly* provide an alternative, acceptable behavior. One could argue that properly playing with the dog would be the alternative, acceptable behavior that follows. So the child is positively reinforced by the dog wagging its tail or otherwise providing pleasure to the child.

If a child breaks something by playing with it abusively, the outcome is loss of access to the object, another natural consequence *if it is not immediately replaced* by an adult or other person. In fact, throwing away the broken toy with a verbal explanation of the causal relationship ("I told you not to play with the toy that way. Now it is broken and we have to throw it away. If you played with it the right way, you would still have it.") is probably an appropriate natural consequence. After several of these episodes, most children will get the picture and modify their behavior.

In general, the amount of punishment should be enough to decrease or eliminate the undesirable behavior without causing a general withdrawal from all other behavior. If you severely beat a child for any and all unwanted behavior, you will soon have a child who does nothing for fear of another beating. A child who wants to experiment with an electrical wall outlet needs a punishment strong enough to deter such dangerous behavior. So a slap to the hand followed by removal from the situation and a strong "no" would be the least necessary response.

Similarly, a child who decides to ignore your request to stop playing and put away his toys can as a consequence receive a mild spanking followed by a cleanup, a taking away of the toys in question, or a time-out followed by cleanup. Note that in the first and third option, there is a negative (punishing) consequence along with a corrective behavior (cleaning up). In the second option, the child's negative consequence is loss of the toys for a specified period. We would want to include the picking up of toys component so the child learns the expected behavior—a decrease in noncompliance to the parent by picking up the toys (or, alternatively, compliance with the parental request).

Another example of a natural consequence would be if a child bullies another child with whom he normally plays. Over time, the bullying behavior will lead to loss of the friend. In this case the punishment is loss of contact and peer time, which, had the bullying child stopped (decreased his behavior), the peer contact would have continued with less (decreased) bullying.

What has the bully learned? Unfortunately, it could be multiple things, bringing up another aspect about linking behavior and outcomes. One would hope the bully learned that bullying behavior was unacceptable, and so now does less bullying. However, the bully could have also learned that if he wants more alone time, this negative behavior is a way to get it. He may also learn about *discrimination* behavior.

In this use of the term discrimination, we refer to the ability to make distinctions. The bully may have learned that there are some kids you can bully and others you cannot. The bully could have learned to become selective about whom he can bully. He may also have learned how to identify new victims and avoid confrontations with those who will not be bullied. Whew! This can get very complicated very quickly. We cannot always know all of the variables that are in play and which consequences are interpreted in what manner.

I offer this example and insight to make the point that learning about this information, which can seem at first pretty straightforward and somewhat simple, is going to lead to many more questions and possibilities as you apply it to your effective parenting. However, it *is* the basis of parenting behavior designed to control and guide children.

Allow me to switch now to a brief discussion of social learning theory as it applies to your parenting. Note that social learning theory argues that children are natural observers and imitators. So let this be a direct warning to parents about *their* behavior as a model, and the behavior they allow their children to observe. If you act in a cynical manner, if you smoke cigarettes, if you curse regularly, expect your child to do as you do. If you think you can act one way and tell your child to act differently, then you are not paying attention here. If you want your child to read, read books in front of him. If you want your child to act politely and in a well-mannered fashion, then act this way yourself. If you are a TV-watching, overweight, sedentary couch potato, your child will be more likely to become a next-generation spud. If you let your child watch R-rated movies, expect R-rated language and behavior. If you let your child hang out with children whose behaviors are questionable, expect the same questionable behavior from your child.

More seriously, if you are raising your child(ren) in an abusive or violent home, you are inadvertently, but actively modeling such an arrangement for their futures. This is especially true for sons who observe a hostile, violent, misogynistic father as he mistreats his wife (and the son's mother) in dangerous and inappropriate ways. Research has shown that these sons are at-risk for replicating this pattern of behavior if they are allowed to remain exposed over their young lives. Over time, the son may learn to mistreat his mother in the same way. So a mother who wants to break the cycle of violence and mistreatment and is looking for a reason beyond the obvious one of personal protection and safety should leave for the sake of her son and any future relationship he may have, as well as any relationship she may have with her son.

A Summary

Classical conditioning, operant conditioning, and social learning theory are the best ways to describe and understand the naturally occurring processes that seem to be responsible for behavior. And they are practical ways to teach educated parents specific skills they can use to raise responsible children.

It is now up to you to review some popular parenting discipline methodologies and approaches of your choosing. Many are available. See if they meet the test of promoting child rearing in a sound theoretical grounding. I will not offer any specific information about discipline strategies other than to urge you and your co-parent to choose one that fits your style. Many books and programs exist for your sampling. I urge you to do your own research and see how these models fit in with your views of discipline. And remember, taking a college course about learning and behavior will help you in many ways and many situations.

Your assignment as a parenting team is to find a program that reflects your values and attitudes as educated, child rearing adults. As long as you both understand how it works and agree to use the system as a team, your children will benefit. Remember that consistency and predictability will help your children. Let us now review some information on corporal punishment.

CORPORAL PUNISHMENT—TO SPANK OR NOT TO SPANK

Viktor Brenner and Robert Fox have studied effects of corporal punishment on young children (under age six). They were looking for validation of a model by Gerald Patterson. His model of antisocial behavior development in children specifically connects inconsistent or overuse of discipline as a first step in a downward spiraling sequence that leads to an antisocial teen. Overuse of discipline means that the predominant parent–child interaction quality is related to negative consequences, including physical punishment. In other words, the child is subjected to constant negative feedback and negative outcomes, and begins to see most of his behavior as punishable.

Brenner and Fox hypothesized that parents who use more frequent punishment would actually see and report more problem behaviors in their children. If, as Patterson suggests, parental overuse of punishment is a specific causal factor in developing behavior problems, then discipline-related problems would "be expected to be a strong predictor of behavior problems even after other factors related to child behavior problems are statistically controlled" (Brenner & Fox, 1998, p. 251).

Brenner and Fox wondered about authoritarian parenting. (Authoritative parenting is not in question.) They hypothesized that "when parents show fewer nurturing behaviors and have lower developmental expectations, their children will exhibit more behavior problems" (Brenner et al., p. 252). For instance, children could be more likely to seek negative attention when parents showed fewer nurturing behaviors. Or children may have more opportunities to act out when parents have lower developmental expectations or do not enforce consistent discipline.

Sure enough, Brenner and Fox found evidence for just those outcomes. For the educated parent, the message is loud and clear. Let us now take up the topic of corporal punishment, or spanking.

Years of research have clearly demonstrated that spanking children often leads to negative long-term consequences. The more negative outcomes are associated with more frequent and severe spanking. These results include later antisocial behavior and attitudes. Excessive use of physical punishments have been linked to adult social and psychological problems and specific problems like depression and anger/aggression management issues. Other research has shown that children who are spanked learn that it is acceptable to inflict pain on others since it has been done to them. It has also been found that children who are spanked are more likely to engage in subsequent aggressive and inappropriate behavior after their punishment. This sets up a negative cycle, as they are then more likely to be spanked again and so on.

Despite these well-known findings, many parents still spank or rely on "the belt" or a "switch." Parents in the southern United States are more likely to spank than in other regions. Younger parents tend to spank more than older ones. Parents who were spanked as children are more likely to spank when it is their turn to parent. Across the United States, 72 percent of parents of 2- to 4-year-olds and 94 percent of parents of 3- to 4-year-olds spank, dropping to 43 percent for parents of 9- to 12-year-olds and 14 percent for parents of 13- to 17-year-olds. Fully two-thirds of all parents use spanking or some other form of corporal punishment. In national surveys, societal trends have shown that whereas 94 percent approved of corporal punishment in 1968, 68 percent approved in 1994.

Many people believe that spanking is more useful with younger children whose verbal and thinking skills are more limited. They are more likely to remember and learn from physical discipline. As children gain competencies, spanking is less effective and less needed since so many other discipline strategies work without inflicting physical pain.

An interesting study on the issue of where parents learn information about spanking was recently written by Wendy Walsh. She also examined whether and how local community attitudes affected the decision to use spanking. Walsh found that more mothers trusted and relied on advice from professional people and parenting books than from family or friends. Interestingly, *hearing roughly the same message,* spanking versus nonspanking parents had different interpretations of what they heard.

From pediatricians' advice, 6.5 percent of spanking parents thought their doctors recommended spanking, while 28.6 percent perceived the doctor to oppose spanking. Fifty-five percent of nonspanking mothers thought their pediatricians were neutral on the subject, whereas 45 percent perceived opposition. After reviewing eight different sources of parenting information (most of which opposed corporal punishment), many of the mothers who spanked heard that it was okay. Nonspanking mothers heard that they should avoid spanking.

What does this mean? It could be that people tend to seek out and remember information that is more in line with their beliefs and attitudes. It could also be the case that many professionals are not clear enough in their messages to parents. I hope that my message is clear—spanking younger children (under age five) can be one of a number of effective discipline strategies. Other means can and should be used along with a spanking. With older children there is much less to gain and more to lose through physical forms of discipline. I do not recommend physical punishment for children six or older. *And if you choose to spank any child, it is your obligation to do it in a manner that is not abusive or damaging.*

An interesting overview and summary of the corporal punishment debate was published in the journal *Pediatrics* in 1996. Across two articles, a point-counterpoint debate played out, with Robert Larzelere concluding that "there were not enough quality studies that document detrimental outcomes of nonabusive physical punishment to support advice or policies against this age-old parental practice" (p. 828). On the other hand, Murray Straus concluded that "so many different studies, using such a variety of methods, almost always show that corporal punishment is related to violence and other anti-social behavior" (p. 842). Regarding the methodological weaknesses argument, Straus maintained that the current situation was like the smoking–lung cancer research connection. Enough cumulative evidence has been assembled, he argued, to make the case between spanking and future violent behavior.

As Diana Baumrind has stated, parents need a full repertoire of varied discipline strategies and techniques. These methods can be applied as needed and can be based upon the situation and important characteristics of the child such as age, cognitive level, and temperament. Parents must employ common sense when choosing to spank. They should never spank because they are angry—this leads to abuse rather than punishment.

If one is to use corporal punishment, I believe that spanking is better than use of a paddle, leather belt, or switch. In part, use of your hand allows for some immediate feedback as to the severity of the punishment. Using other objects does not allow for any subjective assessment of how hard your child is being hit. This can lead to too much error and "accidental abuse." (There is no accidental abuse—whether your intention was there or not, abuse is abuse.)

A Child's View of Spanking

Some researchers have chosen to examine discipline and punishment from the child's perspective. Martin Hoffman looked at how parents' discipline choices affect the moral development of their children. He compared three broadly defined discipline approaches. They were as follows:

Love Withdrawal—a parent withholds attention, affection, and/or approval

Power Assertion—a parent uses physical restraints, spanking, and/or removal of privileges

Induction—a parent explains why a behavior is unacceptable or wrong and emphasizes consequences and corrective behaviors

Hoffman found that the induction method was the best method if your goal was to raise a morally mature adult. In short, a child disciplined with inductive methods is learning not only what not to do, but also why it is wrong and how it affects others. Further, a parent who tells a child what to do to atone for the misdeeds and gives guidance for the future helps to properly form the child's still developing moral standards.

So what do children think? Michael Siegal and Jan Cowen surveyed children age 4 to 18. The children were asked to listen to five different child misbehavior scenarios. They were then asked to choose from four different parenting discipline responses. The choices included an induction strategy, physical punishment, a love withdrawal response, and "permissive nonintervention," or basically no parental response.

Siegal and Cowen found children preferred an induction strategy, followed by physical punishment. The love withdrawal and permissive responses were not chosen by any age group. Four- to nine-year-olds specifically stated that the permissive response was "wrong" or "very wrong." So children, even young children, really do know that parental discipline is necessary and important.

This chapter has a lot of important and complex information. This is probably a good time to put down this book and reflect upon and review the information in the first four chapters. If you feel confused, it means that you are like everyone else who has read these chapters for the first time. The educated parent will stop, reflect, re-read, discuss, and seek out other information to help to digest and understand what is important for him or her. Don't worry; you will "get" what you need to know to be a good parent.

Chapter 5

PARENTS AS TEACHERS: PARENTING INFLUENCES ON EDUCATION

> Parents have become so convinced that educators know what is best for their children that they forget that they themselves are really the experts.
>
> —Marian Wright Edelman

You may have heard that parents are a child's first teachers. This is absolutely true. But the cliché too often seems to suggest that other teachers will follow and then parents are off the hook. In this chapter, I will show you why you will always be an important teacher to your child, and how what you do or do not do will influence your child's level of academic achievement.

Professional educators—schoolteachers—will be the other significant source of influence on your child's level of educational achievement. The influence of teachers is actually reciprocal and to some extent dependent on what your child brings to the classroom. Within the first month of school, most teachers have formed an impression and a level of expectation about your child. By then, they will have noted who comes to school regularly, who is prepared, who has the appropriate materials, who does homework on time and neatly, and whose behavior is learning-friendly. These same teachers also form impressions based upon other information such as your child's previous year's grades and test scores, and his or her family background and the family's level of involvement.

TEACHER EXPECTATION AND SCHOOL PERFORMANCE

Robert Rosenthal and Lenore Jacobsen were among the first to document whether these preconceptions and prejudgments influenced a child's final level of academic success at year's end. In their classic study, the authors told certain teachers that specific (named) students, who were actually chosen randomly, were "intellectual bloomers." By this the authors implied that the children named were to achieve at higher than average levels. IQ tests were given to these selected children and others (for control and comparison purposes). At the end of the school year, the selected students previously identified (who were actually no different in ability at the outset) showed significantly greater improvements in IQ and achievement scores than their fellow students. These same "bloomers" outscored their classmates on reading tests and were rated by their teachers as having more curiosity and interest in learning.

What happened? The teachers, by virtue of the advance (though false) information, formed a higher set of expectations for the select group—they set up a self-fulfilling hypothesis. These students were supposedly brighter and were thus treated differently. The differential treatment was received in such a way that the children lived up to the teachers' expectation. Such students received more effective feedback. They were praised more when they were right, and got more of a break when they were wrong. The teachers actually wound up reinforcing positive work and attitudes, and providing more attention, to the members of the select group. The other children were given less attention and encouragement for their good performance, and their year-end scores reflected this decreased teacher attention.

Although there has been criticism of this study (including questions about the ethics of such a design) and the "Pygmalion effect," as it is known, other similar research has confirmed the key finding, that teacher expectation directly translates into matched performance. First impressions really do matter. Other interesting research has looked at teacher expectation of children in relation to temperament type.

Mary Rothbart and Laura Jones have reviewed the temperament literature and have offered suggestions for applications to education. They have recommended that teacher-education programs focus on the ways that a child's temperament can affect in-school behavior and performance. In their words, temperament variables "have an important influence on how students are viewed and treated by their teachers" (Rothbart & Jones, 1998, p. 480). By having teachers attuned to temperament characteristics, the teacher can apply a goodness-of-fit approach to match teaching methods with student strengths.

One example of how this approach would apply is that teachers can shift focus from "negative attributions" of misbehavior to "active problem-solving." In making this shift, Rothbart and Jones predict that conflict can be reduced and more positive student responses emerge. Suffice it to say that such an approach would be beneficial for both teacher and student, and there is hope that it will be adopted.

Clearly, establishing a good relationship with your child's teachers is a good thing. Bruce Hammond from parentsoup.com, a teacher himself, has written about some commonsense things you can do. These include making your first, and subsequent, interactions with the teacher positive. If you are friendly and supportive of the teacher, the teacher will more likely be supportive of you and your student.

Why are some teachers seemingly overly sensitive and defensive? Hammond reminds us that "teaching is an intensely personal job—teachers are people who are paid to care about the thoughts and feelings of others." Most teachers are in the profession out of passion and a desire to make a difference in the lives of children. Clearly they don't do it for the money. As a result, some teachers have more ego invested, and this leads to taking criticisms personally. Be sensitive to this and your interactions with teachers will be more productive for your child. And that is the point, isn't it?

CHILD MOTIVATION AND PERSISTENCE

What determines how motivated your child will be in school? A number of factors have been examined, and clearly this answer represents another complex interplay of individual, family, and school-based variables. On an individual level, your child's self-esteem and level of self-efficacy are important factors. A child who is convinced that he cannot do math is halfway to failure before the math class starts. Some research has typed children into two categories based upon their responses to challenging schoolwork—mastery-oriented children and helpless children. *Mastery-oriented children* have self-efficacy, the belief in themselves that they have the ability to be successful. Mastery-oriented children have learning goals. They are concerned with learning the material and improving skills. They are not so concerned about judging or being judged by others on their ability. Even when they are not successful, mastery-oriented children believe they will do better next time.

So-called *helpless children* tend to give up quickly when faced with a challenging or difficult task. They are easily frustrated and are quick to self-blame and self-judge negatively. These helpless children are often not different in ability, as determined by test scores. So their differences in success rates are not caused by their ability or lack thereof. They are different in terms of persistence and self-confidence. The helpless child is concerned with performance goals rather than learning goals. By this I mean that they are concerned about looking good to outside evaluators (teachers or parents or coaches), about getting rated positively by others, and by avoiding negative ratings.

When it comes to experiencing failure, the real differences between these two groups comes to light. Mastery-oriented children often believe that they need to work harder or learn a little more and will then be successful. Their self-efficacy allows them to persist and to try harder to learn what it was they lacked to be successful. Helpless children believe that the failure experience means that they lack ability and thus give up on a hopeless (to them) activity. These helpless children lack an inner motivation to persist because their self-doubt and fear of looking bad to others interferes with any desire to try again.

So how do you raise a mastery-oriented child? Well, it actually starts with a secure attachment. Securely attached children will incorporate a sense of security into their explorations, knowing that a parent is behind them. So all of the things we have reviewed on building a secure attachment relationship are the first step. This base will be the foundation for self-efficacy and self-esteem.

Next you want to be sure that your child is allowed to continue to grow and explore the world with supports—scaffolding. In ensuring that your child has the needed tools and opportunities to learn on his own, you ensure that your child will use his natural curiosity and drive. As a child learns and experiments, he or she will gain positive experiences that will build a sense of self-efficacy and a good self-concept. These successes will build upon one another. If your child has a failure or other negative experience, a gentle intervention on your part can turn the negative into a positive. This is done by the parent's explanation to the child of what happened and further feedback about how to be more successful on the next go-around. By showing your child explicitly that it is okay to fail within the context of a good effort, the child will perceive the failure in a less personal way. It is important to then reinforce and encourage a subsequent effort. Again, this next effort needs to be rewarded with feedback from you.

If the outcome of the next try is successful, that will be its own reward. If more difficulties are encountered, you need to determine what the problem is. If your child is simply not able to do the task, it is time to redirect your child to tasks that can be tackled. If there is some skill or technique missing, you can help your child to identify the missing piece and then see how to get it. By repeatedly giving help, advice, and feedback (after your child's try or tries are unsuccessful), your child will learn what it takes to become successful.

A third way to encourage mastery-oriented development is through modeling. When you are working on projects or tasks, allow your child to be part of your work. By actually living a mastery-oriented approach, your child will be exposed to your efforts and your reactions as you encounter success and failure. By sharing your strategies and showing your child an example of perseverance and persistence, your child will learn a great deal about how to handle various situations. Also, by tying in an adult situation that your child is aware of with a situation that your child is dealing with, you and your child can discuss ways to deal with frustration. Too few children are directly taught these invaluable lessons.

PARENTAL BEHAVIOR AND EDUCATIONAL ACHIEVEMENT

As we have already seen, parents play an important role in setting up academic achievement and success. Let's look at several studies that have specifically noted where proper parenting support was lacking. We can draw some conclusions not only from what works but also from what seems to be a problem.

Examining the parenting behaviors of underachieving eleventh- and twelfth-graders in middle-class families, Kaaren Metcalf and Eugene Gaier found that four patterns were associated with poorer performance. Parents who expressed more conflict at home over child rearing and family rules failed to provide a consistent message to their children, resulting in poorer school performance. Parents' behavior that was indifferent or neglectful also was correlated with negative school outcomes. These parents set few or no limits and were uninvolved with their teen's schoolwork.

Similarly, overprotective parents who were rigid, domineering, and perfection-driven did their teens little good. Here it is as if the child/teen was not allowed the freedom to make mistakes or become responsible for his or her learning. Finally, parents who were labeled as "upward striving" also had a negative outcome. These parents were found to be very critical, nagged their teens, and pressured their adolescent to get good marks without other supportive behavior. It is interesting that these patterns mirror the Baumrind parenting styles and outcomes to a great extent.

Another remarkable area of research has to do with the interplay between social class, ethnicity, and parental involvement. Parents who have gone beyond a high school education are found to be more involved with their infants and children than those who did not finish high school. These involvement differences yielded differences in measured IQ when the children were four years old. Most researchers believe that the difference found in parental involvement is stress-related, and not a sign of any lack of caring or concern for their child's development. Many less educated parents simply have more unmanaged stress in their lives, and this stress interferes with their ability and opportunity to interact with their child. When these stressed-out parents do interact, it is more often to discipline than to engage in other positive (to the child) behaviors. You then get a downward spiral of fewer positive or nondiscipline-related interactions, and the infant/child gets less parental attention or avoids the parent and his or her negative attention.

Regarding ethnic differences, Asian American families are noted for their strong support for their children's educational achievement. The child is raised in an atmosphere of high academic expectation, and the parents demand elevated performance outcomes. These children seemingly do well in school in part to please their parents. These same parents also appear to monitor schoolwork more closely than other ethnic groups, and reward good reports, also resulting in more successful academic outcomes.

What can we learn from the parents who are successful in getting their children to achieve at high levels in school? In general, any parent who provides a warm, supportive home environment that supports exploration and self-directed, autonomous behavior will greatly increase the chances of having an academically successful child. Emotional and verbal responsivity on the parents' part is another basic requirement for fostering academic success.

Responsivity in this context means that the parent is engaged and attuned to the child's needs. Responding when a child is in distress (perhaps frustrated by a tough math problem) lessens his stress and teaches coping and self-confidence. Verbal responsivity, or engaging your children in conversation and encouraging them to express themselves, is also important. It is one of the keys to language development, which in turn fuels cognitive development. Better language skills are always associated with higher IQ scores and higher academic achievement levels. These language skills are of course also related to reading.

Parents who serve as models and read often in front of their children encourage reading. As important as the parental modeling is, the benefit gained by children who are read to frequently is also essential. A parent should begin reading to a child as soon as possible, even during late pregnancy. Studies have shown that in utero, children learn to recognize their mother's voice and the patterns of her voice. Pre-born infants whose pregnant mothers read Dr. Seuss books in the two months before birth actually recalled the patterns of the rhyme in testing when they were infants.

Books also provide interesting visual stimuli to infants, which forms the basis for future interest in books and reading. Keeping a child in age-appropriate books is one of the best investments any parent or grandparent can make.

SPECIAL ISSUES RELATED TO YOUR CHILD'S EDUCATION

The question of whether a child needs to be taking special medications to allow him to be able to stay focused and on-task is a special issue for parents. For the treatment of children with properly diagnosed attention deficit hyperactivity disorder (ADHD), the option of taking the drug methylphenidate (brand name Ritalin) should be considered. Much research and hysteria in the media and among some parents has made this issue somewhat volatile. Allow me to wade through the confusion and offer some clarification.

For some children, it has been clearly shown that Ritalin (and other mild stimulant medications) can be a very effective adjunct with other methods and techniques, which together can help a child to focus more, stay on-task longer, and become less impulsive. The fact that medications are often improperly prescribed should not interfere with the reality that they can be a useful, relatively safe way to help improve a child's ability to become successful in classroom settings. These stimulant medications don't actually calm a child down, as was once thought (the "paradoxical effect"). Instead they allow a person to concentrate better and reduce his or her level of distractibility.

Downsides of the medication include some rare but serious side effects, as well as some likelihood of appetite suppression. The appetite suppression can become a problem in a child with an already high metabolic rate or who is a picky eater. In very long-term use, some children have actually matured to adults of a shorter stature as a result. There is also a danger of stimulant-induced neurological damage when a child is misdiagnosed, and actually has a different disorder such as Tourette's syndrome.

In my opinion, the key to helping children with school behavioral problems involves two important processes—accurate diagnosis and proper multilevel treatment. The issue of diagnostics is not as clear-cut as many believe. Among psychologists and pediatricians there is disagreement about what tests should be done, and what variables need to be considered. It is my opinion that only a diagnostic evaluation that is multi-method and multi-measure can lead to an accurate assessment.

Often a child's behavior may have ADHD features, but the real problem is not ADHD. The only way to rule out other factors such as stress and anxiety, family problems, or a medical issue such as Tourette's syndrome as a causal agent is to assess a child in both home and school contexts using various individual measures. One wants to assess attention, concentration, distractibility, anxiety, cognitive factors, and use behavioral rating scales. Once all of this information is gathered and analyzed, then a psychologist can begin to make a proper diagnosis. But this is only half the work.

Once a somewhat accurate diagnosis has been made, then the issue of treatment and interventions must be decided. In my opinion, a treatment package involving parental training, teacher inclusion, child training in cognitive-behavioral approaches, and a double-blind medication trial is the best option. Let's review these one at a time. Parent training would involve a psycho-educational program of information about ADHD and a specific behavior-management plan that both parents become trained in. The goal here is to provide external consistency and structure for the child who lacks internal controls.

In a sense, ADHD can be viewed as a lack of internal control by a child. Whether the lack is due to permissive child rearing or a biological cause doesn't really matter. By establishing and promoting external controls, a child can change his or her behavior and internalize some control. The external controls are structure and consistency from the environment. At home, this means a rule system with consequences that is enforced consistently by both parents. By raising an ADHD child in a consistent environment, the child will quickly learn how to act more appropriately. A similar consistency will be needed at school as well.

Teacher inclusion is therefore also critical. When possible, the teacher will need to assist with completion of behavior rating forms, communicate regularly with the parents, and be apprised of the behavior-management tools the parents are using. The ideal situation would allow the teacher to also use the same management vocabulary and consequences. An example might be a token economy–style reward system for on-task behavior that is used both at home and in school.

A token economy is a behavioral management system that rewards a child with tokens for appropriate behaviors. The same token economy also punishes a child by taking away the tokens when he or she exhibits inappropriate or unwanted behavior. At the end of each week (or every other day), the child can trade in these tokens for some desired reward. Rewards can be favorite foods, books, video games, or even parental one-on-one time. Token economies are powerful motivation systems but must be established correctly to work over time.

Next, the child will need to learn how to control his behavior and to improve his level of concentration. Cognitive-behavioral approaches have the best empirical support in helping children to master their behavior. These approaches are taught and practiced in either individual or group settings with parental inclusion in the training, since the parents will actually help the child to identify when to use the techniques and to be sure they are done correctly. The child learns to identify when his behavior is inappropriate and how to self-monitor for this. The child next learns to stop the inappropriate behavior and to substitute an appropriate one. The last step usually involves feedback and self-acknowledgment for success or to try another strategy to become successful.

Finally, if a child truly has ADHD, a double-blind medication trial should be offered. In a double-blind trial neither the child nor the behavior evaluators (parents and teachers) know when the child is on the medication or when he is taking a placebo. When I did these in my private practice, I had a relationship with a large pediatrics practice. Any child whose parent or teacher wanted a Ritalin trial, and when the pediatrician supported the idea, was referred to me.

To conduct the trial, I had an area pharmacist who would make up seven independent prescriptions, one for each week of the trial. The pharmacist would crush the Ritalin and put it in a capsule, just as he did the placebo. This way neither the child nor the parent could tell what "pill" was being taken that week. At the end of each week, the parents and teachers completed a behavior rating form and turned it in. Parents and teachers could not refer back to previous weeks—each week's rating had to be independent and based upon the behavior observed over the past seven days.

Only the pharmacist, the pediatrician, and I knew which weeks were placebo and which were active medication. (These were randomly determined in advance by me by coin toss, with the only rule being that no less than two or more than five weeks would actually have the Ritalin.) At the end of seven weeks, I could analyze the behavior ratings and compare the scores to the weeks on or off medication. If a real pattern of improvement was observed, the child was recommended for six or more months of drug treatment (along with other interventions). If the results indicated no difference in behavior control, then the child was not given the unneeded medication.

In making sure that your child is properly diagnosed and then suitably helped, you can make a real difference in assisting your child and giving him the best supports to be academically successful. Do not accept a poor assessment or everything else will be suspect. A simple teacher observation is insufficient, as is a quickie single doctor visit. Also, give the option of drug treatment a fair look. Why make an already difficult situation (attaining self-control and reducing distractibility) harder than it has to be (without drug assistance)? For children who do benefit from drug therapy, the improvements are faster and greater. And also know that children will be re-evaluated periodically to determine if the drug used is still making a difference. If not, the drug is discontinued.

A second important special issue is that of disabilities. Children may be negatively affected in their ability to be academically successful as a result of a number of conditions or situations. The grand categories include intellectual/cognitive; emotional/psychiatric; behavioral; and physical. ADHD is actually considered one of the behavioral disabilities.

It is not easy to learn that your child has a problem serious enough to interfere with his success, and likely to be long-term, if not permanent, in nature. Sometimes an immediate reaction includes denial and guilt. Neither of these normal responses will be helpful to your child, however, and you need to move past these as quickly as you can.

IMPROVING THE SYSTEM

How can the American education system be improved? In my opinion, any chance for improvement is directly in the hands of the parents of the children who are to be educated. First, parents must take back their responsibility in the role of educating their children. Parents must set the expectations and provide supportive home environments. Second, parents must keep a loud voice and a forceful say in the decisions made by school boards and state legislatures. If parents cry loud enough (and follow up with their votes), school boards and state lawmakers will get the message and make appropriate changes in financial and other support.

As this brief summary of education-based research has shown, parental involvement and expectations are the first and most important variables that can be bettered. Once our families become less stressed and more oriented toward and able to support achievement, we will have taken a giant step forward in helping all children. Programs that strengthen families, especially those that support parenting behavior in the context of functional marital systems, will allow the adults to then fully support and be involved in their child/teen's school lives. From here we have a chance for real improvement.

After remedying the family front (a surely formidable task), the U.S. education system can be further improved by continuing to increase the amount and level of involvement of parents and family members. Regular appearances and involvement of parents in the classroom speaks volumes about the importance of education to impressionable children. Parental reinforcement and support of teacher authority and classroom discipline will help to restore order that has slipped away in some settings. Parent-teacher conferences every six weeks for 15 minutes are just not enough feedback to make a difference in academic performance. Standing teacher invitations to parents to take part in checking daily homework and ensuring that it is done seriously will surely pay off if heeded.

Lowering the average class size, especially in kindergarten through third grades, is also an important way to instill good early educational experiences. A child needs enough teacher attention to be noticed for his successes. Similarly, it is unfair to expect a single teacher to be sensitive and responsive to 28–30 six-year-olds, each with competing needs and differing ability levels.

Strengthening curricula and raising standards in grading and graduation requirements is the next step. Those who would continue to lower or weaken standards in the name of whatever cause are selling out our weaker students and further widening any education gaps that exist already. Demanding and expecting more will lead to more achievement; anything less will lead to a continued loss of potential in our children.

Alternative school calendars that eliminate 9- to 12-week summer breaks and utilize the entire year more effectively could also help the most needy students stay on track and maintain their progress. Although data are still being collected and analyzed, initial reports suggest that some children might benefit from year-round schooling compared to the traditional calendar and its longer breaks. (Please refer to the Palmer & Bemis article cited in the bibliography for an extensive review of 64 published reports.)

Developmentally appropriate practice (DAP) is the term given to schooling that recognizes and respects that children need to be taught within the parameters of their developmental abilities, with acknowledgment of individual differences. For preschoolers, this means there is more hands-on, concrete instruction, often within the context of games (like play—make it fun) and enactments, also called dramatic play. Recommendations from the National Association for the Education of Young Children cover all aspects of early child education, from curriculum to teacher training to specific developmental emphases.

A few examples that contrast this DAP to more inappropriate practices are in order here. First, DAP goals are sensitive to individual differences in dissimilar children's growth and ability levels. There would be no additional pressure placed on a child who is not ready or lacks the motor skills to successfully complete a certain activity. Similarly, group norms and specific achievement levels are given much less weight in a placement using DAP than in one using inappropriate practices.

A DAP approach also provides growth opportunities in all developmental areas, from the physical to the cognitive to language and social needs. Emphasizing the interrelatedness of development more accurately captures the ability and needs of any child at any time. A DAP education also makes learning fun, giving students an important first impression of how positive school and learning can be. Children in other placements may actually be turned off to school, and this can lead to burnout and noncompliance problems by the third grade.

Does today's child have to have a "formal" preschool preparation? Research reviewed by David Elkind suggests a sound "no." Parents who spend time with their children, who provide resources and proper learning experiences, and who provide ample time for play will likely have their child just as prepared for kindergarten as the child who started in a program for three-year-olds. If a mother or father reads regularly to a child, follows the child's lead with respect to wanting to learn to read and write, goes off on regular trips to the local zoo or playground, and allows for some drawing and other creative expression, the child will be ready for school. Preschool attendance is a good idea if there is a need for more socializing opportunities or if parents recognize that they cannot provide the time and energy needed to do the activities listed above.

Here is an interesting factoid. Danish children do not begin formal education until age seven, and this comes after a preparation of language experience-based education. In France, formal reading instruction begins at age five. Denmark has a 98 percent literacy rate; 30 percent of French children have some sort of reading problem.

HOMESCHOOLING

Is homeschooling right for a child? If you look at who is winning national spelling and geography bees, it would seem so. However, this is a complex issue. A 1999 survey by the National Institute on Student Achievement, Curriculum and Assessment found that the number of reported homeschooled children had tripled between 1990 and 1991 and between 1995 and 1996! Ten percent of all non–public schooled children are taught at home. The estimate for the United States in 1999–2000 was that one million children were homeschooled.

What are your reasons for wanting to homeschool? If it is to protect your child from exposure to a poor education system, you might want to work to improve that system. Protection from "bad kids" or "bad teachers" seems to be a good reason, but I am not so sure. Your child will have to live in a world where one cannot choose all of the people with whom one will associate. At what point do you let your child have the exposure and experiences with all sorts of other people in order to learn how to get along? The longer one is shielded, the more a child falls behind in the normal socialization process. The future catch-up may be harder and more painful than any gain made by having been isolated earlier.

Variables and Issues to Consider

A variety of support and other resources for homeschooling are now available, and quite frankly, a rather large business has quickly grown to provide parents with the tools they need to teach at home. When considering the homeschooling option, there is much to bear in mind. What can and will you do differently than could be accomplished by placement in a public or private school setting? What will you realistically be able to do with your child? How will you structure the days and weeks to be sure that there is the right balance of educational emphasis without going overboard and having burnout, or going too easy and allowing your child to fall behind? How will your relationship be affected by 24/7 involvement and interaction with your child? Will you act differently when you are "mom" or "dad" versus when you are "teacher"? Or will your interactions with your child be "seamless" as you act in the roles of both parent and educator with little distinction made, or noticed, by your child?

Mary Jo Bratton, on her *Backwoods Home Magazine* Web site, suggests that you first write out your reasons for homeschooling and the educational goals you wish to achieve in each subject area. She suggests, up front, that you consider carefully and answer questions such as these:

- Why do you want to teach your own children?
- Do you want to ensure your child's religious training or academic achievement?
- Do you want to ensure your child's individuality, or assure yourself of a continuance of family and ethnic traditions?

You will need to establish educational goals that should focus on some product or outcomes. What do you want your child to be able to do as a result of having been taught the material you will present? How will what you do be different from what could be achieved in a typical school placement?

You need to create a list of specific and measurable educational objectives. You can do this on a subject by subject basis, and relate your goals to those of your local school district. (You will need to contact your local school district to find out about any regulations, grade- or age-specific learning goals, or in-home testing requirements that may be in force.)

You may also want to consider imparting other important values and attitudes needed for success in life. These could include determination and resolve, intellectual curiosity and a commitment to lifelong learning, an appreciation of the aesthetic qualities in the arts and music, and an awareness and tolerance of similarities and differences of peoples of the world. How will you accomplish this? How will you know if you are on the right track?

Homeschooling goals should be sensitive to the needs of the whole child and include physical fitness and good mental health as areas of emphasis as well. A final point involves your knowing your child's strengths and weaknesses. As with the goodness-of-fit model between parent and child temperament, a parent needs to carefully assess whether the parent–child dyad will be able to work together well, and whether your child's education needs are best served by homeschooling.

And let us look at all of the social dimensions of regular school attendance versus homeschooling. Are there substitute experiences for learning to deal with bullies or how to handle gossip? Who will the child associate and play with on a regular basis? Who will attend your child's birthday parties and how many parties will your child get invited to? What benefits are there to group affiliations like being part of a marching band or a service club or a school athletic team? Is it important for a child/teen to work on a school yearbook or go to a prom?

Surely, many of the above activities can have alternate adventures provided for by concerned parents, but they will require more planning and

effort than when these experiences are naturally acquired in a school setting. And what if your child is shy or has some social phobia? Not having
to face this attribute and learning to cope and adjust in more limited settings rather than the world at large will have its price.

There has been research on the social consequences of homeschooling.
Larry Shyers has compared the social adjustment levels between home-
and traditionally schooled students. Shyers measured the self-esteem of a
homeschooled group of children and compared those results with those of
a traditionally schooled group, all between the ages of 8 and 10. On the
Piers-Harris Children's Self-Concept Scale, a widely used measure of
child self-esteem, no difference was found between the two groups.

Shyers also examined how homeschooled children treat other children.
He found no significant differences between his groups in scores on the
Children's Assertive Behavior Scale. Direct observation by trained
observers did reveal that homeschooled children had significantly fewer
problem behaviors, as measured by the Child Observation Checklist's
Direct Observation Form, than traditionally schooled children when playing in mixed groups of children from both kinds of schooling back-
grounds. Shyers believes that amounts and quality of contact with adults,
rather than interactions with other children, is a more important influence
in developing social skills. So on this score, homeschooling with its higher
level of adult interaction, may lead to better child outcomes in the social
arena.

Other reports have found similar conclusions, all showing little or no
differences on social dimensions between home- and traditionally
schooled children. Look for more research findings to be reported as the
trend toward homeschooling continues its growth.

There is a rather big business, growing bigger each year, to help parents
who choose homeschooling. One can purchase curricula, textbooks, other
learning materials, and even teaching and child-management tips. What's
best for you and your child? I would recommend that if you are going to
homeschool, you do some research on Piagetian approaches to education.

Jean Piaget was a prominent child-development theorist who focused
his life's work on the issue of cognitive development. From Piaget's well-
researched theory, David Elkind and others have proposed some general
principles based on Piagetian concepts that can be applied to enhancing a
child's education experience. First, Piaget believed that children learn
about everything by virtue of their personal, hands-on experiences in the
world, a concept called *constructivism.* Only active teaching approaches
would be recommended, with your child being self-directed to explore and

discover, to debate and to reflect rather than to sit quietly and be lectured at by a parent-teacher. So this approach would require that you allow your child to drive his or her own education within the right supports (another example of scaffolding).

Second, Piaget believed that the best teachers were true facilitators of learning. A good teacher, he argued, knows how to observe a child and knows when to ask questions to stimulate further discovery and learning. How would one know whether and what a child is learning? What feedback would be used to help construct such a child's educational environment? Piagetian-trained educators would make use of a portfolio assessment system with multiple measures that go well beyond a collection of test scores, as would be accumulated in a typical public school education. No matter what, it would be essential to monitor progress and maintain a portfolio of samples of work (like completed fraction problems or a book report or a completed work of art). Portfolios demonstrate the attainment of a specific learning goal with examples, and are a great way to determine how your child is progressing. That's why the goals you establish up front need to be measurable, and need to have some stated criterion for success or mastery. Otherwise, how will you know if your child has mastered them?

From these direct observations of your child as a learner, and the portfolio of achievement, the Piagetian parent-educator would set up a "classroom" with activities and game-like tasks that naturally build upon what is already known. Piagetian-based education also would encourage and promote the child's own curiosity, and this would be the motivation for further learning. Here the learning facilitator (you) would again play an important role in providing the necessary resources to allow the child to take an active lead in pursuing further studies about the world and everything in it. Such resources might include regular trips to the public library or monitored time on the Internet.

So a homeschooling, Piagetian-based parent-educator could really provide a qualitatively different environment for learning and exploration that would be right for the right child. But would your homeschooling Piagetian-based experience be significantly better or different from a specialized private-type school environment? Certain schools, such as Montessori-based education centers, would provide much of the same. Further, these private schools would also come with trained educators and a wealth of already established resources that you as a parent would find hard to match.

Ultimately the choice is yours. I urge caution and a great deal of parental homework and research in advance of making the decision to homeschool.

PARENTING BEHAVIORS IN SUPPORT OF EDUCATION

The properly concerned and involved parent should examine this checklist and see what can be done or what can be done better to improve his or her child's academic performance. If some of this looks unrealistic, it may be because you can't imagine making the time for all that could be done. But please don't be swept up in the wave of underinvolved parents and lower your standards. If you don't have the time, try to make it happen anyway. Recall that children see and understand what is important through behavior, not words. If you are serious about your child's education, the more of this you do, the more you will see positive results.

1. Talk with your child *every day* about what happened in school, even if the talk is limited to the time you are traveling home together or the first few minutes when you arrive home. This daily report keeps you informed and allows your child a chance to review and consolidate his day's activities. It also demonstrates that you are involved and care about school. As your child grows into adolescence, it will be easier to talk about school if there have been years of practice beforehand. For teens, a weekly "what's up?" is probably sufficient.

2. Ask specifically about homework. Parents need to know what was assigned and how long the homework will take. Being helpful and supportive of your child's efforts will make your child more likely to complete the homework with a more positive attitude. Your interest and praise for homework behavior will make this undesired work easier for your child.

3. Check the homework when it is finished. Is it done fully and neatly? Briefly discuss what was learned by doing the homework. You may be pleasantly surprised at what is being taught and learned. (If you believe the work is simply busy work or too much for your child, discuss this with the teacher and not your child.)

4. Reinforce your child's appropriate and learning-oriented behavior. Verbal praise and encouragement go a long way. You do not have to give money or food treats; in fact these may not work in the long run.

5. Buy and read books—for yourself and your child. Although you may prefer the classics for your child, any appropriate-level reading material is good. Letting your child choose the material makes it more likely that he or she will read it and want to read more. If your child is into sports, sports books and magazines are fine.

6. See if your child's teacher is available on-line, through e-mail, or has a time he or she will accept phone calls. Contact the teacher to get an indi-

vidual report on your child's status and progress every three weeks or so. It is better to be hearing/reading frequent good news than to be called out of the blue to hear bad news. If the teacher thinks this is too much contact, he or she will let you know.

Although your teen "will just die" to learn that you are in regular contact with the teacher, reassure him that the reports are positive (when they are) and that you are doing your parental duty even if no one else is. Then ignore his protests about your overinvolvement.

7. Be supportive of nonscholastic school-related interests as well. A complete education also involves the social dimension. Facilitation of club and sports participation is important, especially with teens. Helping out on field trips or in-class projects with kindergartners through sixth-graders can be rewarding for parent and child.

8. Involvement in PTA or PTSO groups, as well as parent-teacher school-improvement teams, is another way to demonstrate your commitment to your child's education and its importance to you. This level of involvement allows you the chance to be influential in your child's education on a grander scale.

9. Turn the TV off. TV viewing time robs your child of time better spent on reading or physical activity. Limiting TV and video game time is a challenge for many parents, but to the extent you fail on this point, you are allowing the potential for greater school (and other) problems. A child who knows there is a limit to the TV watching will not be so upset if further limits need to be set as a child who has not had limits.

An "e-publication" written by H. Wallace Goddard and Carmel Parker White, both at Auburn University when their Web site was written, also provides helpful advice. The key to their suggested activities is to make learning fun and interesting. Their work is so complete that I urge you to visit their Internet site. Their valuable suggestions are especially intended for the young learner at the beginning of their school experience (or even before formal schooling), but most of the ideas can be adapted to just about any age.

They offer concrete and easy-to-do activities organized in several broad areas, including making your home a learning place; planning family learning activities; ways to adapt to the needs of your children; and ways to work with other people who will help your children learn and develop. (The site address is found in the bibliography.)

Another Web-based resource (listed in the bibliography) is a summary of a conference report from Parenthood in America, held at the University of Wisconsin in 1998. Ben Benson's presentation focused on six suggestions that can improve performance in both teachers and students. These included: provision of both physical and psychological support; serving as a positive role model; teaching a lifelong learning approach; teaching organization and time management skills; encouragement of child exploration and chance-taking; and teaching children to accept responsibility for their performance and behavior.

Do as many of these things as you can, and you and your child will be the better for them. Educated parents raise educated children. Lifelong learning begins in the home.

Chapter 6

PARENTING AND CO-PARENTING ISSUES RELATED TO DIVORCE

Divorce is more than the *coup de grace* of a stressful marriage.
It is a new beginning that offers people second chances.
—Judith S. Wallerstein

For this chapter, I have altered my format of presenting the research data in detail and then offering guidelines for the best parenting choices. Co-parenting after divorce is an area in which I spent over 10 years in direct, daily service and I believe that the following information will be truly helpful to divorced parents and their children. As so many marriages with children do end, the need for a parenting book to devote a chapter on this topic is obvious. The following is a summary of the information I presented when teaching court-mandated, post-divorce co-parenting classes in Tampa, Florida, in the early 1990s.

Among the references and resources I used to create the course (listed in the bibliography) were publications by the Association of Family Conciliation Courts, which are readily available, a number of good books on divorce and its effects, and my 15 years of experience working with families who faced some of the darkest and most confusing days of their lives.

For your further reading, sections on "divorce effects" in most child and developmental psychology textbooks have excellent summaries of the research database, which as you can imagine is huge. In addition to its size, there is also a lot of conflicting information; some studies' findings are at odds with other studies'. Two popular books by Judith Wallerstein have interesting information. Wallerstein generally believes that divorce effects go on through adulthood for most children, and that divorce is a life-changing, generally negative event for children. More recently (2001), E. Mavis Hetherington, another well-respected, longtime researcher in the area of divorce effects, published her book, *For Better or For Worse.* Hetherington reported that 75 percent of the children she followed eventually were functioning as well as children from non-divorce homes. Who's right? They both are. What you get depends on what you are looking for and how you are looking for it.

Another important book that I found to have essential information is called *Caught in the Middle.* Written by Carla Garrity and Mitchell Baris, who have worked in Colorado in the Denver and Boulder areas, this book explores ways to protect children in the worst-case scenario—extended family conflict at high levels. The one finding all researchers can agree upon is that extended family conflict, without exception, harms children. That is why you have heard it is better to get divorced than to stay (fighting) together for the children. But even this is true *only if* you end the fighting.

RIGHTS AND OBLIGATIONS OF THE PARENTS AFTER DIVORCE

In some states, such as Florida, the legislature has adopted statutes that attempt to keep both parents involved in their children's lives after divorce. Florida calls its policy "shared parental responsibility." Shared parental responsibility (SPR) means a court-ordered relationship in which both parents retain full parental rights and responsibilities with respect to their child and in which both parents confer with each other so that major decisions affecting the welfare of the child will be determined jointly. From the Florida statute itself:

> It is the public policy of this state to assure that each minor child has frequent and continuing contact with both parents after the parents separate or the marriage of the parties is dissolved and to encourage parents to share the rights and responsibilities of childrearing.

Shared parental responsibility designates one parent as the primary residential parent (the one with whom the child spends the majority of time). As the primary residential parent, it is your obligation, duty, and responsibility to facilitate the relationship of your child(ren) with the other parent. "Facilitate" does not mean you have to make the child(ren) do anything, but it does mean that you cannot interfere with or get in the way of contact and interaction with the other parent. Ideally, it means both parents should show and demand respect for each other, and cooperate for the sake and well-being of their children.

The primary residential parent (PRP), by virtue of spending more time with the child and providing the child's legal address, will receive information related to the child that needs to be shared with the other parent. When parents fail to share such information it hurts the child, because access to it can be used by the nonresidential parent as well to develop his or her relationship with the child. And it causes resentment in the excluded parent, who may feel purposefully excluded and devalued as a result.

As the nonresidential parent, it is your obligation and responsibility to fulfill the agreed upon visitation schedule, to stay involved in your child's life, and to remain influential. If there is a child support obligation, it must be paid. If the child support amount becomes unfair or burdensome, you must petition the court for a modification—you cannot just stop paying or start paying less.

The PRP should make copies of the following and get them to the non-PRP parent as soon as possible (by U.S. mail, e-mail/fax, or hand-delivery—but *never by or through the child(ren)*): report cards; school registration information; announcements of plays, fairs, recitals, PTA meetings, bake sales, math/science projects, conference dates, school days off/half-days.

When and if the schools need to place your child for special services (e.g., gifted class or learning disability help), there should be a joint decision. This requires notification and coordination of school conferences for both parents.

Outside of school, the PRP should make copies of the following and get them to the nonresidential parent as soon as possible (never by or through the child(ren)): sign-ups for baseball, soccer, and so on; information about coaching opportunities; practice and game schedules; sign-ups for Scouts, clubs, etc.; car pool schedules; and any other special events (e.g., fund-raisers).

Both parents should be directly in contact about: prescriptions (dosages, refills), all doctor appointments (alternate if possible), medical bills (coordinate insurance, co-pays); optional services (e.g., braces).

PARENTAL ALIENATION BEHAVIOR AND ITS CONSEQUENCES

Among his many important contributions to the field of families of divorce is Richard Gardner's description and identification of what is known as Parental Alienation Syndrome (PAS). PAS is the opposite of the cooperative co-parenting model just presented. Found by Gardner to be a factor in 90 percent of families where there are extended custody battles, PAS is defined as "a disturbance in which children are preoccupied with deprecation and criticism of a parent—denigration that is unjustified and/or exaggerated" (Gardner, 1989, p. 226). PAS is more than just "brainwashing." It is a systematic process involving both conscious and unconscious factors by the "programming parent" that ultimately creates *within the child* (without further parental aid) an obsession to maintain his/her bond with the programming parent at the price of selling out the other parent.

Using psychodynamic interpretations, Gardner details the processes that not only parents but also children undergo in this alienation activity. In terms of the child, Gardner believes that PAS children never stop loving the alienated parent; in fact they maintain a twisted connection through their continued thinking of them through all of the ways that they "hate" that person and often, their extended family as well. One of the surest symptoms of PAS is the child's "complete lack of ambivalence." The "hated" parent is all bad all the time and the "loved" parent is all good and can do no wrong. These poor children are guilt ridden and caught in the worst possible loyalty conflict.

For the programming or alienating parent, Gardner states that a combination of brainwashing and unconscious forces is at play. The unconscious processes are the more insidious and even give the alienating parent "cover" as he or she is really not aware of how these behaviors and attitudes are subtly but surely poisoning the child's relationship with the other parent. One powerful way this plays out is when the alienating parent insists on taking a neutral stance, thus empowering the poor child to make decisions about visitation, but with full knowledge that the child is aware that the alienating parent opposes the contact. Another way alienation works is through inducing guilt in the child, allowing the child to feel bad by visiting the one parent since the child will leave the other parent all alone and abandoned.

Let me finish this section by saying that there is some degree of alienating behavior between practically every parent dyad during and immediately after a divorce. This normal negativity will eventually subside as the parties make their adjustments and move on with their lives. It is when the alienation behavior is raised to a very high level, fueled by conflict and anger, that a child becomes endangered by his or her parents. When PAS is "successful" everyone—each parent and the child—is a loser in the long run.

SURVIVING DIVORCE AS AN ADULT

To a great extent, the way that each parent copes with his or her separation and divorce is a predictor of how well the child(ren) will adjust. If a parent is seen as weak, depressed, and out of control, this scares the child(ren), who is looking to the parent to maintain the family and take care of him properly. In some cases, a child may become "parentified" and take over parenting of younger siblings and serve as a source of support for his or her grieving parent. This is quite harmful for the parentified child and needs to be avoided.

If a parent is seen as coping and adjusting, making progress toward establishing a new family system and schedule, this is a great source of comfort to the child(ren) who is looking for a regaining of security and stability, which was shaken at the separation.

In any event, it is your obligation, as the parent, to look out for yourself during the separation and divorce process. If you need help, get it. Ask family, friends, and others for support and access to resources. If you cannot adjust in a timely manner, you may require the services of individual or group therapy. By all means use these resources for yourself and your family.

Stages of Loss/Acceptance

Mental health professionals are in agreement that all humans respond to loss, whether it be by death or divorce, in a predictable way called stages. Both adults and children go through a similar process of trying to understand and accept what has happened.

The stages of loss and the eventual acceptance of your fate are:

Denial—At first, we can't believe that the divorce is a reality and that it is happening to us.

Anger—After reality sinks in (visit to attorney, served with papers) we begin to feel angry about the divorce happening, especially if we "did not see it coming" or did not want this outcome.

Bargaining—Some attempts at reconciling or working out some arrangement may be tried next.

Depression—The mental stress and exhaustion that we develop from trying to fight off the inevitable leads to a full body response—depression. This can become very serious and, if so, needs professional attention to overcome quickly.

Acceptance—We finally understand and make sense of what has happened. We can then learn our lessons from the experience and move on.

It is as if we must pass through this sequence of levels of understanding in order to put our losses in perspective. From this, we can grow and go on to live a fuller life. We must also complete our emotional response.

How to Grieve, How to Grow

The process of bereavement is the final *emotional* response to our loss. A four-stage process has been identified, modified for divorce as follows:

Shock—At first, we are numb to all of the events involved in the divorce process, and are in shock.

Longing—Emotionally, we wish for the good old times, before the events and behaviors that led to the divorce. This may also be a time when reconciliation thoughts are entertained.

Depression (despair, anger, confusion)—As in the stages of acceptance above, we become emotionally aroused with a jumble of competing emotions as we continue to cope.

Recovery—Finally, we again put our loss into a meaningful perspective and are able to move on emotionally with our lives as an adult and as a parent.

Again, it is the responsibility of the parent to seek help and support from other adults and resources, but *not* from the child(ren), as he or she copes. It is okay to cry in front of your child(ren) as long as you reassure him and show him that your sadness does not interfere with your ability to care for him.

HELPING CHILDREN ADJUST AND COPE WITH DIVORCE

A parent who is on the right track in his or her own adjustment will be more likely to be able to identify and respond to a child(ren)'s needs during this often scary time. Children are quick to give out signals about their status and what they need; however, these signs may be indirect and need translation. The following four areas are usually necessary in helping children adapt more quickly to divorce.

Listening to your child's questions/comments. A child's questions/comments are often asked/stated to elicit a response on two levels. At the surface, the question is a simple one. At a deeper level, there is an expression of concern about an area that the child is unsure of. Here are some samples and their possible deeper meanings:

"Are you going to be late to get me?" OR "Why were you so late to pick me up?" (asked quite angrily). These questions may also be about abandonment fears—will you leave me like dad/mom?

"I don't want anything for my birthday." OR "We don't have to stop at McDonald's today." These comments, especially from a child who used to want those activities may reflect concern about the family finances. Your child is ready to make his/her share of financial sacrifice, but is also worried.

"I'm not going to school and you can't make me." This can be indicative of a child having school difficulties and/or a child who believes there is a need to stay home to protect a parent.

Staying open to your child's needs. Once the child's concerns have been identified, see what you can do to reassure or otherwise settle your child's worries. Encourage him to talk with you whenever he has questions or worries. Try to make time to be just with him, without competing activities. Be prepared to seek outside resources such as therapy, support groups for kids, and time with the school guidance counselor.

Making new traditions and rituals. One sure way to let children see that you are moving ahead as a new family unit is to introduce new ways of doing family things like celebrations, holidays, birthdays, and so on. If you used to spend time with each family of origin at Christmas, the child will now need to adjust to alternating holidays. Start up any new ritual and then let this become the new family tradition for that part of the family. For example, you might read "The Night Before Christmas" on Christmas Eve before putting your child to bed. Or you might set aside an afternoon for Christmas cookie baking and eating and do this yearly. You might switch from fake to real Christmas trees, and you might go off as a family and cut down your own fresh tree. The list is endless. You should encourage your child(ren) to come up with ideas as well and then decide as a family what would be best.

Keeping in touch with the ex–in-laws. The ex–in-laws remain relatives to your child(ren) after the divorce. The usual amount of contact prior to the separation/divorce will be a predictor for what level of involvement is expected and needed by your child(ren). Another major variable in this area is the quality of your relationship prior to the marital problems. Some in-laws insist on keeping a relationship, despite their blood relative's disapproval of such continuing contact; others will cut you out of their photos.

Again, the rule here is what is best for your child(ren). If your children are used to regular and frequent contact with their cousins and other relatives, there should be an honest attempt to keep some of that involvement alive. The same holds for aunts, uncles, and especially grandparents who, in many states, have legal rights of access to their grandchildren. This includes some flexibility with respect to changing visit times to accommodate the "other family's" celebrations. At all times, respect must be shown for these people. Your child(ren) will be the beneficiary of this goodness even if it tears you up inside.

GUIDELINES FOR SUCCESSFUL, TROUBLE-FREE VISITATIONS

Visitations may be one of the most troublesome aspects of post-divorce family adjustment. The nonresidential parent already feels bad—if the residential decision was hotly contested, that person "lost"; if agreed upon, that person has to deal with feelings of being second best or less than equal as a parent. This can also be an opportunity for the PRP to "rub it in" or express feelings of superiority. This should be avoided if you want peace. Consider the following:

Keep open interparental communication. One of the keys to successful visits is that parents are flexible and understanding with respect to potential changes in pick-up times or dates. This requires respectful interparental communication. There should be a minimum need for such talk, but it is inevitable that there will be a need. Take the high road; keep the conversation limited to the topic and do not rehash old complaints.

Make visits positive. For the nonresidential parent, there is the question of what to do during the limited time you have together. It is best if the visit has a positive quality, especially at the beginning. But it is also important to avoid becoming a "Disney parent" who always provides a vacation on each visit. This is unrealistic, too expensive, and will alter your image in your child(ren)'s eyes. Similarly, a weekend visit routine that is all work and no play should be avoided.

Children should wherever possible have rules, a schedule, discipline, and a set bedtime routine on visits. Outings such as going to the mall, a park, or other family event are always acceptable. Discipline must be enforced, even if it causes unpleasant moments on the visit.

Prepare children for visits. It is the obligation of each parent to have the child(ren) ready for transition times. You must be aware of the time so that you can have your child(ren) clean, dressed, and packed (if necessary). The issue of clothing needs to be worked out. Some families keep separate wardrobes; others send clothes each way. Similarly, toys and games need to be selected for safekeeping at each home. Some families have duplicate favorite games, others have certain games at their house as another way to remind everyone that there are now two separate households. If a child is involved in sports, their uniforms and equipment must be forwarded or duplicated. At first, there will be a need to be patient, as some items are likely to be forgotten at one house or the other. Children should not have the additional pressure of being blamed or yelled at for these mistakes.

Maintain frequency and predictability of visits. A fixed, routine schedule is *absolutely necessary* for children under 8 to 10 years of age. The predictability of regular contact serves to give a sense of normalcy to post-divorce life. It is most important to keep your work/life schedule constant as a means of giving security and stability to your child. When changes must be made, make them with as much warning as possible and with a full explanation to your child. Make-up time may or may not be possible. Predictability is important—even if your visit schedule is one day per month.

As a rule, the younger the child the more frequent the visits (although for shorter duration) is best. For teens, it is best to allow them a say in the schedule. You must be flexible to work around their needs for jobs, friends, school, and other teen activities. As a parent, you may feel slighted if your teen chooses to be with friends. This is normal and needs to be respected. Feel free to talk with your teen about how you might spend more time together *and* allow him his teen activities and time with friends.

Although it is essential to keep your agreed upon schedule, there will be times when a change must be made. Work demands, other life events (e.g., illness), and other extraordinary situations can lead to unavailability for keeping the schedule. Flexibility is best accomplished through a history of open communication and with as much notice given as possible.

Visitation Don'ts

There are several visitation issues that spark much conflict in families that fight. *Avoiding conflict is the goal of all responsible parents.* Again, act reasonably and as if you were in the other parent's shoes, and most problems will never happen. Three common issues are reviewed:

Checking on the other parent. Visits are not reconnaissance missions for spying children. It is harmful, inappropriate, and wrong to use your child to find out about activities at the other household. If your child brings up some event or activity, polite listening without questions is the best response. If you hear about some unsavory activity or situation, discussion with the other parent must be delicately handled. Avoiding a defensive response will limit conflict and more likely get you information. Threats or name-calling or calls to your state's child services unit are sure to fuel conflict. Unfounded calls to your state's child services unit are also unlawful and can seriously backfire on you.

If you have concerns about your ex's new boy/girlfriend, talk directly with your ex. Expect to be told it's none of your business (because it usually isn't). If you have concerns about lifestyle issues, discuss these with the other parent without placing the child in the middle, possibly with a trusted third party. These differences may need to be mediated.

Interfering with visits. Some parents fuel discontent, which leads to a disruption in the quality and quantity of visits. It is fairly easy to plant worry or fear of a visit in your child. You can easily cause much grief for the other parent. However, this comes at a cost to your child. More hurt will come to the child than to the other parent. Parental alienation behavior, if proven, will cause a PRP to lose residency or a nonresidential parent to have supervised, more limited visits.

Parents should work together to make transitions and visits with the other parent pleasant and positive. Wishing the child well and acting civilly toward the other parent at transitions makes your child feel more secure.

Another way to (negatively) influence a visit is to let the child know about what they will be missing by being with the other parent. If you are going to some theme park or on a trip, keep a low profile to avoid mixed feelings in your child.

Being on time—what is "on time"? This issue leads to as much sustained conflict as any other. If the visit schedule says pick-up at five P.M., what is late, early, or on time? The general rule is to allow a 15-minute window (allowing for traffic or other likely problems) to be on time. Therefore, 4:45 to 5:15 is "on time." A parent who comes very early for pick-up or to bring a child back from a visit, does so at his or her own risk of waiting. If the change has not been called in and confirmed, it is wrong to come more than 15 minutes early.

If you know you will be late, or some event you are attending is too good to leave, it is appropriate to call to see if the time out can be extended. The other parent is under no obligation to agree—be prepared to leave if necessary. If you know you will be late, if at all possible, call to report your new ETA and give a brief reason for your delay. This is not the time or place to fight about it—you should resolve any difficulties afterward and out of earshot of the child(ren). *Requests for changes need to be kept at a minimum—pick your times carefully.*

PARENTAL BEHAVIORS TO HELP CHILDREN COPE

The following are six suggested parental behaviors and attitudes that have been shown to help children cope.

Allow time to readjust. Don't expect things to settle down quickly; they won't. You may feel that you have reached an adaptation, only to be crying for the next two days. This cycle is not unusual—people tend to plateau, then move forward again in their adjustment.

One old clinical rule of thumb is that it takes about one month per year of marriage (but at least six months) for everyone to settle down emotionally. Each family will have its own timetable based upon how well the parents manage their own grief and can move forward.

Assure children they are not *at fault.* This point cannot be overemphasized. Although children under seven are most likely to feel as if they caused the divorce, any-age child can entertain such thoughts. Parents must take responsibility for the end of their marriage. Children must be assured and reassured that they played no role in the final decision.

Assure children of their security and access to both parents. One of the main causes for a child's poor adjustment is the feeling that his security has been undermined. There is always the question about whether you can be left by the other parent after one has left you. Knowing that they still have a bedroom, clothes, toys, and a routine can help to restore children's sense of security. Each parent needs to reassure the child as needed that they are in charge and that the child does not have to worry about food or shelter.

Similarly, children need to know that the other parent is available, even if only by phone or e-mail, should there be a need for contact. And children need assurance that the other parent is doing okay when separated from them.

Keep a schedule and routine. This point, covered earlier, is related to the security and stability issue. When a child has his own routine, with known discipline and rules, he senses that although some things have changed (through divorce) the world is still the same. This helps children look ahead.

Continue to discipline as always (or better). As mentioned above, one sure way to remind a child that there is stability in the post-divorce world is to keep things as they were before—a theme of continuity in the child's life. A set of rules and discipline reminds the child that he still has to answer to a parent, that he still has to mind, and that the "important" things have not really changed.

If you fail to be consistent or decide to give your child a break because he or she is "a poor child of divorce," you scare your child by giving a second message that things really are different and probably not alright. Guilt or other emotions that prevent you from being tough and consistent must be dealt with quickly. If you yelled about keeping a clean bedroom pre-divorce, you need to yell about keeping a clean bedroom post-divorce.

Keep the children out of the middle. It is sometimes tempting to ask your child to carry a message or make a request of the other parent for you since they will be seeing that person anyway. Avoid this temptation. Children feel burdened when they are messengers. They also feel compromised if the message is negative or leads to a negative response. If you have a message or request, ask yourself—either in person, by phone, by e-mail, or by letter. *These messages should also be kept to a minimum* lest you run the risk of being labeled as a harasser or stalker.

A DIVORCED PARENTS' FAQ

The following common questions and concerns have been asked of mental health professionals by divorcing or newly divorced parents. They may be on your mind:

What Is Co-parenting?

Co-parenting is a child rearing style that is based upon cooperation and respect between biological/adoptive parents, no matter their marital status, over the lifetime of their child(ren). Co-parenting involves:

1. keeping the needs of the child(ren) first and foremost no matter your feelings about the other parent;
2. working out a plan that allows each child enough time to maintain and nurture relationships with both parents;
3. sharing responsibility and decision-making for the child(ren)'s care and needs of the child(ren); and
4. developing a means of communication that is straightforward and child-centered and leads to problem resolution in the child(ren)'s best interest.

Children of divorce who have successful co-parenting in their life have the best chance of overcoming any psychological or emotional problems that could arise from a separation and divorce. Parents who cooperate rather than stay in conflict are truly putting their children first, as all good parents strive to do. *Believe it or not,* parents who were unable to co-parent before the divorce can (and must) learn to do this after the divorce.

How Do I Prepare My Child(ren) for What's to Come?

If you have not yet separated:

- Both parents should prepare together for a joint family meeting and together announce the separation and answer questions.
- Give a developmentally appropriate reason for the separation.
- Tell the child(ren) exactly how he will be cared for and how much time he will spend with each parent.
- Parents need to reassure the child(ren) that they still love the child even though they (the parents) are emotionally hurt.

If separated and in the process of divorce:

- Keep the child(ren) updated with developmentally appropriate information.
- Draw strict boundaries about what is "adult" material and what is not, and do not discuss or share information that is inappropriate.
- Advise as to changes in residency or school, changes in visit schedules, or changes in daily schedules, in a timely manner.

If already divorced:

- Answer questions as they come up.
- Keep the child(ren) updated with developmentally appropriate information.
- Draw strict boundaries about what is "adult" material and what is not.
- Advise as to changes in residency or school, changes in visit schedules, or changes in daily schedules, in a timely manner.

What Should I Avoid to Help My Child(ren)'s Adjustment?

The most damaging things parents can do (and so should avoid) are to:

- Ensure that the child does not have adequate time with both parents.
- Blame the child for the divorce.

- Use the children as messengers between parents.
- Be sure the children are told to not love and not cooperate with any new adults in their lives.
- Threaten to send your child away if he or she misbehaves.
- Point out that you're the good/right parent and the other is bad/wrong (parental alienation behavior).
- Fail to tell your child about any changes until the day the change is made.
- Share your adult worries and concerns regularly (boy/girlfriend troubles; financial worries; job insecurity; feelings of guilt).
- Expect and demand that your child comforts you and helps your adjustment rather than seek professional help or make new friends.
- Become a martyr—give up your life and live for and through your child (and don't forget to remind them of this daily).
- Do anything that undermines security and stability in your child's life.

How Will My Child(ren)'s Needs Change over Time?

This is a question about your child(ren)'s developmental level. Infants (under age 24–30 months at divorce) will simply adapt to the new schedule as if it has always been this way. It is important that there be regular and frequent contact between an infant and the nonresidential parent (two to three or four times per week for several hours). This schedule will eventually need to be changed as the child grows older.

Preschoolers also need regular and frequent contact with each parent, but can also more easily tolerate overnight visits. Until kindergarten begins, more of a fifty-fifty visit schedule can be accommodated. Children this age need to be reassured about their security, need a stable and consistent schedule, and need to be reminded that they are not to blame for the divorce. They are unable to think logically, so you need to be attentive to what they say as signs of what they are thinking, and make corrections as needed.

For school-age children (5 or 6 to 12 years old), a stable and consistent schedule is necessary. Involvement of both parents in school-related functions and work is essential for the child's well-being. Typically children this age are on an alternating weekend visit schedule to avoid disruption of school-related performance. At this age, children begin to think more logically and are more aware of "adult" level conflicts. At this age, they also have "big ears," so be careful to protect them from matters that are inappropriate for their involvement or awareness.

For adolescents, divorce may be quite difficult. They are old enough to understand what has happened, and may also be quick to assign blame to one or both parents, creating a great stress in the parent-teen relationship. Teens can think logically, draw conclusions, and cannot be lied to without severe consequences. Teens are also more likely to insist on having a voice in their residency and in visit-schedule decisions. They are also more likely to act out by challenging authority and/or deal with their depression in self-destructive ways (drug use, suicide, risky behavior).

Is It Really Important to Have Two Involved Parents?

Clearly, yes. The psychological research on effects of divorce on children consistently finds that children do best when raised by two cooperating, concerned parents—even if the parents are not living together. When co-parenting is done right, children have the minimum amount of later difficulties. When hostility and conflict interfere with children's right to have two parents, those children suffer—up to and including suicide. Level of involvement varies from family to family, but it should be determined by the child's needs and not the parent's needs. There is no acceptable excuse for a person to not take part in raising his or her child, except for severe mental illness and drug abuse.

What Do I Do If My Child Refuses to Visit?

By court order, you are obligated to have your child(ren) ready for visitation at the appointed time and place, *no matter what.* In cases of illness or other extreme circumstance, it may be decided that it is best for the child to miss that specific visit time. However, illness alone does not excuse the child from visiting—the other parent is considered to be competent to nurse the child. If the child is insistent about not wanting to leave, the parent who is to have the child needs to determine if it is worth the fight and aggravation to have that visit at that time. It is usually *not.*

If there are no legitimate reasons for missing a visit, the visit should take place. The PRP or custodial parent needs to remind the child that it is time to visit and the other parent needs to avoid hostility or other negative displays in order to encourage the child to come along. The PRP/custodial parent *must not* say or do anything that gives the child permission to avoid or cancel the visit.

If the PRP/custodial parent believes that the child is afraid of abuse, neglect, or another negative outcome during the visit, those issues should be straightened out *prior to the time of transition.* It was difficult for me when I worked with families with these issues to determine the extent to which there was true concern about abuse or neglect by a parent versus a very "reputable" excuse to get back at the other parent. Here is where legal consultation will be necessary—you as the parent can't make the final decision on your own.

How Do I Explain Why the Other Parent Never Calls?

If, for whatever reason, a parent fails to take advantage of his or her visit/access time, it is the obligation of that parent to tell the child why and what alternate schedule will be followed. The PRP/custodial parent needs to stay out of this situation as much as possible.

If the nonresidential parent does not have any contact, the other parent should answer the child's questions truthfully. Do not use this chance to trash the absent parent, and do not cover for him or her. Here are some sample appropriate answers to a child's questions:

"I don't know why your daddy/mommy hasn't called."

"I'll try to get a message to her/him so you can talk with her/him yourself."

"You will have to ask your mother/father why she/he has not been visiting; I can't speak for her/him."

"Maybe we can call grandma/grandpa (parent's parent) and ask them if they can get daddy/mommy to call you."

Do not say:

"You know your father/mother—that's why we're divorced."

"He/she is probably spending all his/her time with the new girl/boyfriend and doesn't have time for you."

"I'm sure she/he wants to see you—I'm sure there is some good reason for her/him to not be calling."

"She/he is probably too busy at work right now."

What Do I Do If My Child Wants to Change Primary Residency?

At some point it is inevitable that this topic will come up. Don't take it personally. Usually, the child is trying to make things "fair." He or she believes that at some point a switch needs to be made so that parenting time can be made equal. Children need to be reminded that they are being raised by both parents even if they spend less or more time with one parent.

No changes should be considered for at least a year after the new living arrangements have been finalized. Everyone needs an opportunity to adapt and adjust without pressure for immediate change. If after awhile the current arrangement is not working out well, a change of primary residency may be considered. At adolescence it may make more sense for same-sex arrangements for primary residency (boys with fathers, girls with mothers). These need to be assessed on a case by case basis, always putting the child's best interest first.

What Do I Do If Child Support Isn't Being Paid?

Seek out legal remedies but *do not interfere with visitation.* It is clearly the responsibility of the designated parent to pay his or her support fully and timely. If irresponsibility or disrespect for a court order is shown, you have to live with it until it can be corrected. Judges are sympathetic to the receiving parent, and they will penalize the irresponsible party. There is usually a court-supervised office that can help you as well. It is clearly tempting to withhold visit time as penalty for not paying the child support but it is not right (or legal) to take care of this by yourself.

What Is the Role (If Any) of a Stepparent/New Boy/Girlfriend?

The answer to this question is not easy. Every family situation is unique. Under the best of circumstances each parent needs to show respect for a new adult in the child(ren)'s life. If the new boy/girlfriend was the presumed cause of the separation/divorce it may be quite difficult to get past that issue. Therapy may be needed to sort through the mix of emotions.

If the adults can get along in their communication, it is usually best to recognize that this new adult will be a parent figure. He or she is *not* a replacement parent. Children should be allowed to determine what that new person is called, but Mommy and Daddy should be subtly discouraged. However, if the child wishes to call the biological/adoptive mother "Mommy" and the stepmother "Mom" (or the equivalent for fathers) it is clear that the child has made a distinction. Biological/adoptive parents should be reassured that they are not being displaced or minimized.

In many successful family situations, only the biological/adoptive parent handles disciplinary issues. This is generally a good rule. In other successful families, a stepparent assumes a limited number of duties/areas of authority and is backed up by the parent.

Finally, in some families, the stepparent has the full authority and backing of the parent. This needs to be monitored, as the other parent may disagree with decisions and values/attitudes. This resolution is *not* recommended.

How Long Does It Take to Get Back to Normal?

It depends. Every family's situation has a number of variables that can make the adjustment back to normalcy harder or easier. If both parents cooperating and conflict is minimal, the adjustment will happen more quickly. Insofar as the parents can't or won't cooperate, or can't or won't back down from their conflict, the children and adults will be dragging out the necessary and eventual adaptation for longer than was necessary.

The psychology literature suggests that the first year is an important predictor of long-term readjustment. If you can establish stability, maintain discipline, keep a trouble-free visit schedule, and create new "split family" rituals, you are on the right track.

Do Kids Ever Adjust to the Back-and-forth Time?

Most do, some never do. Transitions are a particularly difficult time in that there is, in a sense, a weekly replay of the divorce-caused feelings of isolation/rejection/separation. Transitions may at times be harder on parents than children. Some sensitive children may show repeated behavioral problems or emotional displays at transition, and later settle down. It is important to respect your child's feelings and be ultra-patient at these times.

As time goes on, most children will accept and adapt to these exchanges. Some find it helpful to have a calendar that gives predictability and shows clearly that they will eventually be reunited with the other parent. If a schedule is followed consistently there is a better chance for adjustment.

What Do I Do If I Can't Get Cooperation?

If you are trying your best to be positive in your interactions and you are flexible and open to necessary changes, you have done all you can as a cooperative co-parent. The primary reason for a lack of cooperation is unresolved anger/blaming from the divorce. Some uncooperative parents need therapy and time to adjust. Others are just ornery and combative. This is a personality problem that you can't fix, but can try to avoid.

If you cannot find a solution or resolution with a difficult former spouse, you may try several options:

1. Ask for their resolution of the issue(s) in dispute.
2. Ask if they will meet with a trusted third party.
3. Ask if they will attend mediation. (This may be required—check your final judgment or ask your lawyer.)

What usually *will not work* is:

1. Badgering and nagging
2. Name-calling and accusations
3. Threatening a return to court over every dispute

REMARRIAGE AND LATER POST-DIVORCE ISSUES

Depending upon how close you are to the time of separation or divorce, future situations may not be so clear or important. However, at some point in the future, there is a real possibility that you will decide to remarry or enter into a "domestic partnership" with a new person. These events can be a positive sign that life goes on and that you are ready to move ahead. For your child(ren), there may be some confusion.

As previously mentioned, one or both parents will eventually decide to begin dating. It is the opinion of many that first dates and meetings with others occur during times when your child is with the other parent, and it is considered best for children if they are not introduced to a number of different people over a short period of time. Therefore, when you believe that the new person will be a presence in your life for a while in the future, you may then set up a meeting between your children and the new person. Try to plan a time-limited activity with a beginning and an end so there is an out if needed.

The immediate questions that arise are: "How do I know how long this relationship will last?"; "How many is too many new introductions of people?"; "How should I introduce this person?"; and "What questions will my child(ren) ask?" for a start. As with all of these scenarios, the answers will depend upon your child, his or her age and developmental level, and the level of post-divorce adjustment that has been reached at the time this situation presents itself. Try to be honest and make your point at a developmental level that is appropriate for your child.

Another area of potential trouble that arises after the divorce has to do with loyalty issues. In most families, children have preferences for one parent or the other depending on what they need or want (this is actually related to attachment patterns as discussed in chapters 2 and 3). These preferences can extend to the post-divorce family configuration and grow stronger. The upside is that you have a child who may be well-bonded and protective of that parent's interests. This may be seen with a child who defends that parent's behavior to others who may attack the parent when he or she is not present. It can also be seen in sibling fights when the siblings are on "opposite sides."

The obvious downside is that loyalty conflicts can force a child to choose between parents—a choice he cannot ever truly make. Loyalty issues often arise after a parent has begun a new, serious relationship with a boy/girlfriend. The child believes that it would be disloyal to the biological parent if he or she begins to like or care about the new person/potential stepparent. These issues are best dealt with openly and directly. The caring, loving parent knows that it's necessary to reassure the child that it is okay to have more relationships despite the fear of hurting the other parent's feelings. A parent should never set up the situation to force a child into a loyalty test, since this causes great psychological distress.

It is also certainly possible that you may begin a new relationship and become seriously interested in a new person, only to receive flak and opposition from a child or all your children. This child may try to make you miserable or otherwise act in ways that show his or her disapproval. Often, this is related to a loyalty issue, but it can also be representative of a child's hope/wish that you may reconcile with your former spouse. Obviously, the child can maintain a reunion fantasy as long as you are unattached. Once a relationship looks serious, the child realizes that the divorce is truly final. That issue must then be addressed.

Other times, the child may not want you to bring in an outsider since he or she has adjusted to the new family unit. The child may fear yet another disruption and all the anxiety and uncertainty that go with change. You must decide what is important to you both as a parent and as an adult, and tell your child(ren) your feelings, again at a developmentally appropriate level.

Some of my most difficult court custody cases involved the issue of disrupting a post-divorce adjustment situation owing to a change-of-life situation. If a parent remarries, gets a job transfer, or has to leave to care for another person, there is a major problem with respect to access for the parent who will live too many miles away to maintain the original schedule.

The legal issues to be resolved here involve a number of criteria, including the best interest of the child. Psychologically, this issue presents *another major disruption* and should, if at all possible, be avoided. This can mean that a parent delays a job/career move, "forces" a new mate to stay put, or decides against an obligation or responsibility, all for the sake of the child. This is a major sacrifice for the parent, but also a necessary one if the current adjustment has worked out and the child(ren) is doing well.

Settling Conflicts without Going Back to Court

One simple rule, which if followed by both parties, will keep most of your conflicts to a minimum and usually leads to an end to legal disputes—*keep your child's needs first.* If both parents can remove themselves from the emotional confusion, and focus on what the child(ren) need(s), most resolutions become obvious. You may need to talk out these issues with a trusted third party in order to get a more detached, rational perspective of the situation.

One way to maintain conflict from the past into the present and future is to continue to fight the divorce issues. If you live in the past and continue to bring it up, you will never get past that part of your life and you will continue to keep your child(ren) in the middle. If your ex was always late and lateness becomes a problem at transitions, it does not help you to remind that person of this character flaw. Instead, you should focus on a solution such as agreed upon transition times that are earlier (to make up for the lateness) or some other alternative.

If you wish or need to replay some old unresolved issues, try counseling. You may include your ex in "divorce therapy" if it is that important to you, assuming that person is willing. If he or she is not willing, go by yourself. For now, I offer these three activities to help you to minimize conflict:

Try out new ideas on an experimental basis. Often, there is a legitimate disagreement over some issue for which there is no "right" way or solution. I often suggest to families that they try each of their proposed solutions on an experimental basis in order to see what is best for a child. For example, some families believe that children should not have overnight visits during the school week as it disrupts their schedule. Others argue that it is more important to have physical contact and family time (including overnight stayovers) than to maintain a schedule. One way to resolve such a situation is to try both solutions for one month each and monitor the child's response in as fair a way as possible (*not* through the child directly, but by teacher report or other family member report).

Ask a trusted third party to help resolve your dispute. When you are in conflict or disagreement, and you both believe that your position is best for the child, it may be time for a third party to bring a fresh perspective. This individual may be a professional (therapist, counselor, clergy) or a respected friend or family member. The problem with a friend or family member is that one person may believe, or secretly hope, there is bias. If this is the case, don't even bother—you must seek professional intervention. (Most smart friends will know to run far away and fast if asked to be placed in the middle of someone else's family battles.)

A competent third party can hear each of your positions, ask questions about your child's needs, and help you both to see what is best for your child, even if it is not best for you. If you truly have your child's interest at heart, there is little need for further discussion. At that point, you *must* do the right thing.

Attempt civil mediation to resolve disputes. Many recent final judgments now include a mediation clause. This means that each party is required to attempt mediation before they are allowed back on to the court docket for modifications. This change is an attempt to limit post-divorce modification cases, which paralyze the court system. It is also used to encourage divorced parents to work out their problems between themselves more often, which leads to better, more personal solutions.

Civil family mediation involves each parent meeting together with a trained, certified mediator. That individual may be an attorney or mental health person (by training) who is in a position to help you reach a cooperative, mutually agreeable solution. Mediators are *not* arbitrators, nor are they serving as lawyers or psychologists when they are mediators. You reach a shared, mutually agreeable resolution with their assistance.

Much data suggests that families handle their problems better when resolved through mediation. Many families prefer a mediated settlement to a court order by a judge who doesn't have time to get to know that individual family's needs and resources. Judges are happy to have less pressure in their work when more families reach mediated settlements. And your children are happy because their parents have stopped fighting.

In the chapter on fathering, we will review the research on how fathers can stay involved and influential in their children's lives. We will also review the very important role of the mother, who serves as a gatekeeper for access to the children in most post-divorce setups.

Finally, many good books are available for children to read in order to help them understand and learn to cope with some of the confusion that comes with the territory. Four sources that I recommend are:

Brown, L. K., & Brown, M. (1986). *Dinosaur divorce: A guide for changing families.* Boston: Atlantic Monthly Press.

Gardner, R. A. (1983). *The boys' and girls' book about one-parent families.* New York: Bantam.

Ricci, I. (1980). *Mom's house, dad's house: Making shared custody work.* New York: Collier Books.

Rofes, E. E., (Ed.) (1981). *The kids' book of divorce.* Lexington, MA: Lewis. (This book has 20 children, age 11 to 14 as essay authors.)

All are typically available in public libraries and can be purchased at most bookstores. Please remember that divorce is hard on everyone. Whatever can be done to ease the pain for children must be done.

Chapter 7

DAY CARE

Who takes the child by the hand takes the mother by the heart.
—Danish Proverb

Placement of a child in a day care setting is one of the most important decisions a parent can make. For this chapter, day care means caregiving for a child by people other than a parent in either the child's home, the caregiver's home, or a day care center placement. This care is provided during daytime hours, usually because parents are unavailable owing to outside work. Almost 60 percent of children were in some day care placement each week in the United States according to a 1997 Children's Defense Fund survey. This works out to 7.7 million youngsters under the age of five in day care at that time and each year the number increases.

There are many variables to consider in reaching a decision on whether to place a child in day care. These include:

- whether it is best for a parent to stay home until the child reaches a certain age or developmental level, or continue in an outside-of-home career;
- whether a child is better off cared for at home with a provider who comes to him, or whether a child is better off taken to another setting with many other children; and
- whether a full- or part-time day care placement is best for a child even if there are parents or other family at home or otherwise available to care for the child.

We will look at the very diverse research results in this field in an effort to help you make the best choice possible in your family situation.

REVIEW OF RESEARCH ON THE EFFECTS OF DAY CARE PLACEMENT

First, educated parents need to know that the research on day care effects is a very mixed bag. Some studies look at attachment outcomes as a main source to decide if day care exposure is good or bad for a child. Others seek to learn whether a certain amount of time spent in day care causes problems. Other studies look only at socialization effects or cognitive development results. Added to this lack of a standardized way to approach the issue are the political agendas of some of the researchers and the funders of the research.

Many people have a vested interest in the outcome of this research area. Some research groups have found one set of results and later reversed their interpretation of their findings. The U.S. federal government has funded many of these studies to aid in establishing public policy. We will review private day care, but also know some of the research has come from Project Head Start. We will also review what the educated parent can do at home in order to make the day care experience better for the child.

It is important that every parent be aware of these findings, and that they make an informed decision in the best interest of the needs of the family. Is it better to have a stay-at-home parent even if the family financial situation is weak? Does one parent need to sacrifice a career for the sake of the children? Can a family "have it all"—a strong quality of life supported by two incomes *and* healthy, functional children raised in large part by outside caregivers? Do children benefit from greater financial resources overall, made possible by two working parents? In addition to the psychological studies, other factors such as family values and personal parental competencies must be considered.

Other research that has examined parental attitudes toward the day care decision is important to note here. In an ongoing National Institute for Child Health and Development study that we will review in more detail later, it was determined that parental attitudes and the quality of care the parents deliver *at home* are more important variables than those found in a day care setting. Similarly, having a positive attitude about *both* parenting and outside work achievements has been associated with positive day care outcomes. Finally, the full agreement and support of both parents for the day care decision helps to ease any guilt or regrets. This allows for both parents to do a better job of parenting when they are with the child in the home.

In a similar vein, there has been some, though limited, recent research on the stability of day care placement arrangements. For many families, once their day care dilemma is resolved, conditions change and disrupt the placement. Reasons for this disruption can be that a parent has changed jobs or job locations, or the day care center makes changes such as raising fees or closes for a two-week period for staff vacation purposes. This is a real-world scenario and cannot be avoided.

To the extent that it is possible, the best thing parents can do in these circumstances is to get their child placed in the next-best reliable setting. The well-prepared parent will try to always have some contact with a possible backup placement, although this is a lot to ask. The consequences of not having a day care backup are lost time at work and/or a hodgepodge of temporary arrangements while you search for your next semipermanent setting. Further, creating some potentially problematic, but not life-altering, instability for your child is another worry.

Since this can be a confusing situation for caring, educated parents, it is most important that the research in this area be reported as objectively as possible. It does no good for a study team to ignore some data and emphasize other findings that support its political or social agenda. If there are data to show negative outcomes, it must be presented fairly so that parents understand the costs associated with day care placement. It is even better if the variable can be isolated so that corrective actions can be taken to lessen such negative effects. If there are data that show beneficial effects, parents should know what their child could be missing by being raised solely at home. Such findings should be disseminated widely so all child care providers can have the tools to do the best possible work with their young charges.

Research Finding Negative Effects on Children

Beginning with work by Jay Belsky in the mid-1980s, some psychologists first viewed day care as a potential attachment disrupter, thus leading to many potential problems for a child for years after. Belsky was among the first to point out that infants in day care were more likely to avoid or ignore their parents when observed in the Strange situation. It seemed clear that early and extensive day care exposure was related to higher rates of insecure attachments.

Belsky and his associates concluded that 20 or more hours per week in day care constituted a risk factor for insecure attachment patterns. Belsky also reported that children who began full-time day care placements before 12 months of age were also more likely to be classified as having an insecure attachment relationship. He and others thus opened a debate that continues to be waged today.

In response to Belsky's work, a number of studies were conducted to either support or challenge his findings. In support of the Belsky team results, a piece by Karl Zinsmeister in 1988 ("Brave New World") was particularly negative in its review of select articles on day care outcome. Zinsmeister has written frequently, compellingly, and articulately since then about the dangers and risks associated with day care. I require my students to read his articles because they paint a personal view. His use of individuals' stories to make his point is powerful, even if they are single-case examples.

One of Zinsmeister's first examples of day care dangers was related to health issues. Going beyond hygienic matters, he argued that most day cares were breeding grounds for infectious disease. He also argued that day care children get sick far more frequently and this in itself poses a health risk for later development (Zinsmeister, 1988). Many parents must bring sick children to day care in order to meet work demands. At certain times of the year, with colds and respiratory infections, the situation can get very bad.

According to Zinsmeister, the American Pediatric Association reports that "infants under one in group care have eight times as many colds and other infections as babies cared for by their families" (Zinsmeister, 1998, p. 41). Infants' immune systems are not well developed. Infant behavior contributes to transmission in that such little ones are putting everything into their mouths. The Centers for Disease Control (CDC) warned that "diaper changing is the highest risk procedure" associated with day care. In the 1980s, the American Academy of Pediatrics recommended that "large groupings and groups with turnover among the children ought to be avoided when children are young" (Zinsmeister, 1998, p. 42).

Some studies have found that children in day care centers suffered 50 percent more infections and four and a half times as many hospitalizations. Increased day care transmission of ear infections alone is a cause of great concern. This has implications for future hearing impairment as well as increased surgical corrections for prevention.

The other health issue of concern is the recent decline over the past 30 years in the physical motor skills of children. It is argued that the day care environment often does not provide enough physical outlets for large–motor skill development. Children are also less likely to learn important physical skills and games from older playmates than they did a generation ago. Since most day care settings isolate children by age-determined peer groups, there is less transmission of physical skills and information across age boundaries. So where children once learned from such older playmates, their access is restricted or very limited.

In a perfect world, begins Zinsmeister's 1998 article, "there would be an abundance of intelligent, well-balanced, devoted individuals willing to attend lavishly and patiently to the demands of strangers' children.... These dream workers would all be willing to provide their services so cheaply that there would be little or no strain on family finances. And they would remain with the same family year after year, meshing perfectly with child, parents, and surroundings" (Zinsmeister, 1998, p. 26).

Zinsmeister then goes on to give numerous instances and examples of how there is no perfect world, and day care is never better than raising a child at home. His stories are taken from both parental and professional observations and experiences. "[P]urchased care is rarely more than a stopgap," he argues.

Among his more provocative stories include accounts of parents who were often surprised by what was actually going on with their children. Many stories involve in-home day care. In one account, he relates a mother's shock at discovering her valued and trusted provider "sleeping on her sofa while 11 children (she had informed me that she only cared for five) wandered aimlessly around in front of the blaring TV. Another time, on an unannounced visit, I found that the "highly recommended" licensed day care provider confined seven preschoolers to her tiny dining room. I found them huddled together, leaning over a barricade to watch a TV program showing in the adjacent room" (Zinsmeister, 1998, p. 27).

Zinsmeister refers to the Metropolitan Toronto Social Planning Council survey of 281 day care homes. He cites this as an example of the way things are, with the situation no better or worse in Toronto than in any other large city. His summary: quality was a mixed bag. Some centers "were genuinely stimulating" and a very few were "out-and-out abusive." The majority, by and large, provided care best described as "merely indifferent." He concluded that day care for most children was an understimulating experience.

Zinsmeister also has many accounts of disrupted attachments. He cites examples of insecurely attached children wandering aimlessly in homes and centers for hours on end. In one in-home example, he reports the not unusual account of a child protesting when the parent comes to pick up the child. The small child has attached to the day care provider and does not want to leave her to go home with his mother. This is difficult for all involved—parent, child, and provider.

At day care centers, Zinsmeister worries about the effects of "musical caregivers." It is not unusual for children to be cared for many different providers, thus creating unpredictability and instability. These factors are negative for very young children and infants. Stability of staff and its relationship to attachment is an important factor to know about. We will address this further later in this chapter.

Zinsmeister accuses parents of simply settling for these outcomes. He argues that parents have lowered their expectations and make compromises "by the millions" every day. He goes on to quote from Deborah Fallows, author of *A Mother's Work.* In her book she presents 18 months of observations from many different day care centers in Maryland, Washington, D.C., Texas, and Massachusetts. Fallows discovered "no abuse, relatively little dirt, and adequate physical conditions in most centers...." Zinsmeister adds, "she nonetheless found the average child's experience frighteningly empty" (Zinsmeister, 1998, p. 28).

It is a major criticism of day care on Zinsmeister's part to decry the neglect and understimulation of children in day care. He recounts Fallows's stories of

> children referred to by their teachers as "little boy" or "hey little girl," of activities that cater to the group average but leave quiet toddlers behind, of desperate notes pinned to youngsters' coats in which parents plead for extra attention or special comforts.... There is much tedium, much bewilderment, many unconsoled tears.... In a situation that human biology guarantees no natural parent would ever have to face (four to ten same-aged youngsters per adult), tired teachers do what they can to get by. (Zinsmeister, 1998, p. 29)

Zinsmeister also cites William and Wendy Dreskin's book, *The Day Care Decision.* The Dreskins operated their own nonprofit, "very high quality" nursery school and then day care center in the San Francisco area. They began with a half-day preschool, and then expanded into a full-day operation. To their dismay, the Dreskins "began to notice changes in their children."

Full-time day care, it was asserted, led children to begin to withdraw, become aggressive, or just cry a lot. They noted that some children's behavior regressed, and other children had more negative attitudes when placed for longer periods of time. Of note, "the parents changed too" (Zinsmeister, 1998, p. 30). The Dreskins reported that parental involvement fell off, and interest in the child and his or her activities waned over time. They noted frazzled parents and confused children at the transition times.

It is also Zinsmeister's contention that provider–children ratios can never be adequate for proper child development. There is always the problem of "lack of individual attention." He reports that the federal government's National Child Care Survey showed that among centers caring for one-year-olds, the average group size is currently 10, and the child–staff ratio is nearly seven to one. The validity of these numbers may also be questionable.

No matter, the needs of infants require great amounts of time per child. Zinsmeister argues that if a caregiver just keeps up with changing diapers, cleaning up after, and feeding needs for just four babies, there is little time left for stimulation or other one-on-one activity needed for development. Such is the reality of day care.

Research Finding Positive or Non-harmful Effects on Children

On the "other side" of this debate, research by K. Alison Clarke-Stewart, who reviewed a number of studies through 1989, found an alternative interpretation of the Belsky-side data. She found in her review that an average of 36 percent of children in day care (with working mothers) became insecurely attached. However, 29 percent of children of non-employed or part-time working mothers also developed an insecure attachment quality. Why is this? Some possible reasons include:

- Mothers who are less happy with motherhood or who dislike child care responsibilities could be more likely to pursue full-time employment;
- Mothers who must work full-time and carry child care responsibilities are overstressed and tired, leaving these mothers unable to be as sensitive and responsive as is needed for secure attachments.

Clarke-Stewart also found a number of "moderators and mediators" of day care effects. She examined the data in the areas of day care, child, and family factors in three key domains. Those domains were emotional insecurity (attachment disruption), sociability and aggression in children, and intellectual/cognitive development.

Clarke-Stewart found that the "type, stability or quality" of day care did not predict attachment quality. In fact, child variables like temperament were more important than any day care variable in predicting emotional security. She also found that family variables such as maternal desire to work or stay home were also significant, as reviewed above.

On the issue of reports of disrupted social development and increases in aggressive behavior among children in day care, Clarke-Stewart found that day care actually promoted positive social development for many children. She argued that some of the increased aggressiveness in children might be a by-product of the caregivers' desire to promote independent behavior. Parental variables tend to reinforce the child care experiences; often the parents themselves act in ways as to allow for more aggressive behavior. So we see a pattern of more aggressive-like, noncompliant behavior as a result of less constraining caregiving in day care and at home.

In the area of intellectual and cognitive development, day care and preschool experiences seem to positively contribute to at least short-term gains on measures such as IQ. Note that these gains cannot be attributed solely to day care/preschool exposure because of the many home variables that also play a part in these outcomes. It was suggested, however, that in this area, "parents are augmenting the day care effect (rather) than that they are causing it" (Clarke-Stewart, 1989, p. 271).

More recently, the National Institute of Child Health and Development (NICHD) has studied 1,300 families in 14 different cities in the United States to look at day care effects as well. This ongoing study found that the more time children were placed in day care, the less sensitive their mothers were toward them at 6, 15, and 36 months of age. Children spending the most time in day care were also found to be less affectionate toward their mothers at 24 and 36 months of age. These correlations were relatively weak, but did emerge.

It must also be pointed out that at-home parent–child interaction quality is always a factor that must be considered as well. One cannot make a complete causal relationship between day care time and parent or child relationship quality on the basis of day care exposure alone. This is a complex, multi-determined phenomenon. Much more research is still needed.

Nina Koren-Karie has examined preexisting emotional differences among mothers and their choice of day care. Mothers more likely to choose day care centers rather than stay-at-home care alternatives were found to score as insecurely attached, as determined by the Adult Attachment Interview test. Yes, *the mothers* were insecurely attached as rated by the adults' recall on the AAI. They are at-risk for setting up further insecure attachment patterns with their children as presented in chapter 3. Perhaps they are more willing to place their children in day care since relating to their children in a more secure fashion is too difficult. Or it is possible that these mothers believe that others might do a better job in raising their child than they believe they can do.

In another recent report by Barry Schneider and his team in Canada, a review of 63 studies was completed. In this review, the focus was on attachment patterns as they relate to children's peer reactions. This report, reviewed in chapter 3, also sought to identify "variables that moderate (influence) the relation between attachment security and peer relations." Day care is one influence along with parenting and attachment that interacts to determine child outcome. Day care provides experiences for children to practice with each other. A secure attachment can minimize any negative effects that may occur through day care experiences.

The topic of peer interaction as it is related to day care was explicitly studied by the NICHD Early Child Care group in 2001. Children begin to show differences in peer relations by age two. These peer relations can be a critical dimension in their attainment of social competence, and for other relationship issues. The NICHD group looked at children's experiences with other children in the child care setting and experiences with their caregivers.

It is believed that child care experiences play an important role in developing social competence and peer-relation skills in two ways. First, children get to experience many different children and see how they relate with each other. From a social learning view, we would expect that children in day care settings observe and model many behaviors. They are able to be "more sociable and engaged, more playful, and more affectively positive with other children." Other studies have in fact found that exposure and interaction with peers allow for better communication and better political skills like sharing, cooperating, negotiating, and compromising.

A second mechanism for improved social competence is by the nature of the relationships children form with their adult caregivers. More "sensitive and responsive behavior" by adults is associated with less negative and more positive peer interactions. In addition to the sensitive caregiving outside the home, it was also found that maternal sensitivity and child variables like cognitive and language skills predict social competence. Taken together, this means that one must look at both family and day care influences when one seeks to understand how peer-relation and interaction patterns develop.

The NICHD researchers found "consistent, albeit modest, relations" between child care experiences in the first three years of life and children's peer competencies. Another interesting finding by the NICHD group was that levels of maternal sensitivity were related to peer skills. "Mothers who were more positive and responsive, and less intrusive or hostile, in play" had children who were more "socially skilled" (2001, p. 1495). This further underscores the need to consider family and day care influences.

There is also research to demonstrate positive effects of day care placement on children. For example, a research group led by Carolee Howes has shown that children who have formed insecure attachments at home with parents can form secure attachments with stable day care providers. Also of importance, these children were later more socially competent than insecurely attached counterparts who did not have the benefit of a more secure attachment.

So it is possible that good day care can actually compensate for poor parent–child attachments in the home! The Howes group has also reported that training day care staff specifically in attachment promotion behavior as part of an overall day care quality-improvement training package resulted in definite positive attachment outcomes for their charges. This can be another variable for the educated parent to consider when choosing a day care setting.

The Children's Defense Fund report of 1997 also asserted that having children in high-quality day care settings (specifically those with well-trained staff) leads to fewer delinquency or other antisocial behaviors in later life. Also, these children were more successful academically as a result of their preschool preparation exposure.

Good-quality day care also has been associated with enhancement of children's language development, improvement in specific cognitive skills, and a better adaptation to new settings. These children are more autonomous and secure, leading to increased social competencies and more self-confidence.

Belsky has since reevaluated his data and the work of others, in light of criticism leveled at his earlier work. He is now in the group that believes that day care done right can be an acceptable experience. In his words, when infant day care "is of high quality," there is less likelihood of negative developmental outcomes. However, in a 2001 article, he reiterated that "early, extensive, and continuous" day care experiences can lead to child behavior problems. These problems include aggression and noncompliance behaviors.

DAY CARE DONE RIGHT

What is day care done right?

Most psychologists would agree that the following conditions are necessary for a high-quality day care experience, and thus lessened chance for negative outcomes to the child placed in such a setting. These are: proper attention levels for each infant; appropriate developmental opportunity and encouragement to interact with adults; proper safety and health regimens; regular family communication and interaction; and trained and professional stable caregiver staffs. Let us look at these in turn.

Infants especially need significant and ongoing attention paid to them. They are in constant search for new experiences and require adults to provide them with proper stimulation. A small caregiver-to-infant ratio is a must. Although each state provides guidelines and mandatory ratio requirements, few are as stringent as the ratio recommended by the research. For infants, a ratio of two dependable, trained caregivers for every five infants is the ideal. For toddlers, the number can be doubled to one caregiver per five preschoolers. Having this amount of adult attention makes sure that children's needs are met and that chances for quality interactions can take place regularly over the course of a day. Spreading adult attention across too many infants does not allow for the needed one-on-one time such children require.

Enabling a child to actively explore his or her environment and to have enriching experiences in doing so is also essential. A child needs to be stimulated in all ways developmentally—physically, cognitively, in language, and socially. Infants especially need specific toys that help them to explore the world in ways that provide both sensory and physical/motoric stimulation. Language exposure is also key, with the best environment having children exposed to interactive conversation, songs and sing-a-longs, and age-appropriate games. Toddlers require the same developmental opportunities, with the level of supervision needed to ensure safe exploration and activity.

Health and safety regimens are also regulated by states. An ideal day care placement truly practices hygienic routines such as frequent hand washing by staff, accident prevention and child-proofing, and a safe, protected area for play and physical explorations. Food preparation and general housecleaning must be done "by the book." Climbing apparatuses should be child-safety approved, and they should be clean and on a surface that is soft and can provide a good landing spot. Nutritional needs are just as important. Snack times with healthy alternatives, and proper hydration through the day are essential.

Regular family communication and interaction are also important. Reports to the parents about the child's behavior and progress are important so that parents are aware of developmental changes (e.g., toilet training status) or problems that might emerge. For example, biting behavior may begin, and such negative behavior needs to be dealt with as a team—

parents at home and the day care staff must work together to stem this behavior.

It is also important that parents are welcome at the facility at all times. A parent who knows he or she can drop in at any time can be fairly sure that all is well. Having the option to come by and see what is happening can be very reassuring, and it is more reassuring to actually stop by periodically. If there are field trips or other special activities, encouragement of involvement and participation by parents is also a good way to bridge the home–day care gap.

Finally, a well-trained and prepared day care staff is equally important for an ideal day care. Staff stability is another issue. If a day care has rapid staff turnover, this can be confusing for infants and young children who need the security of knowing and expecting the same faces each day. Expecting a staff of college-trained caregivers at $7 per hour is unrealistic, but the more such staff is educated in developmental and educational practices the better the child outcome. Again, many states require ongoing continued education–type training for caregivers. These in-service trainings often cover items such as health and safety, attention levels, and developmental skills training as listed above.

Day care settings that employ high school students or very young staff may be offering a mixed situation. In exchange for their youth, enthusiasm, energy, and willingness to learn, you lose experience and stability as these young people often move on to other jobs or are otherwise forced to leave because of competing activities. All things being equal, an older, more experienced and patient staff is better for a child.

Some day care placements offer profit sharing to valued staffers who remain on the job in a year to year, reliable, and dependable schedule. If these staffers are responsive and sensitive to children, and experienced, they alone can satisfy the four conditions just reviewed. Of course, the more quality that can be delivered, the higher the expenses will be—and so will the weekly fees. In urban settings, good day care placements can run to $200 per child per week—that works out to $10,000 per year.

Finding the Best Day Care Placement

So what can you do if you cannot afford these ideal day care settings? There are many caring and nurturing people in the day care industry. They work hard to provide the necessary supervision for the many children whose families require this help. Before placing your child, personally check out the potential setting. Look around for yourself. Are the children and the rooms relatively clean? Are the children interacting and showing positive emotions?

Examine the food preparation area. Check for child-proofing of electrical outlets or other potentially hazardous situations. What toys are available? Are they in good shape? Are there enough to go around? What outside activities are provided for? Is there room to run and jump and climb in a safe way, either outdoors or indoors? The educated parent can make up a checklist of criteria to look for.

Ask about the staff training and how long the staff has worked in their jobs. Ask about the most recent training or continuing education that was received. If you can get as many positive answers to all of these inquiries as possible, your child will be in a better position. If a day care fails on many of the above points, look around for another place.

Basically, you want to be sure the day care isn't dangerous or potentially harmful. First and foremost, you want to look for adequate supervision and safety. This is accomplished in part by the staff-to-children ratio. Other health matters such as proper food preparation can be discovered by checking for a posted inspection certificate or through a phone call to the local government health agency responsible for day care supervision and oversight.

Of equal importance to me is the level of stimulation in the environment. A good outdoor or open indoor space for physical activity and a wide variety of age-appropriate toys are a must. In the NICHD study even mediocre day care was not found to "cause" harmful effects in most children. The same study reported that the observed attachment problems were more likely the result of maternal-child issues than day care experiences. Steady, stable care in a less than ideal place was better for children than an assortment of different providers that parents had to assemble on a week to week basis.

Diane Adams has reported on the "mazes" that parents must run in order to find proper day care. According to Adams, these mazes are cost, regulations, and quality. Cost is often a first if not primary consideration for any family. Governmental and private sector approaches to aid working parents have been tried, tinkered with, and teased. The unfortunate truth is that every family must budget what an acceptable cost is and then go from there. Tax credits and deductions only go so far.

As for regulations, the parent maze is related to amounts of training for workers, child-to-caregiver ratios, and age-limit restrictions. Constant tinkering and revisions to these rules have created confusion in many states. For parents, the issue is in learning what the rules are so one can choose a day care that is functioning legally and safely.

The final maze of quality goes back to earlier comments about stimulation levels, safety, and nutrition. Here a parent must ask many questions, get referrals from friends, monitor the child's responses, and be involved where possible.

ATTACHMENT SUPPORTS AT HOME

What can you do as a parent to promote healthy attachment so that any potential negative day care effects will be minimized? Recall the work of Marianne DeWolff and Marinus van IJzendoorn, reported in chapter 2 in the attachment section. To review, they found six key parenting variables to be associated with optimal attachment bonds. They are:

Sensitivity—the prompt response level of the parent to the child's signals/needs

Positive attitude—expressions of positive emotion and affection toward the child

Synchrony—the structuring of reciprocal interactions with the child, matching parental behavior to the child's mood and activity level

Mutuality—the coordination of mother and infant to the same activity or event

Support—watching for the child's signals to provide emotional support for the child's activities and behavior

Stimulation—the active direction of behaviors and stimuli to the infant

Let's revisit these, with some added information on what you can do to make these criteria a reality for your child. Sensitivity is the same as responsivity in this context. Making and taking the time to become aware of your infant and child's needs is a start. Is he a hearty breakfast eater or are mid-morning snacks best after a "light" first meal. Can you tell when a good mood is going south owing to your child being overstimulated or tired out? If you can't do this at first, you will soon learn with more interaction time.

Talking to your child and nurturant touching (hugs and kisses and back rubs) are additional important concrete signs of your love and affection. Children need to be praised and acknowledged, sometimes for something special they have tried or accomplished, sometimes for just being there. Your positive attention and interactions will bring positive responses in return and increase your emotional bondedness. This can solidify a secure attachment.

Matching parental behavior to your child's mood and activity level are also important in establishing attached behavior patterns. Is your child more active when first awakened or after awhile? When is the best time for physical play or a visit to a park? When is the best time for a quiet activity like reading a book or singing together? Try to chart you child's daily rhythms when you're caring for him. See if you can get a report about activity level from the day care provider for the times you are not together. Most children get into somewhat predictable cycles of activity levels, moods, hungry times, and quiet times. Try to match your interactions with your child's cycles.

Coordination of mother and infant to the same activity or event is also important for your infant's well-being and connectedness to you. Playing a sing-song game like patty-cake or the itsy bitsy spider song are reassuring to your child who now has your total interest and attention. You can also eat a meal together, alternately taking bites or drinking a beverage.

Providing emotional support for your child's activities and behavior is similar to some of the above behaviors. Watching your child's efforts will lead you to know when to step in and help with a frustrating situation and when to stand back and allow your child to learn to persevere and overcome problems. And praising success or a good effort are parent behaviors that go well beyond infancy and attachment establishment.

Proper stimulation helps your child grow into the next level of developmental ability. Making sure your child has age-appropriate toys and activities that keep him interested. A child's natural curiosity and desire to explore will be aided with the right supply of materials and opportunities for activities that match your child's internal drives to learn about the world. You don't have to spend thousands of dollars to provide the right implements. Many parenting Web sites and magazines have more detailed explicit information about proper stimulation. Equally important is the need to not overstimulate your child. Overstimulated children are actually quite stressed-out and overwhelmed, since they cannot sort out everything they are experiencing. The end result can be that a child will shut down and avoid you.

In a February 2002 study, the health aspect (as addressed in the Zinsmeister review) was again taken up. The *Archives of Pediatrics and Adolescent Medicine* reported that two-year-old children in day care have twice as many colds as two-year-old stay-at-home children. But looking longitudinally, when these children were in elementary school (ages 6–11), the day care children had one-third fewer colds than their stay-at-home counterparts. By adolescence, the difference disappeared.

The research group concluded that the day care exposure to germs was actually beneficial in the long run for helping to develop immune system responses. So having more respiratory germ exposures early on made for better defenses by the grade school years.

SOME CONCLUSIONS

So what can be concluded by reviewing the above? The educated parent should feel free to further explore the reference material and to sort through the limited data I have presented. Again, within the framework of your family values and needs, and your parental competencies, you can make an informed decision on what is best.

In my child psychology class, I always require my students to read Zinsmeister as well as the more "pure" psychology research. I have at times set up a pro- and anti- debate for class discussion. I then always have as an exam question the following: "A mother asks your opinion about placing her young child in day care. What would you tell her? Reply, citing the research, and give her a decision one way or the other." In the real world, they and I cannot tell you what to do. Instead, I offer the following from my perspective to help you make your decisions.

Issues to Consider before Placing Your Child in Day Care

What you do at home with your child, for whatever amount of time you have, can affect whether or not day care will help or hurt your child. If you make time to have quality interactions that promote secure attachment behavior, your child will be better off. This secure attachment foundation will allow your child to function better in day care if needed. As long as the day care is at least of good quality, few negative effects should emerge.

If your parent–child interactions at home are few and of an undersensitive or nonresponsive quality, your child will likely form an insecure attachment with you. This can be made into a more negative outcome if the child is then placed in a poorer quality day care setting. At the least, an insecurely attached child will have a more difficult time in day care than a securely attached one. However, it is also possible that an insecurely attached child can benefit from a "corrective" attachment experience in a quality day care setting.

Your attitude toward the day care–placement/work-outside-the-home issue will affect the decision as to whether to use day care. Parents who stay at home but are resentful of their loss of employment do no favors for their children. Similarly, a situation with a miserable, conflicted parent who hates to go to work and feels perpetually guilty every time the child is dropped off will not lead to a positive outcome for the child. Full agreement by both parents who then are supportive of each other and the child makes for the best decision, whether it is staying at home or placement in a day care.

Quality of day care is a very important criterion. The better the quality of day care, the more positive effects demonstrated by the child. Social competency and other healthy child outcomes are clearly associated with day care staffers who are well-trained and who are in smaller caregiver–child ratios. Quality day care experiences can enhance a child's development in the physical, cognitive, and emotional spheres.

The amount of time spent in a day care placement has been shown to negatively correlate with maternal sensitivity toward the child and the child's level of affection toward his mother. Working mothers have more insecure attachment relationships with their children, but this can be due to non–day care caused reasons. If your child is in day care because you don't want to be with him, a negative outcome is more likely. But this will not be due to the day care exposure.

Parents who are unsure of their parenting or otherwise feel unsupported are more likely to have children with problems. Getting some parenting training or other sources of support should be a priority. When a mother and father are in agreement in their reasons and decisions as to where children will be raised, the children will be better off.

The decision to have children in day care should be reviewed annually. Do the benefits of a two-career situation with day care help outweigh the drawbacks of day care for your children? It may be that one parent can alter a schedule so that day care time can be minimized. It may also be decided that financial sacrifices while the children are under five are worth the trade for at-home care with a parent who wants that experience. Only you as parents can decide.

Chapter 8

STRESS AND ANXIETY IN CHILDREN

It is not what you do for your children, but what you have taught them to do for themselves that will make them successful human beings.

—Ann Landers

An unfortunate fact of life in the twenty-first century is that stress levels have increased across all segments of our population. While most would agree that high stress levels are part and parcel of the adolescent experience, increases in chronic stress have made their way into childhood as well. You might argue that most children historically have been stressed-out. But I would argue back that children in the past 100 years, in industrialized countries, have seen significant efforts paying off to reduce chronic, or ever-present stress levels. Chronic life stress would refer to living in such a manner as to always be on guard, to feel a lack of safety and security, to suffer multiple losses, or to have few moments of rest and unfettered play.

A rise in diagnoses of anxiety-related illnesses in childhood is all the proof I need to make my case that stress levels are increasing. Children are diagnosed with a number of anxiety disorders, as we will see. All of these anxiety issues have negative effects on a child's development.

As Nancy Ryan-Wenger has pointed out, one big concern for parents about childhood stress is the toll taken on a child's body. Stress-related *psychosomatic symptoms* include stomachaches and headaches, but can become more severe if the stress is chronic and elevated. Then the symptoms can be hypertension, ulcers, and recurrent abdominal pain (RAP) in otherwise healthy, normal children. If a child has a chronic health condition, recurrent stress can cause or exacerbate bronchial spasms (asthma), hyperglycemia (diabetes), or joint pain (juvenile rheumatoid arthritis).

Psychosomatic symptoms have been shown to develop in childhood as a result of stressful (nonsupportive) family and social environments, stressful life events, and ineffective coping strategies. So a child living in an underorganized, chaotic environment is set up for stress when then faced with other life events and a lack of role models and experiences with coping mechanisms that work.

Psychosomatic symptoms may be reduced or eliminated as a result of changing or eliminating the stressors, changing the perception of the stressors, or changing or improving coping strategies. In other words, as we will see in this chapter, parents have some control in modifying a stressful child's world. Their impact can be by direct changes (changing schools, ending family conflict) and stress management approaches. Such approaches would include modeling appropriate responses to stress and actively talking with children about how to cope with their problems.

ANXIETY DISORDERS IN CHILDREN

Let us now look at anxiety effects on children. *Separation anxiety disorder* (SAD) is a type of anxiety disorder specifically limited to children. A diagnosis is based upon excessive anxiety responses about separating from known people or surroundings. For children under four this is somewhat normal, and so the amount of anxiety must be great in order to be diagnosed with SAD. Three to 5 percent of children (under 12) and about 2 percent of adolescents have SAD at any time.

For many children, treatment with anti-anxiety medication is typical. The drug imipramine is often prescribed, and research on its effectiveness is generally positive, but far from convincing. For parents who prefer a nondrug alternative, there is a cognitive-behavioral model to help children. Andrew Eisen and his group have described a parent-training program that allows for parents to aid their anxiety-affected children to cope in a variety of settings without medication.

For most parents of anxiety-affected children, there are three situations that are usually also present. These are parental overprotection, excessive reassurance behavior, and negative parent–child interactions. As you might infer, these collateral conditions support and maintain the anxiety problems and can also hinder efforts to improve the children involved. As such, parent-training programs address these issues and minimize the likelihood that the three factors will interfere with a child's progress in overcoming his or her anxiety.

Both the parent and child are trained and are allowed role-playing and other rehearsal strategies that give them more control over potentially threatening and anxiety-producing situations. Parents become coaches and facilitators in helping their child to use the new skills they have practiced when they are really needed. This is one way that a parent can actively teach coping.

One such cognitive-behavioral model credited to W. K. Silverman involves the four-step process summarized by the acronym STOP. *S* is for Scared, the first step in recognizing an anxiety response. *T* refers to Thoughts, specifically thoughts about what is causing the anxiety and thoughts about the anxiety. *O* is for Other thoughts, the newly acquired self-talk and coping methods the child is to use to deal with the anxiety. *P* is for Praise, the last step, which encourages the child to praise himself for trying to cope and deal better with the anxiety situation.

Armed with this process, and with the knowledge that a parent is there to help if needed, a child can be successfully trained to apply this coping skill in a variety of situations, thus allowing for a more adaptive and less dysfunctional response. These cognitive-behavioral models have been shown to be easily learned and generalizable with practice.

STRESS AND CHILD DEVELOPMENT

Many anxiety-based issues are tied to long-term stress. Let us now explore three areas where children are subjected to stress on a daily basis—the home, schools, and the outside world, through the culture and media environments.

What can concerned, educated parents do to help their child? The short answer is to do all that is possible to provide structure and stability, providing security and safety, which is after all a respite from stress. Further, the educated parent must teach and model healthy, adaptive ways to cope with whatever stress remains.

To begin, *stress* is the term used to describe the body's (mental and physical) reaction to change. Every living animal is made to handle stress and you cannot live without some stress. Stressors, whether positive or negative in variety, are responded to in a similar way physiologically.

As part of life, every child will experience different stressors every year. Problems can emerge when too many of these events happen too quickly together over time. Please refer to the stress rating scale I have adapted from the work of David Elkind at the end of the chapter. It is like ones you have probably seen for adults, based upon the pioneering work of Thomas Holmes and Richard Rahe. *As a parent, your task is to organize your child's life situation in such a way as to promote stability and minimize losses and major change.*

Marianne Barton and Charles Zeanah have studied stress effects in preschoolers. Typical preschooler responses to stress include regression, attention-seeking behavior, social withdrawal, and changes in the way the child plays. In this age group, play allows a child to retreat into a less stressful reality, and it also allows a child a chance to replay some of the stressful situations and allow for mastery of or a simple desensitization to the stressor. When under stress, even preschoolers' play can be negatively affected. Play will be of shorter duration, be less flexible and more rigid, and less creative.

The research has indicated that the following are now normal stressful events for the preschooler: maternal employment, day care, and birth or adoption of a sibling. Beyond the norm, divorce effects, hospitalization episodes, abuse/neglect, and loss or lessening of parental contact are documented stressors that impact the preschool-age child negatively.

Preschoolers' stress responses can be helped or mitigated by individual variables such as gender (girls handle stress more adaptively than boys); intelligence (smarter children cope better and can maintain their focus better); and temperament type (difficult-temperament children often show more behavior problems). Protective variables for preschoolers include a structured and stable life (stability is especially important in coping with divorce), access to attachment figures, and the quality of the parent–child relationship (securely attached children function and respond best).

Ways to help a preschooler cope more effectively are with:

1. information (telling children what is happening and what to expect lessens anxiety in a situation);
2. ventilation (allowing an opportunity and the means to express their distress, such as play);
3. rituals surrounding a stressful event (allow for a sense of control and mastery);
4. maintenance of routine (the need for stability and predictability as discussed previously); and

5. cognitive change (for older preschoolers, the ability to learn problem-solving and other behavior modification strategies).

Susan Sears and Joanne Milburn have looked at the research on school-age stress effects. Common school-age stressors include: (1) school-related issues (anxiety about school, general test anxiety, teacher conflicts, peer problems, learning disorders, parental pressure to achieve, failure experiences); (2) siblings (relationship problems, rivalry, jealousy); (3) parental problems (alcoholism, abusive/neglectful behavior, loyalty issues surrounding a separation/divorce); (4) personal issues (dental and medical visits, responses to violent/inappropriate TV programs, low self-esteem); and (5) peer problems (teasing, bullying, competition, and comparisons).

One particularly problematic stress consequence for children is recurrent abdominal pain (RAP). RAP is diagnosed when meeting the criteria of three episodes of pain (usually in the navel region) occurring within three months and affecting the child's activities. A literature review by Lisa Scharff reported that RAP rates in children vary from 9–25 percent of a population, depending on age, gender, and geographic location. RAP has also been called an "abdominal migraine."

RAP may actually have an underlying physical cause (like an ulcer or intestinal obstruction) but is often psychologically caused. In some children, the pain reported is considered an exaggeration of what would be expected when there is a physical cause identified. Anxiety and acute stressors are the primary triggers of a RAP episode. Fortunately, a combination of medical intervention, parent training, and relaxation training for children has been found to relieve many of the RAP-afflicted children. Unfortunately, this problem persists in a sizeable minority of children even after medical problems have been ruled out or attended to. In addition, this minority can also develop a wider variety of somatic symptoms over time.

What can parents do to help with any of these stress and anxiety problems? Parents can be accepting and encouraging, set realistic goals and expectations for their child, teach and model active learning and problem solving, and reward interest in appropriate child pursuits like learning and academic achievement. Being accepting and encouraging is an obvious starting point. When children feel loved and accepted for who they are, they can develop a sense of self-esteem and self-value. These feelings and beliefs can serve as stress inoculators and as a foundation for coping skills and the notion that the child can handle whatever issue is needing to be faced.

Setting realistic goals and expectations also make your child's life more manageable. A child who wants to please his parent needs to believe that he has a chance at accomplishing that goal. If a parent sets the bar too high or lets it be known that the child has no chance to achieve success, then the child will give up and be left feeling that he is unworthy or a failure. These feelings add to a sense of distress and will cause more difficulties for the child in other stress-related areas of life.

Regarding the third helping behavior, parents can and should help their child identify sources of stress and anxiety, and then discuss and teach ways to cope. Such coping strategies can include learning a relaxation response or a cognitive restructuring, where the child reinterprets a situation or an outcome in a more manageable way. We will review some parent-training programs that deal with childhood stress prevention and treatment later in this chapter.

As for rewarding interest in appropriate child pursuits like learning and academic achievement, a parent in this case is simply organizing the child's life around age-expected behavior. This is likely to lead to many successful and positive experiences as the child is in "his element." As was seen in chapter 5, parental guidance around educational pursuits is essential for child achievement. But again, children need to be supported to do their best. The bar cannot be set at "honor roll or bust."

Robert Hendren has described the consequences of teen stress. Adolescent stressors typically include: (1) physical-related changes (hormonal influences, puberty, secondary sexual characteristics like breast development or penile changes, increases in sexual feelings and general heightened sexuality); (2) other individual changes (feelings of moodiness or emotional instability, gender role changes, sexual orientation issues, new and enhanced cognitive abilities, identity formation issues, increased desires for autonomy and independence); (3) family-related changes (different relationship with parents and siblings, parental discord or divorce); and (4) peer-relation issues (peer pressure, conformity pressures, different cultural expectations).

Adolescent stress disorders include depression and suicide, substance experimentation and abuse, and eating disorders. Suicide rates for teens have tripled since 1950. Increased social pressures coupled with decreases in support from adults add to the mix. Body image changes and self-esteem issues related to identity and family relations are another source of stress that can lead to depression.

Fascination with illicit substances, be they drugs, alcohol, or nicotine products is natural. Although experimentation with these substances is common, it is not universal. Much research has been conducted to determine causes of teen attraction and experimentation. The following is a very brief summary of hundreds of articles in the area of causal agents.

A teen's likelihood of experimenting is related to: (1) opportunity (more supervision = less chances; less supervision = more likelihood); (2) quality of peer relations (a group of delinquent, conduct-disordered teens will more likely be a gateway to experimenting with substances than association with appropriate-acting teens); (3) self-esteem (a teen with low self-esteem is more likely to engage in such behavior to fit in or be accepted than one who feels more in control and better about himself); and (4) parental/family value systems (teens of churchgoing, nonsmoking, nondrinking parents are also less likely to try illicit substances). Also recall the Wills et al. study of temperament effects presented in chapter 3.

Eating disorders often emerge in adolescence, especially among females. Young women are especially vulnerable as a result of a mix of variables that include identity issues, body image, cultural messages and modeling, and personal-control issues. A teen who is already depressed or has low self-esteem or problems with effective emotional expression is more at risk than others. Eating disorders are multi-determined by an array of individual, societal, and family-related factors. Stress is not a documented primary cause.

Teens are most likely able to benefit from cognitive-behavioral approaches to coping and stress reduction because of their increased cognitive abilities. School-based curricula that teach coping strategies, such as peer mediation programs, can be beneficial for many adolescents. I believe parents should support and encourage their teen's participation in these school-based programs where available.

Eugene Arnold has listed stressors that all children and teens in today's society must learn to deal with effectively. Arnold's list follows here. Regrettably, abuse tops his inventory. *Abuse* at the hands of caregivers is a significant source of stress and anxiety and leads to long-term negative consequences. The abuse can be from exposure to family violence as well as physical, sexual, mental, emotional, or verbal abuse aimed directly at a child. *Threats of violence,* such as fears of terrorist attacks, local crime, or school-related concerns are also problematic. Schools also provide stress in the form of *competition.* Competition to succeed, to avoid failure, and to be successful can all get out of hand.

Larger issues include *poverty, parental absence,* and *parental illness or death.* Poverty is a chronic stressor which can touch every aspect of a child's existence. Parental absence for whatever reason (travel, separation/divorce) is always experienced as a loss. Parental illness and death can also tax a young child. A parent who is severely depressed is not only less available to a child, but also can create doubt in older children and teens about their potential to develop in a similar way. Death is the ultimate loss for a child or teen. How a child grieves, and the timing of such a loss has vast implications for the level of stress to follow.

The research news on childhood stress and anxiety is not all depressing or discouraging. Research is underway to fully examine protective factors and aspects of resiliency, the ability to cope and grow in spite of the odds being stacked against a child/teen.

Some definitions are in order here. *Risk factors* are elements that increase the likelihood of a later emotional or behavioral disorder as a result of such exposure in development. Examples would include parental mental illness, poverty, or difficult temperament in the child.

Protective factors are the characteristics of a person or their environment that limit or reduce future problems based upon their exposure to risk factors. Examples of protective factors are having above average IQ, gender (easier for girls), family socioeconomic status (SES) (being middle or upper class), and good physical health. Protective factors are usually placed in three broad categories: positive temperament qualities; supportive family situations; and positive external (to the family) support systems that encourage and reward the child/teen to continue adaptive and healthy responses. This last category includes a good school experience with caring and responsive teachers.

An example of a general protective factor is found in the work of Arnold Sameroff and Michael Chandler. These researchers first spoke about a *continuum of caretaking casualty.* This continuum is related to family environment, specifically the quality of the family situation that a child is reared in. At one end of the continuum, one can find a family scenario that promotes good development and overall health. Such an environment would include educated parents, financial resources, and authoritative parenting. On the other end, one would find poverty, family stress, violence, and substance abuse. Depending on which environment a child enters, there will be more or less risk for that child to develop problems. Some have said that this continuum is a precursor to resilience.

Resiliency, as I will discuss this term here, is an individual factor, different from protective factors, which can also be environmental or external to the person. Resiliency is a "summary factor" or a construct based on multiple variables after the fact. So resiliency can only be determined *after* a person has been exposed to risk factors. A resilient person is one who has minimized or escaped from the expected negative outcome.

Judith Kimichi and Barbara Schaffner have grouped resiliency profiles by developmental period. They have found that resilient infants are cheerful, respond positively to people and objects, are alert, and are otherwise of easy temperament.

Resilient preschoolers also have easy-temperament characteristics. Additionally, they are independent, play well and often, and show self-directive behavior and autonomy, but also know when to get help. They are effective communicators and have good frustration tolerance.

Resilient children (ages 5–12) are good in school, relate well with their teachers, have great peer relationships, and have well-developed coping strategies. Resilient teens are energetic, involved, achievement-oriented, responsible, and caring. They have developed a sense of personal responsibility and a belief in themselves and their abilities. They are well-developed socially.

Family characteristics associated with resiliency include low conflict in the home environment and having a middle-class SES. Resiliency is also associated with competent, authoritative parents and properly spaced siblings (two to three years between births). All of these home qualities may also be viewed as stress inoculators for children.

DAVID ELKIND'S HURRIED CHILD MODEL

In David Elkind's book *The Hurried Child Syndrome,* he presents some patterned ways that children will likely use to cope with stress as it gets to be overwhelming or seemingly out of control for the child. *Free-floating anxiety,* also called "unattached uneasiness," is when a child feels anxious for no apparent reason. Such a child may act in a way indicative of an attention deficit problem. Headaches, restlessness, and irritability may also be seen. A child suffering from free-floating anxiety is likely to be diagnosed with an anxiety disorder problem.

Some children will adopt a *type A personality,* much like the adult version, where the child becomes quite competitive and aggressive. Under stress, type A children will try what they can to overcompensate and over-control to make up for their perceived (and stress-inducing) lack of control. Physical correlates of this type include stomachaches, gastrointestinal problems, and the beginnings of hypertension. While there can be some positive gain from a type A response in that these children tend to over-achieve and even excel, it comes at the price of underlying insecurity and a lack of a sense of satisfaction or accomplishment.

A third interesting stress response is seen in children who train and specialize at a high level of intensity in art or sports. Called *premature struc-*

turing, this stress response occurs when a child sacrifices normal growing up in order to be involved at a high, even professional, level in some endeavor. An example might be gymnasts who train from ages as young as seven or eight for hours each day, even sometimes living away from their families in order to achieve maximum benefit from coaching. Such a child is at-risk for burnout and a kind of midlife crisis at 17. Certain parts of his emotional or personality development may be delayed as a result of missing out on normal developmental experiential opportunities. The stresses from being separated from normal family and social experiences coupled with an intensity and focus on a limited aspect of his identity (a gymnast or pianist or skater or tennis player) can create later adult dysfunction.

Related to the premature structuring notion is another stress-related phenomenon called *achievement-by-proxy*. Achievement-by-proxy (ABP) is a term used by Ian Toffler, Penelope Knapp, and Martin Drell to describe how "ambitious parents could potentially damage their children by overstressing them and pushing them." In their research, they have found that supportive parental behavior for high achievement is one thing. But social and financial benefits from the child's achievements should be a bonus, rather than the main motivation for the adult.

In cases of ABP behavior, the adult goes way too far. The benefits of the child's achievements become primary goals for the adult, not a derivative of success. The parent's will takes over. The child will be caught up in the excitement and believe that he is doing the behavior for himself. You know you have gone too far as a parent when you are making risky, short-term choices that may hurt the child in the long run. One can easily turn over parenting decisions, even custody of a child's life, to a coach or mentor.

For instance, parents and other adults may encourage or condone such dangerous behaviors as disordered eating (as with ballet dancers and some gymnasts) or continued exercising or training with a serious physical injury. Looking ahead to a gold medal, future endorsements, or a lucrative contract blinds some parents to the "right thing" for their child.

Educated parents, argues the Toffler group, must be aware of "danger signals." These would be the rationalizations adults may have in pushing for greater success or achievement from their children. Ways for parents to protect their children include:

- always seeking to balance the child's goals with appropriate developmental expectations;
- practicing responsible parenting by watching out for children and their ability to handle pressure;

- questioning one's "parental motivations" by asking whether you are doing this for your child or yourself; and

- being honest with yourself about any "hidden agendas."

Elkind's premise in *The Hurried Child Syndrome* is that many parents are guilty of rushing their children into maturity and adulthood faster than normal development dictates. High levels of parental pressure for success and achievement can start at birth, as some parents must place their child on a four-year-long waiting list for a prestigious preschool or kindergarten. The parental intentions may be good, but the outcomes can be disastrous for the child. A recent example just played out in New York and Colorado.

As told by *New York Times* reporter Erica Goode, a mother was so intent on providing the best for her son that she did all she could to promote his educational opportunities. These included enrollment in an on-line high school at age five, and coursework at the college level at age six. This super-gifted child was even "documented" through testing. His mother had an official IQ score for him of 298, and paperwork to show a perfect 800 on the math section of the SAT.

It turned out that this quite-above-average child was improperly coached before the IQ test (rendering the score invalid). The SAT score was actually earned by a neighbor's child and altered by the mother to appear as her son's. This would have been an interesting experiment in fooling the system if it did not have such a bad ending.

The child, it was reported, began to develop emotional and anxiety-related behavioral problems at age seven. When enrolled in a new school for exceptional students in Colorado, he at first did well. But soon after, this child refused to do schoolwork, had behavioral outbursts, and became suicidal. He was placed in a residential psychiatric facility and then in foster care. The boy was removed from his mother's custody, as reported in the news account, amid charges of her failure to supervise her son properly and playing a role in substantially impairing his normal development, as well as interfering with his psychiatric care. As of this writing, this parent's and child's futures were uncertain.

I recount this story not to condemn the mother but to issue a warning to other parents who might become consumed by a belief that they must go way beyond the norm for the sake of providing the best for their child. The outcome of such irrational behavior is an inordinate amount of stress and pressures placed upon a child who will never be developmentally able to handle such expectations. Trying to please a parent is a powerful motivator and wish for children. Adding improper expectations, engaging in ABP behavior, or raising the bar so high that it cannot be attained is both unfair and counterproductive.

Children may be hurried in a "developmental" way, as in asking children to perform in ways that are precocious or above their level of developmental ability. They may also be hurried in an "energic" manner, as in living in a rushed, totally planned out daily routine.

For example, take the child who must be awakened at 6:15 on Monday morning and must get ready (dressed and schoolwork packed up) and eat breakfast in order to leave with Mom or Dad to be dropped off at day care by seven A.M. Then the child leaves for school at 7:45 and spends the day there until picked up and returned for after-school care. There, the child may have a 30-minute window for homework before heading out to tennis lessons or karate. Then Mom or Dad picks the child up at six P.M. to rush home. Sometimes dinner is eaten at home and other times at a restaurant. After arriving home, the child must finish any remaining homework or possibly make time to practice piano or clarinet for 30 minutes. Other nights it's time to work on the book report or science project, where parental patience might be stretched to its thinnest. Then it's bath time and time for bed. On Tuesday, you do it all over again. It's an exhausting regimen with little time for play or spontaneity, unless it has been built into the schedule (that's a joke—you can't schedule spontaneity).

What are the overall consequences of hurrying children? Well, all of the health problems, as a start. But children also suffer from attachment disorders (not enough time with parents), suicide thoughts and behaviors (mostly in adolescence), and other acting-out behavior (from oppositional or resistant behavior with authority figures as a child, to crime and drug/alcohol abuse for teens).

How do parents contribute to this stress? To begin with, many families are in distress. There is a lack of stability, whether it is found through inconsistent schedules and home routines, decreased levels of contact with extended family members who once were a source of security and stability, or simply a hurried lifestyle where every family member is too busy and common times (like the proverbial dinnertime) are too few. Other parents wind up stressing their child(ren) when used as "surrogate selves." The surrogate-self child is living the childhood experience that the parent was unable to have. There is a real desire on the child's part to make the parent happy and to please him or her, adding to the pressure experienced by a child in this position.

Other parents inappropriately depend on a child to be a source of support, or even a confidant, as they have few others they can turn to in times of need. In multi-sibling families, oldest children (usually female) can become surrogate parents—they assume responsibilities for supervision, feeding, house cleaning, and general parenting duties. When a teenager is placed in this position it is "no-win."

In family-therapy circles, such children are said to be *parentified,* meaning that they have assumed the psychological responsibilities for their siblings. They are acting in a way as to be prevented from normal teen development. Additionally, such a scenario often leads to hard feelings between the siblings. The younger siblings will question the authority of one of their own and may form alliances against this "extra parent."

The parentified teen will lose out on more normal sibling relationships and have to deal with home stress that may interfere with school achievement or social opportunities, which in turn will be blamed on the siblings' needs. Many teens will willingly take on this parenting responsibility. They do so to feel important or older, but mostly to help out a parent in need. In this way, the child becomes an equal to the parent—another negative outcome for the child/teen who is not yet grown up.

STRESSORS RELATED TO SCHOOL

Parents also have the obligation and responsibility to know and be aware of the stressors affecting children from school. Here I refer to system pressures, not those caused by nightly homework or teacher personality conflicts. In far too many U.S. school districts, outcomes assessment has taken priority over learning outcomes. Schools (teachers and administrators) get measured on the basis of a grade or score. Often these grades or scores have arbitrary standards or meaningless (but measurable) criteria such as attendance rates or tardiness. Then there are regularly administered standardized tests upon which monetary rewards are linked to outperforming peers in the district.

The result is that schools decide to "teach the test" in order to win, and every campus has increased anxiety. Schoolchildren become very well aware of the meaningfulness of these test results, either from direct instruction by the teacher or from the pervasive anxiety brought about by the state mandates. Competitiveness has its place in the world as a way of making improvements, but schools are not one of those places.

As a parent you are obligated to participate in these decisions. You vote, so you can influence your state priorities and the membership of your local school board. PTA or PTSO meetings are a place to begin to get involved in telling the schools your opinion and pointing out the unintended consequences of trying to fix an ill-defined problem (e.g., "poor schools") with simplistic and wrongheaded solutions.

Yet another school-based area for creating stress in children that Elkind has pointed out is the issue of sex education. Here the concern is about both developmental readiness and the question of content of information. At what age does one begin this discussion in the school? Is first grade too soon? Is third grade too late? Given the very different rates of child growth, how can any school system gauge when a child is ready for this information and how much information should be presented.

Children and teens, very naturally curious about the topic, can also become easily confused and conflicted via mixed messages. If the teacher discusses the topic of safe sex and explicitly (how else can you do this?) teaches about condoms and their use/misuse, is he or she advocating or endorsing safe sex as an approved teen behavior? What about free condoms being readily available in guidance counselor offices? If such condom availability limits the spread of disease and unintended pregnancy (as the supporters rightfully argue), is the availability also a promotion for teen sex (which the detractors would contend)?

I will not get into this debate further, except to say that sex education is rightfully an obligation of parents. Since many parents have abrogated this responsibility it has gone to the schools, where parents have a diminished say about content or timing of information. Parents need to regain their ownership of this value-laden topic. The argument that "they will do it no matter what, so they should have safe-sex information" is lame unless you are saying that your teen (or even preteen) is so out-of-control and beyond your supervision ability that you've given up.

CULTURAL AND MEDIA-BASED STRESSORS AND CHILDREN

Finally, our children are bombarded with all sorts of mixed messages through media and culture. Watch and surf broadcast and cable TV for any three-hour period. What messages are portrayed about sexual behavior? What modeled behavior is there about fashion and clothing? How is cigarette or alcohol use depicted in the movies on TV? Can you stand to watch an hour of so-called pro wrestling? How do these images and communications conflict not only with other TV content but with what you are trying to encourage and establish as a parent?

Violent content on TV has been an especially prevalent and well-publicized problem. Researchers such as Aletha Huston have tracked the effects of such exposure. She and her group have found that TV viewing encourages and models antisocial behavior in child-age viewers. In fact, the effect has what are called interactive factors, and is cumulative as well. That is, the amounts watched build on previous amounts watched, and their total effect grows stronger with subsequent viewing of violent content. The Huston et al. study reported that children who watch a lot of TV are likely to act more aggressively in other areas of their life, and children who are aggressive already, are drawn to view violent content. Other researchers (e.g., a study by Ronald Slaby and Leonard Eron) report that children who watch many hours of violent content are often bullies in their peer interactions, and more likely to retaliate in a physical, aggressive manner when attacked verbally or otherwise.

A 2002 study published in the prestigious journal *Science* and widely reported in print and TV media outlets, found support for the TV viewing–aggression link as well. Although the main focus of the study was on factors influencing children's mental health, this longitudinal research was able to document a correlation between amount of general (not just violent or aggressive content) TV viewing at age 14 and aggressive behavior in adulthood at age 20. This correlation, which is *not* a valid indicator of causality by itself, was weak but statistically significant. In general, when a researcher finds a significant correlation it is a case of "where there's smoke." Additional research is needed to see if "there is fire," but something is going on to relate the two variables.

This study is an interesting example of what happens when the media decide to report a finding of a complex nature with a stream of sound bites. In fact, aggressive behavior in adults is an intricate, multi-determined phenomenon and there is no way that one can pin such a specific behavior on TV. What else could have been involved? Perhaps lack of parental supervision and/or interaction was a significant contributor to the later behavior. It is easily understood that in such a scenario the lack of parenting is related to both increased TV viewing *and* the greater likelihood that a child would have been in situations where aggression was learned. So what the correlation may really be pointing to is that lack of parental involvement leads to more aggressive behavior when teens grow into adults, even though it was TV viewing time that got the bad press.

While it probably is the case that there are many things going on other than the TV time and parental quality (to name two variables out of many), TV viewing time is in the mix of factors that contribute to adult aggression. That's all that can really be concluded. How much, in what way, or whether TV exposure "causes" aggression still cannot be said with certainty. We are left with a strong circumstantial case that remains to be proved.

Exposure to physical violence on TV is even of concern in cartoon fare, where violent acts are portrayed at a rate of 25 per hour according to the National Coalition on Television Violence. Mutant Ninja Turtles and now Power Rangers are often involved in destructive and aggressive types of behavior, so these viewing effects, whatever they might be, start when children are relatively young.

Joanne Cantor has reviewed and written extensively on the topic of media and violence and its effects on children. She has devoted one stream of research to uncovering how media violence causes increased fear reactions in children. Cantor has found that college students vividly recall being frightened by movies or TV as children, and how those effects were longer lasting than one might guess. She has also written a book for parents (*Mommy, I'm Scared*) where she has offered information on how to teach coping responses to children following exposure to violent media content. I recommend it for your further reading.

Sexual and violent content are the norms for most movies worth seeing to a teenager. What exactly does a PG-13 rating mean? Does it matter if a teen sees an R-rated movie? If you have cable TV, it is almost a certainty that R movies will be viewed. MTV programming is laden with content aimed at young adults, but how much does your child or teen watch? Yet it's hard to completely blame the producers of MTV content as they are not the ones who control the remote at home.

From music video content to lyric content, what songs does your child listen to? Have you ever heard a five-year-old singing about losing her virginity? I have. Did the child understand the lyrics? Probably not, but she will some day, and sooner than you think. Or what about six-year-olds rapping about "bitches and ho's" or running away from the police?

And then there are video games. The level of violence in many games is obscene. Many different methods of killing are graphically portrayed, as are the results of the aggressive behavior (e.g., a still-beating bloody heart ripped out of a chest). There is now a rating system for parental guidance, but the shrewd marketers have used this to make a game more desirable for preteens and teens by way of its "badder" rating on the box. (The Entertainment Software Ratings Board, or ESRB, has created a tiered rating system. The "E," or everyone, rating may contain minimal violence, general mischief, and mildly crude language. The "T," or teen, rating is intended for those over 13 and can have violence, mild profanity, and suggestive themes. "M" rated games, for the "mature" crowd of 17-or-older players, have graphic violence, serious profanity, and sexual themes. In 2002, the ratings percentages for games were: 63% with an E rating; 27% with a T rating, and 8% with an M rating; 2% were rated EC (early child-hood)).

As of this writing, the video game "Grand Theft Auto III," or GTA3 as it is known, is among the most popular in sales. GTA3 sold two million copies in the first three months of release in North America alone. What is in this "game"? Well, you as the player work for the Mafia and can earn points for carjacking, running down or shooting the carjack victims, and generally act aggressively against every virtual person on the screen. These virtual victims include police, innocent pedestrians, and even elderly bystanders. Not satisfied with the excessive violence, there is also a sexual, misogynistic thread woven into this garbage. You can also earn points (actually expressed as "money") by stealing back the money you paid out to pick up a prostitute by either beating her up or killing her.

GTA3 as well as other strong-selling video games have made it to a list of "software to avoid" for impressionable youth as compiled by the National Institute on Media and the Family. Who is buying games like GTA3? Primarily adolescent and young adult males. Why are they attracted to these destructive themes instead of more constructive alterna-tives? That is a question we must all ask. For parents, be sure you know what your child/teen is playing on his PlayStation or Nintendo. If you allow violent content within a gaming scenario, you need to reflect on why you allow it. You also need to strongly consider limiting the amount of time your child/teen is exposed to the repetition of violence.

The arguments from the research against unlimited exposure to the video game violence are similar to those with TV content as follows: it models aggressive and hostile behavior; it normalizes such inappropriate behavior through reduction of its revulsion through repetitiveness; it sexualizes and objectifies the female characters; and it desensitizes the player to the real consequences of violence in real life. The argument that video games are not reality is legitimate. Some studies have suggested that the people most affected by such exposure are those who already have some psychological problems; "normal" children are actually affected little if at all.

To what extent does a player make the distinction between "the game" and reality, and how does repeated exposure translate into actual behavior or attitude change? There are no clear answers. The fact is that such com-plex questions cannot be cleanly answered with the research tools we have available. So the trends in research and a little common sense must guide the educated parent.

The Internet and Children

And now we turn our attention to the Internet. Although Internet saturation into our homes is still not complete, it is only a matter of time. As with TV and video game research, there are no clear-cut studies one can point to for direction. This is another example of where good old parental common sense is called for. Trying to shield your child from any Internet time would be quite difficult—it will be found in schools and preschools. If you work at home or just want the possibilities that the Internet offers, you will have it in your home or home office.

Some initial reports focused on overuse of the Internet and its potential for disrupting normal social and peer relations. The thinking behind this was that many children might choose to e-mail a friend rather than meet face to face. Or a child/teen might assume an "e-persona" and get lost in various chat rooms where truth and reality are as ephemeral as electrons. Such a removal from real-life social settings would lead to lost or inappropriate social skills over time.

There are also the worries about sexual predators or others out to exploit children. Accidental exposure to inappropriate content is another concern. Purposeful searching can also lead to trouble, as when a child or teen seeks to learn about bomb making or deviant sexual practices.

Professional presentations have encouraged parental caution, and there are uncertainties about how children will be impacted. For example, Jennifer Bremer and Paula Rauch have noted the attendant risks of unsupervised Internet usage. These include exposure to inappropriate material, predators in chat rooms, and other abusive experiences. At the same time, these authors hold out hope for the positive side of Internet access. They believe that properly used, Internet time can be a great asset in educational pursuits, be a source of enhanced self-esteem, and serve to "offer information about medical and mental health treatment, diagnoses, and support networks." Again, the key is in proper supervision.

Support and encouragement for children's use of the Internet has come from an unlikely coalition, as seen in survey results by the National School Boards Foundation (NSBF), the Children's Television Workshop (CTW), and Microsoft Corporation. As posted on-line in 2000, this report refuted claims that "the Internet isolates kids," and it found that there are no gender differences in usage.

The report states that "families are overwhelmingly positive about their experiences in cyberspace. The survey by the NSBF contradicts previous reports that the Internet negatively influences young users. Parents, in fact, want their children to use the Internet, especially for educational activities, trust their Net use and feel the Net is generally safe" (National School Boards Foundation, p. 1).

The NSBF sought to update and add data to the ongoing debate about Internet use. Based on interviews with a random sample of both parents and children, the study is worthy of a closer look. Some key findings as posted:

- Ninety-five percent of those surveyed said that family interactions had increased or stayed the same with the Internet at home.

- Parents trust their children's use of the Internet and generally believe it's a safe place. Most parents forgo the "watchdog" role for a "guide" role, adopting a commonsense, balanced approach to their children's Internet use. Parents monitor the sites their children visit, limit their time spent on-line, and set other rules about usage. (Sixty-seven percent of parents surveyed said their role is as a guide to good content.)

- Parents and children report that the Internet does not disrupt children's everyday habits and normal, healthy activities. (Eighty-five percent of parents whose children use the Internet said their children spend more or the same amount of time reading books.)

- Girls use the Internet as much as boys (50% of 9-to-12-year-old girls are on-line, compared with 46% of boys; 73% of 13-to-17-year-old girls use the Net, compared with 70% of boys). However, girls are much more likely to go on-line for education, schoolwork, entertainment, and games.

- Schools have an opportunity to help narrow the gap between the technology haves and have-nots, with schools providing significant Internet access for students who otherwise would not have access (in families with incomes of less than $40,000, 76% of 9-to-17-year-olds who use the Internet say that they log on at school; in African American families, 80% of 9-to-17-year-olds say they log on at school).

- The main reason cited by parents for buying home computers and obtaining home Internet access is for their children's learning/education (45%).

Gary E. Knell, president and CEO of the CTW, added that, "This study validates our commitment to provide high-quality educational content to families on the Internet. Early exposure helps build literacy and other cognitive skills. Parents and children should be encouraged to go online together where they can learn, grow and bond."

The NSBF has developed and is promoting guidelines to help schools and families use the Internet safely. Their guidelines, adapted below from their posting, recommend:

- parents and teachers pay as much attention to highlighting good content as restricting bad content;

- development of a plan to help schools, teachers, and parents educate children about safe, responsible Internet use (e.g., put computers in rooms that are shared, teach children not to give out personal information, participate in an on-line safety program);

- foster appropriate use of the Internet among preschoolers and other young children;

- helping teachers, parents, and children use the Internet more effectively for learning (e.g., suggest education-related Web sites for parents and children to visit together, offer after-school tutoring on-line, provide teacher training to integrate the Internet into lessons);

- use the Internet to communicate more effectively with parents and students and stimulate parent involvement (e.g., post exemplary student work on-line with teacher comments, create a school Web site, encourage parents to e-mail teachers); and

- engage the community by encouraging computer and Internet training, and hosting forums to discuss children's use of technology for education.

In 1999, Bob Affonso posted another positive review of the Internet and children (www.sierrasource.com/cep612/internet.html). I recommend its reading (and a look at the Bibliography for more information) for the educated parent. Among the highlights of his report, adapted in summary:

On reviewing reports that Internet use has a negative influence on individuals and their social skills:

- A Carnegie Mellon University study found Internet use to lead to small but statistically significant increases in misery and loneliness and a decline in overall psychological well-being.

- The HomeNet project studied 169 people in Pittsburgh during their first years on-line. Subjects reported keeping up with fewer friends as their Internet use increased, spending less time talking with their families, experiencing more daily stress, and feeling more lonely and depressed, even though interpersonal communication was their most important reason for using the Internet.

- The Annenberg Public Policy Center in Washington, D.C., found that a majority of parents in computer households feared the Internet's influence on children, owing particularly to its wide-open nature and interactivity. Parents also believed that their children needed Internet access and its educational benefits.

- At one large university in New York, the new-freshmen dropout rate rose in relation to the investment in computers and Internet access. Dropouts apparently increased owing to the fact that 43 percent of them were staying up all night on the Internet. http://www.sierrasource.com/cep612/addicted.wav

On the issue of the Internet being "addictive":

- Some studies suggest addictive behavior patterns among heavy Internet users following criteria often used to define addiction. These include: (a) using the computer for pleasure, gratification, or relief from stress; (b) feeling irritable and out of control or depressed when not using it; (c) spending increasing amounts of time and money on hardware, software, magazines, and computer-related activities; and (d) neglecting work, school, or family obligations.

- In disagreement, others argue that the symptoms seem more related to general personality disorders rather than real computer addiction. Others challenge the findings of the on-line survey studies because of sampling problems and demographic inequalities.

On the question of the Internet and children:

- Referring to the HomeNet study, it was found that teenagers are much heavier Internet users than their parents; they were more likely to use the Internet to play games, to listen to music, and to meet new people.

- In their dealings with technology, youths are portrayed as either victims or criminals. Both are incorrect stereotypes.

- The Internet can assist social skills development. There are many opportunities for children and teens to interact on-line in productive and positive ways including on-line magazines where one can write, share, and communicate ideas.

- Children can become attracted by the intrinsic opportunities of the technology of computers and the Internet at the expense of other more appropriate activities such as homework or normal social interchange. Most children seem to innately correct the problem of overuse.

- The HomeNet study recommended that parents limit and monitor their children's Internet use and encourage family interaction by installing the computer in the living room, rather than the basement or a child's room.

Affonso concludes, "despite the alarm, research indicates most children are doing fine.... [O]verall, technology can be considered a positive enhancement to growth." Affonso and others claim that children on-line are "reading, thinking, analyzing, criticizing and authenticating—composing their thoughts." In other words, they are engaging in desirable cognitive activity.

Jakob Nielson and Shuli Gilutz, as reported by Steven Levy in *Newsweek,* have found that children (age 5–11) aren't as naturally able to run through and navigate Web sites with the ease that adults often wish they had. For example, many children don't scroll, apparently unsure that anything not visible is there or important. In particular, children respond to Web ads differently, being unable to distinguish between a banner ad and the content below it. On a positive note, it was found that children were aware of privacy issues. They knew not to give out names and other contact information, and that the Internet could be a very dangerous place. So they are listening to concerned adults.

In June 2002, regulators from the Federal Trade Commission (FTC) reported their concerns regarding child and teen access to gambling Web sites.[1] David Ho has reported that the FTC found that 20 percent of "popular Internet gambling sites" had no warnings for minor access, or had blocks or screens that could be penetrated easily. The educated parent needs to be very careful as on-line gambling is very addictive and the financial consequences to families can be quite costly. With children, one worry is that such gambling experimentation may be the seed for a later full-blown addiction. In the absence of FTC policies that would not violate first-amendment rights of the site owners, parents must be the ones to safeguard and protect their children from this ready source of trouble.

To its credit, AOL has pioneered the importance of parental controls that can limit many purposeful and accidental exposures to unwanted content by children. Many other software packages are also available. These are probably a wise investment.

However, not all would agree with this advice. Sara Bushong has reviewed and reported on several Internet safety practices, including filters. She argues that these can't be considered any kind of guarantee and there is no substitute for parental guidance. Similarly, Geoffrey Nunberg has written about shortcomings and problems with filtering software. His argument goes beyond issues of protecting children, but the sentiment is valid. There is nothing better than direct parental supervision and monitoring of use.

PARENTING MEASURES TO REDUCE STRESS AND IMPROVE COPING

Given all of the above, what can the educated parent realistically be expected to do? Should you throw away your TV set? Is moving to a cave a good idea? Can homeschooling shelter your child from the world's evil?

Let's begin by reviewing what we have just explored. Knowing the underlying problems can help us determine what specific and general approaches should be applied and carried out. Here is a list of eight recommendations, in the order reviewed in this chapter.

1. Structure your home life to be as organized and well-managed as you can make it. Your home can be your child's safe harbor from the outside stress and turmoil.

2. Model and actively teach coping strategies as your child brings home problems from the world.

3. Make a schedule for your child that is reasonable and allows for downtime and spontaneity.

4. Minimize large life-change situations where possible. Staying in one house in one neighborhood is a good thing for children. Keep all large changes to an absolute minimum when you can control them.

5. Set realistic educational goals and expectations. Support all of your child's school-related efforts and activities.

6. Try to never hurry your child—energically or developmentally.

7. Don't live your life through your children. Their life is theirs, not yours.

8. Monitor what your children listen to on the radio and TV, and what video games they play. Never let your child/teen be unmonitored on-line.

APPENDIX: STRESS TEST FOR CHILDREN

Directions: Circle the number associated with each event that your child has experienced in the last 15 months, then total the points.

If the total score is at 150 or below, your child is experiencing "normal" stress levels. If the total is from 150–300, your child is at-risk for minor behavioral or physical stress-related problems. If the score is above 300, your child is at-risk for *serious* changes in physical health and/or behavior. Excessive stress/changes need to be addressed as soon as possible to avoid long-term problems.

Stressor	Pts	Stressor	Pts
Parent dies	100	Parents divorce	73
Parents separate	65	Parent travels often	65
Close family member dies	63	Personal injury/illness	53
Parent remarries	50	Parent loses job	47
Parents reconcile	45	Mother begins working	45
Family member's health changes	44	Mother becomes pregnant	40
School problems	39	Birth of sibling	39

New teacher/class change	39	Family financial change	38
Close friend illness/injury	37	Starts/changes activity/sport	36
Fights with siblings	35	Bullied at school	31
Sibling leaves home	29	Grandparent trouble	29
Wins award/recognition	28	Move to new city	26
Move across town	26	Get/lose a pet	25
Trouble with teacher	24	Schedule change with caretaker	20
Change of school	20	Family vacation	19
Change of friends	18	Summer camp	17
Change in sleeping habits	16	Birthday party	12
COLUMN TOTALS:		GRAND TOTAL:	

Note: This version is adapted from Elkind (1981). Holidays with typical full-family involvement (e.g., Christmas, Hanukkah, Thanksgiving) are not included here, but are found in other stress scales for children.

NOTE

1. David Ho, Associated Press; posted on-line June 26, 2002.

Chapter 9

FATHERHOOD

> Most American children suffer too much mother and too little father.
>
> —Gloria Steinem

The role of Father in the American family has undergone many changes over the past—both recent and distant. Fathering has become a major topic of research in the social sciences, with over 10,000 published studies on the topic of father influences on child development! Michael Lamb, who has researched father influences and effects since 1975, has tracked the evolution of the father role. In work he cites by Joseph Pleck, the past two hundred years have seen four primary roles for U.S. fathers. Fathers have changed from being moral teachers to breadwinners to sex-role models to nurturing co-parents. To some extent, the contemporary father tries to fulfill all four roles in many cases.

SOME HISTORY: A REVIEW OF RESEARCH ON THE IMPORTANCE OF FATHERS

It was the 1980s when research on fathering hit full bloom. The first reports of increased involvement of fathers, and increases in time spent on child care, began to creep into the contemporary literature and news. These "new fathers" were described as caring and nurturant and emotionally sensitive to children. These initial reports also touted the newly discovered research relationships between father involvement and greater intellectual and emotional development in their children. A movement toward embracing androgyny, allowing men to explore their feminine side, also came about.

In Lamb's review, these nurturant fathers were men actively involved in the daily care of their children. True parenting behavior, as of the 1980s, was considered to be a "central component" of the definition of a good father. But it was the 1970s, paralleled by the broadening societal support for feminism, from which this fathering definition emerged. This nurturant role was not a replacement but an add-on duty. Men were still to be bread-winners and sex-role models in family life.

As the role of fathers changed in society, the research approaches to learning about fathers' roles evolved. In the early 1900s through World War II, Lamb notes, Freudian perspectives dominated the scientific litera-ture. For Freudians, a father's role was to be not only a good provider, but also a psychological rock within the family. This was especially true as Freud's theory emphasized identification processes as a key for both boys' and girls' healthy development.

For Freud, boys learned how to be men by incorporating their father's beliefs, attitudes, values, and sexual orientations, all by age six or so. In a process termed *identification,* a boy resolved his internal psychic struggles to form a unique personality by coming to see his father as *the* role model. In this psychodynamic view, a father's masculinity was a key ingredient in developing a healthy son. If there were a father absence or a dominant mother in a family, that scenario would lead to a possible homosexual out-come in the son. (In those times, homosexuality was considered a disorder or personality abnormality to be avoided.) So to be sure that a son devel-oped a healthy, "normal" personality and sexual orientation, strong fathers were needed.

Girls' relationships with fathers were also important in the psychody-namic model. Similar internal, unconscious psychic forces that shaped boys' personality development also occurred in girls. For girls the proper, healthy outcome was identification with Mother's femininity after a pro-cess involving an attraction to the father and the strength and power he represented (the so-called penis envy phenomenon). Much was written about such Freudian notions, most of which is now viewed with historic interest, as little of his work is scientifically validated.

Of note, research begun in the 1960s did lead to an interesting conclu-sion about the role of fathers in gender typing. It was found that a boy's masculinity was dependent upon a strong father role model, while a girl's femininity was less tied to parental example. Boys with weak fathers and powerful mothers are much more likely to exhibit feminine behaviors. Fathers who are dominant and who set limits and enforce structure are more likely to produce masculine sons.

In Lamb's review, he further notes that the next areas of research to emerge were on the topics of father absence effects and maternal deprivation. Paralleling World War II and major losses of family intactness, research demonstrated the need and importance of attachment, considering only the role of mothers. The father absence literature repeatedly showed that boys were worse off for life if separated from their fathers.

In the 1980s and 1990s, American society began to recognize the huge costs associated with single-parent families and for a generation of children growing up without an involved father. Perhaps the exclamation point of this national discussion occurred when the TV character Murphy Brown, on the show with the same name, was going to have a baby and be a single mother by choice. Even Vice President Dan Quayle got into the fray. The debate was on, although way too much mudslinging and ad hominem attacks interfered with a fully meaningful resolution of the issue.

In fact, both the early maternal deprivation and father absence studies were methodologically flawed. Put simply, the results of most of this work were overstated and inaccurate. Later research was an improvement, but researchers soon concluded that their approaches were too simplistic to yield truly meaningful results. However, these efforts helped lay the groundwork for the next wave of research.

We are now in the most modern and enlightened period of fatherhood research. Lamb and his group have set the stage for the next generation of research. Stating that we have learned as much as could be known from the previous models, Lamb believes it is time to go to a more complex level of analysis. His solution is to better define the parameters of parental involvement and their impact on child development. He has proposed that all new research in this area focus on any or all of three component parts—engagement, accessibility, and responsibility.

By engagement, Lamb means that such research examine "actual one-on-one interaction" time, excluding "time spent sitting in one room while the child plays in the next room." Believe it or not, some older research would count proximity as father time. Accessibility refers to being available and nearby. The above exclusion of sitting in the next room *would* count as accessibility time. As long as a child knows the father is available and near, he is accessible. Finally, responsibility refers to a parent in charge. Activities such as going to the pediatrician—from making the appointment to going to the office and then getting the prescription filled—or doing things beyond baby-sitting or helping would apply here. All too often, fathers do not act and are *not* seen as responsible for child care. They are merely mother's helpers.

Ross Parke, another prominent fathering researcher, has also joined in the discussion about future research directions and needs. Akin to the responsibility parameter, Parke talks about the "managerial" functions of parents as a key variable to examine. These managerial functions are likely more important to the welfare of a child than the amount of direct time spent in one-on-one stimulation. That's because the time spent by children in their world (the toys they have, the clothes they wear, their health and nutrition needs being met) is far greater than the actual parent–child interaction time on any given day.

The managerial role extends to nonfamily socialization experiences as well. Where does the child go to school? Who are his friends? How much time does a child get to play with these friends? Parke's data suggest that fathers are still only minimally involved at this managerial level of child rearing.

Parke's other important contribution on this issue is a call to again be sure to look at the father's impact and influence relative to the developmental stage of the children involved. How do father interactions change as the child grows? While much research has carefully documented father time with infants, the other life stages have been under-researched. Parke has also proposed that research look at the developmental level of the father. Older first-time fathers act quite differently than do younger first-time dads. Similarly, issues related to career and marital satisfaction/security are related to paternal age and developmental status.

It remains to be seen how this new framework will go forward. What is certain is that researchers are well aware of the complexity of these research queries and the need for more sophisticated approaches and techniques to tease out the relationships between father variables and child outcomes. These are exciting times for social scientists who work in the fathering research area.

FATHERHOOD: DEFINITIONS AND IMAGES

What does it mean when we say fathering? Is there a "job description"? Is fathering a truly different type of parenting? How is fathering any different from mothering? How does one learn to be a father? Does it matter to a child if there is a father in his or her life, and what if there isn't? We will explore next the special role of fathers in child development as revealed in the research literature.

To begin, *fathering* is the term given to describe the special and specific traits and behaviors that men bring to the child rearing experience. In a 1995 review of fathering by William Marsiglio, he pointed out that there have been significant changes in the amount of men's participation in child rearing in the past 50 years for several reasons. These include increases in the number of women in the workforce, changes in family demographics (more divorce, more stepparenting, more single-parent homes), and the impact of studies that have documented the father role in child well-being. In fact, changes in relationships between men and women have both helped and hurt the cause of fathers.

Karl Zinsmeister, as our conservative voice, has written on the fate of fatherhood in U.S. society. He is especially attuned to how men–women relationship issues have impacted fatherhood. In his opinion, the core issue is a simple one. He writes, "The heart of today's fatherhood breakdown isn't between fathers and children. It is between fathers and mothers. Quite simply, too many men and women are at sword's points. The damaging flight of men from families, and from their children, is to a considerable degree just a side effect of the breakdown in comity and long-term commitment between men and women" (Zinsmeister, 1999, p. 44).

Zinsmeister believes that today's fathers are caught up in a still-unresolved gender war. Women's changed attitudes about the need for men in their and their children's lives have dramatically impacted a man's place. Women can support themselves, terminate unwanted pregnancies, and get different sources of support if they choose single parenting. This has led to "a prevailing background of sexual separatism." This has impacted the societal view of marriage as well. Zinsmeister quotes the journalist Paul Taylor: "When marriage atrophies, so does fatherhood. And so does society."

So Zinsmeister argues for "a more humane and practical path." This path is one of a renewed commitment to monogamous, long-term marital commitment. It asks men to allow women more control and say when children are younger, but "make sure they (the fathers) do not become shirkers and slackers" (Zinsmeister, 1999, p. 45). He states that men need to address women's concerns and needs for professional and career goals, but to make sure that motherhood is a worthy profession to consider as a full-time option as well. In closing, he adds, "Fathers and mothers who take up their awesome childrearing duties as distinct, overlapping, interdependent partners will find success and happiness within easy reach" (Zinsmeister, 1999, p. 45). And in so doing, so will their children.

William Doherty and his team have delineated four tasks as needed for a responsible father. They are: providing financial support; providing care; providing emotional support; and establishing legal paternity. This definition was derived as part of a federal government project we will review later in this chapter. It is part of a general policy shift by the Bush administration seen as controversial by some since it promotes marriage and two-parent families. James Levine and Edward Pitt, cited by the Doherty group, have also more clearly defined "responsible fathering." A responsible father does the following:

- He waits to make a baby until he is prepared emotionally and financially to support his child.
- He establishes his legal paternity if and when he does make a baby.
- He actively shares with the child's mother in the continuing emotional and physical care of their child, from pregnancy onwards.
- He shares with the child's mother in the continuing financial support of their child, from pregnancy onwards.

When you think of fathers, what images are brought up? There are, of course, the stereotyped media images of fathers. You could think of 1950s TV stars like *Father Knows Best*'s Mr. Anderson or *Leave It to Beaver*'s Mr. Cleaver. Perhaps Dr. Huxtable, the 1980s father in *The Cosby Show* comes to mind. Then there is the 1990s bumbling Homer Simpson. In fact, the media have portrayed fathers from the all-knowing, in-charge fathers of the fifties to the hardly-adult Homer Simpsons of the present, with all sorts in between.

Since the 1970s, movies like *Mr. Mom* (a parenting role-reversal story), *Kramer vs. Kramer* and *Three Men and a Baby* began to portray men in a more sensitive and nurturing light. In these and other movies like them, the men were often initially reluctant and downright inept before growing into their fathering roles, which by film's end, were readily and happily accepted. In these feel-good movies, one could sense a longing in the audience for their fathers to be as caring and competent as the on-screen men. TV's Dr. Huxtable came along about this time as well, as did the men of *Full House,* another popular TV show with "new father" types in charge. All of these cultural/media models also helped to redefine the father role in U.S. society.

In the twenty-first century, TV has a given us a new model like Bernie Mac, a surrogate father who each week has to balance the burdens of responsible fathering with his personal needs and struggles. Each episode of his sitcom has Mr. Mac resolving a dilemma in a caring positive way, despite his initial brusqueness or annoyance regarding the children's demands and needs.

Marsiglio, among others, argues that the media have often portrayed a "good dad/bad dad" dichotomy. On the good-dad side, there is the nurturant, caring, and involved father—the modern, new millennium dad if you will. The bad-dad side is the picture of uninvolved sperm donors, who are there at conception and gone. Or the bad dad is the never-married or now-divorced deadbeat who refuses to make visits or child support payments. Clearly both sets of fathers exist. In combination with the media portrayals, there is the idealized cultural image of fathers as nurturers or breadwinners/providers.

FATHERS AS CHILD CAREGIVERS

What do we know about fathers as child caregivers? For one, we know that fathers interact differently with their children than do mothers. Fathers tend to roughhouse more and engage in more physical play with both boys and girls. Fathers will bounce infants, throw them in the air (and catch them!) and engage in serious tickling. Mothers on the other hand, are more likely to interact in play in a less intense and less physical manner. Fathers tend to produce more arousal in their children when playing than mothers. It is also true that mothers are more likely to interact with their babies around child care needs (diapering, feeding), whereas fathers are more likely to come around to engage in play or some sort of supervision capacity. It is the case that there are no known innate gender differences in how fathers relate to their infants, nor do infants respond differently to fathers than mothers owing to any genetic predisposition. The differences we do see are due to socialization effects.

We also know that fathers are more involved with their infant children when happily married and when their wives are encouraging of their increased level of participation. Infants typically will form secure attachments with their fathers in the last half of their first years, especially when the fathers spend increased amounts of time and are sensitive and agreeable to the caregiving role.

In a surprising finding to some, fathers easily become quite skillful at all of the many activities required of a quality caregiver and attachment object. They can learn to diaper, clean, bathe, feed, and soothe infants as well as most women. Once involved and attached, fathers also can serve as the secure attachment base from which their infant and toddler offspring can explore the environment. In one interesting study of 44 toddlers by Mary Main and Donna Weston, they found 12 children securely attached to both parents, 11 securely attached to their mothers but not their fathers, 10 securely attached to their fathers but not their mothers, and 11 insecurely attached to both parents. The infants who securely attached to both parents showed less fear and more socially appropriate behavior compared to the other groups.

Other research has also shown that children with secure attachments to both parents fare better than those with a secure attachment to only one parent. These children are less anxious and withdrawn, do better in school, and have fewer problems in adolescence. As Main and Weston point out, secure attachments to fathers (in addition to their mothers) strengthen the security and stability of children, and can compensate for the negative effects expected when there is an insecure attachment with their mothers.

Work done by Ross Parke also underscores the fact that fathers can and do act sensitively and responsively to their infant children. He and others have documented that fathers can be competent caregivers, especially with infants. A 2000 report by the National Institute for Child and Human Development, Early Child Care Research Network summarized what happened with fathers when their children were 6, 15, 24, and 36 months of age. Through interviews and direct observations, it was determined that certain factors were predictive of a father's ability to practice daily care activities or demonstrate sensitivity to his child's needs. The NICHD study found that fathers were more involved in direct caregiving when the fathers worked fewer hours and the mothers worked for longer times outside the home. They also found that younger fathers and fathers of boys were more involved. In addition, fathers with less "traditional child-rearing beliefs" and who had more reported levels of marital closeness were found to be more sensitive to their child's needs in play situations.

A look at fathers' interactions with preschool-age children reveals that they are no different than most mothers. Developmental expectations and choice of disciplinary strategy are the same when comparing mothers' and fathers' self-reports. Similarly, both fathers and mothers express high levels of concern regarding child aggression, and equal "puzzlement" about children who are socially withdrawn.

Henry Biller has written on the importance of including fathers in child care and child rearing, and active co-parenting. He argues for a partnership in parenting, stating that such cooperation is "an important ingredient in the child's development of positive attitudes toward both males and females" (Biller, 1993, p. 48). Biller also emphasizes how fathers are major contributors to children's development of self-control and moral standards. The father as "role model, limit setter, and communicator of positive family values" is a key aspect of "paternal nurturance," which positively shapes children (Biller, 1993, p. 92).

POST-DIVORCE FATHERING ISSUES

Level of engagement between father and child is routinely found to be associated with appropriate fathering behavior. Even among divorced fathers, one sees a relationship between connections and involvement levels. One study has shown that fathers with joint custody (where "visitation" is a constant) pay full child support at 90 percent compliance rates. Seventy-nine percent of fathers with visitation rights pay child support, compared to only 44 percent who pay without visitation privileges.

The post-divorce fathering research base has two generally accepted premises: (1) children benefit from the involvement, caring, and economic support they receive from fathers, and (2) a father presence is important across different aspects of child development. A survey of post-divorce effects on children provides a variety of outcomes. Work by E. Mavis Hetherington and her group and Judith Wallerstein and her group have generally concluded that fathers are important to a child's post-divorce adjustment status. Father contact in most research studies has been found to play an important role in reducing child behavioral problems, improving child self-esteem, and other positive outcomes. However, there are also research findings to suggest that father absence was not associated with negative outcomes.

Inge Bretherton and her team investigated 71 sets of mothers and preschool-age children, all described as "well-functioning." Their research focused on questions related to how mothers and children perceive post-divorce co-parenting by fathers, as well as attitudinal measures. Among their findings:

- Mothers held fathers in low esteem for two or more years post-divorce.
- Mothers were able to separate their negativity from their children's more positive views.
- Many mothers reported improved parenting and child relations post-divorce (somewhat relieved to have the father out of the way).
- In a measure using child-generated stories, many reported family reunification.
- Mothers prefer father absence; children want more accessibility and contact.

Given other data indicating that both mothers and fathers have negative views of each other, the goal of co-parenting seems harder to achieve. The Bretherton team acknowledges this and argues that post-divorce parenting education needs to address and correct these perceptions.

What does the research indicate about the factors associated with future levels of father involvement in the post-divorce family? The emotional stability of the father *and* the mother, as well as the parental perceptions and beliefs about the quality of parenting are important. The sex of the children is another variable—men are more likely to stay involved and return regularly for sons. Other variables include the father's economic well-being as well as the amount of encouragement and support he receives from others (extended family and friends) to continue his father-ing role. Finally, the quality of the co-parenting relationship is a variable as well. Parents who can work cooperatively and with little or very reduced conflict are the pairs for whom continued father involvement is most possible and likely.

The relationship that fathers have with their co-parent is directly related to father involvement levels. A father's role and his role identity have been shown to be highly influenced by the support and encouragement received by the mothers of their children. Fathers are clearly more committed to their roles when their fathering is valued and supported by their co-parents, especially after divorce. The previously cited Bretherton findings are appli-cable here as well.

Nonresident fathers' attitudes toward fathering are affected by a number of variables according to the research base. These include the consequent family status of the father (being single, remarried, and/or having stepchil-dren). In general, a remarried father has reduced involvement with his children from the first union as a result of the time he now invests in the new marital relationship. In some cases, however, remarriage to a woman who is committed to the importance of fathers will serve to increase the level of involvement with the man's children. So again, the marital support variable has been shown to be an important determinant in father involve-ment.

Other nonresident father variables that have been explored in research include the characteristics/qualities of the ex-spouse/ex–co-parent. Resi-dent mothers are typically the gatekeepers to child access, with much con-trol over the when and where of child contact. Remarriage by the resident mother may also serve to reduce a father's access, as the family situation becomes more complex and more likely to express or harbor conflict. It is a generally accepted research finding that women gain even more control over their children's lives when they are not living with the fathers, especially in the case of children under six. Some fathers give up rather than fight for their parental rights in these circumstances.

A nonresident father's social status and education are also variables to consider. More-educated fathers have more-positive father attitudes in general, and likely played a more significant pre-divorce role in their children's lives. They may see themselves positively in the role of father, have established a father identity, and are able to continue to participate in their children's lives even after divorce. Hetherington has reported that fathers who see their lives becoming more complicated or who are experiencing pain at the loss of their families may then disengage and limit their involvement in their children's lives as a result. Supports and other mental health–style resources for these fathers are needed in order for them to reengage.

FATHERING AND INDIVIDUAL GROWTH

For the most part, fathers are still underinvolved in domestic labor activities, and that impacts on their and their wives' parenting. Some more recent studies show that women do two to three times as much work at home than their mates, and this is an improvement in comparison to the state of affairs 40 years ago.

A study by Alan Hawkins and his group has proposed that all adults have a psychological need to develop a caring attitude, particularly in developing an interest in guiding and establishing the next generation. There is a developmental need, termed *generativity* in the work of Erik Erikson, for men to make an ever-expanding commitment beyond themselves to help nurture the next generation as they grow into adulthood.

Within the context of a family, men can typically develop this generativity need through four processes. The first is by socialization effects that arise from having a child. When men become fathers, there is a new sense that their lives are now changed from a more egocentric and self-centered perspective to one of caring for another, in a way far different from care and support commitments within the marital relationship. In this way, the birth of a child can awaken or bring into awareness the adult man's generativity needs.

A second family-based process that can change fathers is that of a change in the man's "possible self," defined as a new or revised view of who he is and what he can or would like to become. An image of an ideal father may be to become increasingly involved in the life of his child, and so the father will match his behavior to his ideal. The danger here is when there is too large a gulf between this ideal image and what is actually doable. In that case, a father may dismiss the ideal and give up on any chance of changing. For others, however, the desire to become that possible self is a constant motivator that leads to better and better fathering.

A third possible family-centered process to increase a man's generativity response is the theory of role-person merger. As with the possible self, in this case the father engages in behavior to fit the role; in merging with the role, attitudes and beliefs follow. According to the Hawkins group, "the extended and permanent relationships between parents and children in intact families provide a powerful context in which fathers can be transformed through involvement in their children's lives" (Hawkins, Christiansen, Sargent, & Hill, 1995, p. 47).

The fourth process is a social learning one. In this take, Albert Bandura himself, author of social-learning theory, has said that as a "father's involvement and skills in the activity (child care) increase, social, symbolic, and self-evaluative rewards assume the incentive function" (Hawkins, Christiansen, Sargent, & Hill, 1995). In other words, a father can be readily self-reinforced to grow into the role by watching society's models (e.g., the social and symbolic media images) and then experiencing and appreciating the fulfillment and rewarding nature that his fathering behavior brings to him. These rewards are personal, from feedback in the parent–child interactions, and societal, through positive feedback and role matching from friends and extended family.

Kerry Daly has argued that there remains a lack of preparation and a lack of role models for men in the father role in American society. He says two questions are truly difficult for most men to answer—How do you learn to be a father? and What constitutes a "good father"? As a sociologist, Daly also believes that we are continually remaking the father role because it was discovered that parenting opportunities "fell short" of the level of involvement that most men preferred or wanted with their children. For this and other reasons, fathering is an "emergent identity" which is continuously shaped and reshaped from a variety of inputs.

Daly also recognizes the role of the media in shaping our definition of fathering. Using social learning theory as a base, Daly argues that men learn about fathering through modeling and imitation of role models portrayed on TV and in the movies. Models can be symbolic, as those portrayed in films and shows, and concrete—watching and observing actual fathers and what they did and do. In his study of 32 men whose average age was 34, Daly found that three themes emerged in response to the question of who served as important father role models. In general, men had a difficult time in identifying any specific person. When talking about their own fathers, they discussed how their fathering behavior was different from their own father's behaviors. Second, many fathers have used a selection of important fathering behaviors or attitudes from a variety of sources to create a personalized model to follow. Third, the men in his study emphasized the importance of being and becoming role models for their own children, seeing that their fathering would impact their children's lives.

On this last point, the men in Daly's study expressed some anxiety about "doing it right" in light of no clearly identifiable or definable father role models. The intergenerational continuity of fathering and father behavior was nonexistent in his sample. The fathers in his study were choosing to create a new fathering model rather than to pass on the models of their past, which were lacking in different ways. For the men in his study, the current fathers were rejecting the fathering they received as a potential role model for their behavior. Specifically, these men had respect for their fathers but did not want to repeat their fathering ways, in particular the amount of time spent (too little) with their children. As a result, it can be concluded that many of today's fathers are caught in the position of having to create a good fathering ideal from different sources of modeling. These men are generating new standards for who a father is in the hope that they will impact their children in a more positive way.

In further support for the argument that men have unclear ideals or ill-defined father models, Hawkins has pointed out that research has shown that some men have lowered father expectations as a result of being negatively compared to mothers, so that their father efforts are seen as inadequate. The men are thus relegated to several specific, but less-than-equal parent functions, namely to be a playmate, a substitute caregiver (basically a baby-sitter for when Mother is unavailable), or to resort to the out-of-family role of provider and breadwinner. In this view, fathers are second-class parents whose parenting contributions pale in comparison to the quality parenting that mothers provide. While this is true in some situations, it does not have to be, or to remain that way.

Demographic changes have also led to large recent increases in the number of single-father homes. In post-divorce situations, fathers are more likely to have a successful home situation with sole custody or primary residential status when they were very involved and invested in their children in the pre-divorce family. Fathers who fear future litigation or a contesting of their custody do experience more problems, both with their children and intrapersonally. Further, receiving child support from the mother can be a truly validating experience for the father as parent, not to mention a source of additional resources that can make life less stressful. Finally, studies of post-divorce single father–headed families find that some child problems may arise as a result of inconsistent visitation with the mothers. As in the reverse scenario (fathers not consistently visiting when mothers have custody), children are more likely to express their displaced anger at the residential parent, even though that parent cannot control the other one's behavior.

Rebekah Coley has recently reviewed the fathering literature and has added some findings about men who are low-income, unmarried, and/or minorities. These classes of fathers are often not those found in the majority of research on fathering. As you might imagine, there is a definite need for accurate studies with these men, as their numbers are significant and noteworthy. Their impact on a large number of children is equally worthy of examination. It is also true that many stereotypes and myths abound, and these need to be addressed and dismissed as necessary.

Coley's review finds support for much of what we have just reviewed from studies that have used married and middle-class men as subjects, but some special situations and findings are deserving of mention here. (Much of the research she reviewed is also available on-line through a federal government Web site (www.fatherhood.hhs.gov). I urge all interested readers to spend a few hours reading this wealth of information.)

One interesting finding was the data in support for disadvantaged fathers' effects on children's cognitive and socio-emotional development. Coley found "the most consistent findings concerning father involvement and children's outcomes in low-income, minority, and unmarried-parent families focus on children's cognitive and educational attainment... with links between the strength of father-child relationships, father's nurturance, father-child activities, and parenting style and children's cognitive development, school achievement and academic attainment" (Coley, 2001, p. 749). Coley also reports that the data on social and emotional development have a general positive flavor, but are not always "consistent."

Another result of note is that not all of the research findings out there, many based on mothers' reports, are accurate. As Coley found, "listening to the views of poor, minority and unmarried fathers themselves provides a very different picture" (Coley, 2001, p. 746). In fact, research she found by Nelson, Edin, and Clampet-Lundquist reported that "disadvantaged fathers wanted what most parents want for their children: to do better than they themselves had, not make the same mistakes, and carry on their name and heritage."

For me the significance of the Coley review is that all men apparently want to make a difference in their children's lives. For the disadvantaged, there are way too many obstacles (some self-made, unfortunately) that interfere. But if policies and opportunities can be more father-friendly and supportive, things can change.

HOW FATHERS AFFECT CHILD DEVELOPMENT

What happens when fathers are not around? There is a large database around the topic termed "father absence effects," which can answer this question. Sara McLanahan and Julien Teitler reviewed these data in 1999. They reported on three categories of findings in the literature. We will look at two of them. The first of these is related to economic deprivation and instability. In fact, they report that "children who live apart from their fathers do less well than children who live with both parents because they have lower financial resources" (McLanahan & Teitler, 1999, p. 91). Wide-ranging factors like quality of housing and the negative general effects of poverty are at play here as well—less money translates into more problems to overcome.

When one applies statistical analyses to the data, income effects between intact and single-parent families become more clear. Six percent more children/teens in single-parent families drop out of school than do those from "intact" (nondivorced) families. When one accounts for the income variable, the number drops to 3 percent. The same effect is found with categories like teen birth risk.

A second category reviewed by McLanahan and Teitler is that of low-ered levels of parental resources as expressed in decreased amounts and quality of parent–child interaction time. In single-parent families, especially post-divorce, the father is often perceived by the child(ren) as having left the family regardless of the actual reasons or situation. Removal of a father reduces the family's normal co-parenting "checks and balances" as well. The effect of this is that children are no longer "buffered" from any negative effects that may emerge from a single mother who may now discipline inconsistently or otherwise engage in dysfunctional parenting behavior as a result of her higher stress levels.

Similarly, single mothers are more likely to suffer depression and higher levels of stress as a result of the never-ending parenting demands that are hers alone. Maternal depression or high stress leads to decreased quality and quantity of parent–child interactions and this has negative consequences. Loss of consistency in discipline and the home routine are also found at higher rates in single-parent (mother-) run families. Single mothers are found to "exercise less control" of their children. A father presence can make a big difference.

The McLanahan and Teitler review then looked at how the post-divorce parenting changes affect a child's well-being. They examined "how much the effect of family structure decreases after controlling for measures of post-disruption parental involvement, supervision and aspirations" (McLanahan & Teitler, 1999, p. 95). Their findings: higher drop-out rates and teen pregnancies were related to loss of family structure. The level of interparental conflict was also related to child outcome—less conflict leads to better child rearing results.

Taking all of the above together, the loss of a regular father presence leads to a loss of parental resources. This loss of parental resources leads to a number of negative consequences for the child involved. McLanahan and Teitler concluded that "on average, children who grow up with both biological parents do better" (McLanahan & Teitler, 1999, p. 99). These results are obtained "across multiple outcomes and multiple data sets." They also found that a stepfather cannot replace or fully compensate for the absence of the biological father.

Other research supports the findings above. Nancy Dowd's 2000 review of other father-absence/single-parenting data led her to conclude that fathering biological versus step or unrelated children leads to "quite significant" differences. Further, the outcomes for children of single-parent homes are about the same as those from stepfamily arrangements. Step-parenting, although very common, still requires more research to understand how those dynamics play out. Many stepfamily scenarios are complicated by the presence of two father figures. Competition, loyalty issues, a desire to avoid conflict or problems, and disagreements about the children are all factors to reconcile between two fathers.

The psychologist Vicky Phares completed an extensive review in 1996 of father effects on child development. I will report some of her findings here. She found positive effects, especially for boys, upon intellectual development and academic achievement. In studies regarding cognitive achievement factors, she found that: (1) fathers who were more nurturant to their sons had sons with higher IQ scores and higher scores on tests of verbal ability; (2) more restrictive fathering was associated with sons' lower scores on cognitive tests; (3) both preschool-age boys and girls who did better on verbal and IQ tests had "highly involved" fathers; and (4) a father's highest education level is positively correlated with boys' and girls' IQ scores, especially when measured at ages 7–15.

Regarding educational outcomes, the research reveals that: (1) a father's communication style with high-achieving girls is related to higher overall global self-worth feelings and significantly higher levels of academic competence; and (2) fathers reported higher academic expectations for preschool-age children, with both fathers and mothers expecting higher performance from daughters than sons.

Phares also reviewed divorce and interparental conflict research. Her findings are consistent with what has been presented in other parts of this book. For example, one study "showed significant associations between marital disharmony and children's psychological functioning, especially when overt parental conflict is assessed." In related work, it was found that in some studies a father's reports of conflict and child functioning did not produce the expected associations. In those cases, some have speculated that fathers may be less aware of family functioning or less willing to admit to conflict or child behavioral problems. Others dispute that finding and state that fathers' perspectives are "legitimate" and that perception of the conflict and its effects is merely different. The overall conclusion reached in this review is this: "There is fairly consistent evidence that interparental discord is associated with higher children's emotional and behavioral problems" (Phares, 1996, p. 240).

So what can be said about these studies?

APPLYING THE RESEARCH TO YOUR FATHERING

After such a review, we now need to make this information relevant to your life as a parent. Remember that my purpose in writing this book is to provide you with a basis upon which you can make educated decisions about your parenting. I hope I have made an overwhelming case for the importance of fathers in the lives of their children.

If you are a mother reading this chapter, you now know why a father is important to your child's development. Whatever you can do to encourage and support your child's father to be actively involved will likely be rewarded by way of children who are better off in a variety of ways. If you are a father reading this chapter, I hope you know more about your importance in your child's life. I also hope that you will be motivated to develop your generativity needs and to become an even more responsible player in your child's life.

Let's begin by going back to Lamb's three components of parental involvement. I believe that many men are involved at the engagement and accessibility levels. Many men are there for their children as coaches in both boys' and girls' athletic pursuits. There are now more than a handful of fathers at PTA or PTSO meetings I have attended. You can probably generate many examples from your life experiences as well. These changes are both welcome and wonderful for the children involved. But in my opinion they are still not enough.

It is in the responsibility dimension where the work remains to be done. Although I bristle at every report, it is still true that women in U.S. society are in charge of children. Not that there's anything wrong with involved mothers and women, but there is a problem if it is at the cost of excluding men. In some cases, I do believe that men are purposefully excluded, and this needs correction. However, it is far more often the case that men either allow the exclusion or even welcome the relief from the responsibility.

Who really raises children in the United States? We know that mothers bear the lion's share of infant and preschool-age children's child care. The luckiest children get some father time with Dad in the role of Mother's helper and baby-sitter. Who teaches and supervises in day cares and preschools? Who teaches in elementary school? Who supervises and monitors after-school programs? In U.S. society, until middle school (about age 12), both boys and girls are raised by women. Sure there are some exceptions, but these are so novel that they make network news. I refer here to reports in April 2002 of men acting as "mannies" or male nannies. It was as if some families had allowed aliens to care for their children.

The irony is that women continue to fight for more opportunities to raise children. It is women who worry about whether they can have it all, translated as being able to have a career and significant mothering/family time. How many fathers have complained or worried about having it all? Not too many, because having it all is defined very differently. For men, having it all is plenty of time for career pursuits while married to a good woman who will bear and have responsibility for the children that come. Household tasks and the home quality are issues for women to resolve. Yes, many men will help out with household work, but the data don't lie. Women still do two to three times more work in domestic chores. Only a small percentage of men are the primary responsible partner for home management work and obligations.

Am I ignoring the division of labor or the old societal model that worked for many apparently quite well? No. It is still the case that every family unit has to decide how it will be organized and run. If a family decides that the father is the breadwinner and the mother is the domestic engineer/child manager, that is fine. However, even in this scenario, men need to be more assertive in their role as father. By this I mean men need to be more directly involved in child rearing activities and decisions, the managerial functions discussed by Parke. Is this fight worth it? I think so.

Why would a man *not* want to have more of a parenting role? Why would a father *not* want to be as involved and influential as he could be for his children? I am afraid I can easily come up with dozens of reasons that have "selfish" written all over them. If a man were a more complete father, he would probably have less time for his hobbies, his TV, sleep, and sports interests to name a few. And there would be less time for work and career. For many families, that could be a worse outcome, because they depend financially upon the father's wage-earning ability. I do not wish to father-bash, but to encourage more men to do more.

If you're married and already in a groove and a lifestyle that is functional, a change like this would have to be done very carefully or you risk turning the apple cart upside down. And remember, mothers *are* the gate-keepers who control access and availability to children even in intact families. Why should a father bother? I think you should try because your children will be better off for your increased level of participation and responsibility in their lives. And you will be a better and more complete person.

(A disclaimer is in order here. I was *not* this complete father figure either. I did many more domestic chores than my father, but never 50 percent worth. I knew what I would have to give up, and I also knew what I had to gain. My reasons for not doing more were multi-determined as are everyone else's.)

The research is about as clear as it can be regarding men's ability to do all of the tasks required of a good parent—they can. It seems as if there is a lack of desire that in part is fueled by lack of readily available information. I do see some signs of more awareness. There are occasional public service announcements that promote responsible fatherhood, but these 60-second messages can't deliver anywhere near the full message required.

So what will it take to make significant changes? From the research just reviewed, there are several starting points one can take. I also know there are many barriers and obstacles to overcome. It is also the case, as always, that there are no simple solutions to complex issues. But we can spend a few paragraphs in a what-if scenario, can't we?

Let's get past the major issues such as the women-as-gateways-to-children and an ill-defined father role to follow. (An interesting discussion of this topic can be found in a 1999 book by Francine Deutsch, *Halving It All*. Deutsch reviews a variety of different issues and challenges in discussing maternal issues related to co-parenting within the overall context of marital equality.)

I begin with a list of several simple correctable obstacles, which I will address in no particular order of importance. They are important, but different, barriers for different men. Let's begin with definitions of who "real men" are in U.S. society and how that influences behavior. Then I'll make a brief mention about how men who work with children are falsely stereo-typed. Finally a simple lack of quality and quantity time spent with chil-dren is a very easy barrier to overcome.

Is a "real man" one who diapers babies? Do "real men" help first-graders with homework? Do "real men" act in caring and nurturing ways with small children? What if you do these things? Are you then less of a "real man"? I always thought some sort of breakthrough in cultural images of men and children was made when Arnold Schwarzenegger became a teacher of tots in *Kindergarten Cop*. I mean here was the slayer of *Predator, Conan the Barbarian,* and *The Terminator* wiping noses and looking out for a room full of five-year-olds in a still masculine but sensitive man-ner. If Mr. Schwarzenegger could be nurturant and caring, couldn't any wanna-be macho man do the same?

All kidding aside, it will take more portrayals of men whose societal credentials are established to allow more everyday, real men to take on the important obligations of child rearing and child care without prejudice. More men are needed by America's children both in the home and outside.

This raises the other large concern about the motives of men who might want to work with young children. As unfair as it may be, men who really do teach in elementary schools for a living always have a cloud of suspi-cion. Is he a pedophile? Is he on a "gay recruiting mission"? Such ques-tions persist even though they are unfair or outright ridiculous. Men more in touch with caring and nurturant emotions, with more feminine gender-role characteristics, do exist. They are normal and their motives are beyond reproach.

When I conducted child custody evaluations on a regular basis (1989–1995), it was almost unfair to fathers when it came to an informa-tion questionnaire I had each parent complete in order to determine the extent to which they knew their children. Time and time again, fathers could not answer questions about the name of the child's pediatrician, the child's developmental history, a list of three friends' first names, or prefer-ence questions like naming a child's favorite foods, TV shows, or toy the child most wanted for his or her next gift. Mothers, on the other hand, could easily recite a child's birth, weight, length, and Apgar scores, tell me the child's ear infection history, and report a child's favorite color or almost any sort of personal information I asked about.

What did I learn from this experience? That men have to find ways to become more engaged and involved. This means talking to your child, playing with your child, and watching your child interact with others. And these needs are present from infancy until adulthood, they just change as the child develops. So this is my final obstacle I would like to see overcome—lack of quality engagement and knowledge about children.

These child custody survey findings were my own informal research sample on the lack of father engagement or responsibility. Yes, these interviews were with divorcing fathers. For some, perhaps the divorce came about because of the father's family absence or lack of involvement. But these were contested situations, so outside of the percentage of cases where the men may have just wanted custody to get even with an ex-wife, there was a desire to be the primary parent. I can tell you the men seemed sincere in their efforts and were generally embarrassed by their ignorance of their children's daily lives and preferences.

If I get the time someday, I would like to administer a revised form of my child custody evaluation questionnaire to fathers in stable marriages who believe they are engaged and involved. How do you think they will fare?

There is also hope for fathers, from of all places, our federal government. The Web site I cited above in reference to Coley's fine work is the home page for the Fatherhood Initiative. People can argue that this initiative is more of a ploy to get more paternity suits settled and more child support paid so that welfare costs will decrease. But it is and can be so much more. Everyone will win when men take up their responsibility and obligations. This will happen when government and workplace policies, and women in their lives, support them and allow them to.

Here, from the Fatherhood Initiative (fatherhood.hhs.gov), is a report summary titled "Responsible Fathering," by William J. Doherty, Edward F. Kouneski, and Martha Farrell Erickson of the University of Minnesota, written in September 1996:

> A consensus is emerging that responsible fathering means establishing paternity, being present in the child's life (even if divorced or unmarried), sharing economic support, and being personally involved in the child's life in collaboration with the mother. The research literature on fathering has been long on empirical studies of specific fathering behaviors and notably short on theory and the bigger picture. And while innovative programs to promote better fathering have multiplied in the past decade, they are often not connected to either research or theory. This report summarizes the research on factors that influence fathering and presents a systemic, contextual framework that highlights multiple interacting influences on the father-child relationship: father factors, mother factors, child factors, co-parental factors, and broader contextual factors. A principal finding of this report is that fathering is influenced, even more than mothering, by contextual forces

in the family and the community. A father who lacks a good relationship with the mother is at risk to be a non-responsible father, especially if he does not reside with the child, as is a father who lacks adequate employment and income. On the other hand, this contextual sensitivity means that fathering can change in response to shifts in cultural, economic, institutional, and interpersonal influences.

The principal implication for fathering programs is that these programs should involve a wide range of interventions, reflecting the multiple domains of responsible fathering, the varied residential and marital circumstances of fathers, and the array of personal, relational, and ecological factors that influence men as fathers. In particular, fathering programs should:

a. involve mothers where feasible and, especially for unmarried fathers, families of origin;
b. promote collaborative co-parenting inside and outside marriage;
c. emphasize critical transitions such as birth of the child and divorce of the parents;
d. deal with employment, economic issues, and community systems;
e. provide opportunities for fathers to learn from other fathers; and
f. promote the viability of caring, committed, and collaborative marriages.

Believe it or not, I read this Web site *after* I had written about 95 percent of the material in this chapter. I had heard of the fatherhood project but had never gotten around to looking for it. This summary captures the essence of my message.

Chapter 10

SPECIAL PARENT–CHILD ISSUES

Adoption is not about finding children for families, it's about finding families for children.

—Joyce Maguire Pavao

In this chapter, we will address some special-circumstance issues that many, but not all, parents may face. Some of these issues are not typically included in parenting books, but I believe they are too important to exclude. The issue of adoption can be problematic in some families. Its effect on parents is addressed more fully in other books and publications, and if this matter personally affects or interests you, you should pursue additional reading. The topic of children who are chronically ill or have life-threatening illness is one that all parents pray they will not have to confront, but fate has its own plan. This sensitive and often terrifying matter must be dealt with straight on—it cannot be deferred or denied. Finally, the issue of death itself, and how a sensitive, responsive parent can use the eventual passing of family, friends, and pets as a teachable moment about life and death for a child will be reviewed.

For all of these issues, let me endorse the idea that professional help is available and should be used when needed. Problems related to adoption are especially common, and many mental health professionals have the expertise and experience to resolve your family issues before they get out of hand. Similarly, help with children in life-threatening or disabled conditions should be sought and utilized. It is good that in the United States, every region has people who can help families with these issues. Support groups are an especially helpful forum for parents to share ideas and solutions to common issues. Parents deserve any assistance available as they work to make their child's life the best it can be.

ADOPTION OF CHILDREN

The decision to adopt children represents a major step in the life of a family. Some parents adopt because of infertility issues, others out of a heartfelt desire to make a difference in the life of a deserving child. Most of the parenting matters we have reviewed thus far equally apply to adoptive as well as biological parents. However adoptive parents face several issues that are unique to their situation.

Arguably the most special circumstance arises when an adopted child develops into adolescence. A primary psychological task for healthy development in the teen years is identity discovery and formation. In the case of children adopted as infants, almost all are told of their status in the preschool years (based on current standards). The issue of their origins naturally emerges or reemerges in adolescence.

To me this is an expected, if not welcome, sign of normal growth, as questions about the circumstances around one's birth are a likely place to begin to think about one's identity in the world. (It should be mentioned here that identity formation processes start earlier in development than the teens, but reach full activity as a normal developmental task at this time.)

Searching for Biological Ties

The search for a child's birth parents raises anxiety in almost all adoptive families. Some parents worry that their child is unhappy with them and is off to find a replacement. Others are concerned that the child may find out some facts about the birth situation they hoped would remain hidden. Helping a child search for his or her birth origins could lead to discoveries that might be hurtful. Still others fear some future competition for the main role of parent in the child's or teen's mind, even though almost all adoptive children know that "your parents are the people who raised you."

No matter your fears or worries, if an adopted child/teen feels a strong urge to learn about his or her personal birth history, it should be allowed. If your child/teen is comfortable enough to bring up the topic directly with you, you should feel both proud and encouraged. That child is securely attached to you and you will most likely not be replaced by anyone. For your adopted teen to trust that you will help out with the search indicates that your role and place in his or her life is well established.

Having said that, neither should you be too worried if your teen chooses to not share this desire for searching with you. Rather than jump to the conclusion that your teen is unhappy, unattached, or dissatisfied, the more likely reason for not telling you is out of respect and protection of your feelings. In this case, your teen is more likely trying to diplomatically balance his honest desire to learn of his origins with his keen awareness that this sensitive issue could be seen as some sort of betrayal of trust or source of hurt.

A 1999 study by the Center for Adoption Research at the University of Massachusetts, provides a glimpse into the possible future for parents of adopted children who will decide to learn about their biological origins. This study followed 345 adult subjects (most in their thirties) as they engaged in, or recently completed, a search process for their "birth families." They also surveyed how those contacts were received and perceived. It is my opinion that much of their work applies to older teens as well.

What motivated adults who were adopted as children to search for their biological parents? As you might expect, the research suggests that people who were adopted search for a variety of reasons, among them: identity-related motives, the need for factual and/or medical information, curiosity, and a need to "fill a void in one's life." Reasons for searching were found to be related to many variables such as level of psychological functioning, the adoption experience, and expectations about the search and its results. "Altruistic motives" such as letting the birth mother know that things turned out alright were also stated as reasons for their search.

The UMass group created three categories of reasons for searching and followed up those people who searched: in order "to fill a void" or "to find a sense of belonging"; in order to "gain a better self-understanding"; and as fact finders wanting to gain medical or other information.

In the UMass survey, the subjects as a whole scored within normal ranges on various psychological tests, but within this normal group there were differences in level of functioning. Subjects who searched in order to fill a void had lower scores than the others on measures of self-esteem and life-satisfaction, and they generally felt worse about adoption. In this study, a correlation between self-esteem and feelings about adoption was borne out. Of note, however, was that this finding was found among the females only.

In this survey, the majority of subjects said that they were not sure about the kind of relationship they wanted to have with their birth family. Of those who did have an idea, 17 percent wanted to establish a close friendship, 6 percent a loose friendship, and 5 percent a parent–child relationship. A full two-thirds of the searchers met the member of the birth family they wanted to meet, which in most cases was the birth mother.

Often the fears of hurting adoptive parents were misplaced, as the most frequent reactions of the adoptive mother to being told of the search were "being supportive" (64%) and "being understanding" (61%). A small minority of the participants felt that the search had a negative effect on their subsequent relationship with either adoptive parent. The most frequent reactions of the father to the telling was "being understanding" (68%) and "being supportive" (55%). As with the mothers, the majority of those surveyed felt that searching had not changed the level of tension with, openness with, and closeness to their adoptive fathers.

Talking about adoption while teenagers and quality of attachment best predicted whether participants told their adoptive mother and father about their search activities. Those who felt more securely attached to their mothers and fathers, and felt more comfortable talking about adoption with them, were most likely to tell their adoptive parents about their search.

Adoptive parents may, understandably, feel that their child's interest in searching is an indication of some failure as parents or a sign of ingratitude on the part of their child. They are often afraid that the child's contact with his or her birth parents might weaken the child's attachment to them. The UMass report showed that these beliefs and fears are unfounded; search and contact activities were not related to quality of attachment problems with adoptive parents, and by and large did not cause problems in the parent–child relationship.

So what can be learned from this important study? I believe several points are worth highlighting. For one, the fact that in most cases there was a "happy ending" suggests that searching in and of itself is not damaging to relationships. A second result leads to the topic of open adoptions. How were adults able to find information about once sealed, "confidential" adoptions? They were able to do this through agencies created to allow for future reunions, one of the recent developments related to open adoption policies.

Issues Related to Open Adoptions

There is no universally accepted definition of "open adoption," but it usually refers to birth parents and adoptive parents receiving and acquiring knowledge about one another. In some cases, the birth parents, almost always the mother, may actually choose the new family. In open adoption, families get medical/genetic information about the birth family and other information that "might help in dealing with the emotional issues that often accompany adoption."

From the National Adoption Information Clearinghouse (NAIC) factsheet on open adoptions, I present this summary:

> Formal open adoption is a controversial idea. It raises questions to which there are not yet clear answers. Will a child raised with knowledge of two sets of parents grow up confused? Will adoptive parents feel threatened by the intrusion of the birthparents? Will the child/parent relationship be able to develop in a healthy and normal way? Will the birthmother want to reclaim her child? Will she make unwelcome visits and phone calls? When the child is older, will he choose his birthmother over his adoptive parents? Can open adoption really be successful? Those experienced in working with open adoption say that problems are likely to occur when the birthparents and adoptive parents have an ambiguous agreement as to how open the adoption will be, or if they have a clear agreement, and then one party oversteps the bounds. Adoption social workers also disagree about the degree of openness that is desirable in adoption. Some agencies encourage the birthmother to play a prominent role in the child's life. Others limit the amount of personal information...exchanged between the prospective adoptive parents and the birthmother. There are also agencies that allow the birthmother and the adoptive parents to decide how much and what kind of future contact they will have with each other.

It is my opinion that open adoption processes, although well-intended, are too risky. As cited above, a number of questions arise as do potential arguments. What if the birth parent opposes the choice of school or religious upbringing of their biological child? Do birth parents have any say after the adoption is final? I believe the rights and welfare of most children are best addressed through sealed, confidential adoptions. Although this can cause anguish for birth parents, I believe this is part of the cost that is paid when they make the altruistic sacrifice of surrendering a child they know will be better off raised by others.

By making a clean break with no further connections, the new family can operate without worry or threat of interference. They are owed this basic right of parenting. Similarly, the birth parents can start the next chapter of their lives as well, knowing that the decision to tell others about their child will be made by them and them alone should they desire.

When the adopted child is a teen (with parental permission) or adult, if he or she wishes to search I am more understanding of that scenario, as explained previously. I fully support groups that match information from birth parents who decide if they wish to be found. (If a birth parent wants confidentiality, that desire should be fully respected and kept.) If a teen/young adult wants the information and it is accessible, so be it. But the searcher should also know that there are no guarantees that every birth parent wants to be discovered. That eventuality should be considered, prepared for, and respected as well.

Telling Children They Are Adopted

The issue of disclosure of the adoption status to children is addressed next. For most infants who are adopted, parents are advised to, and will, tell them of their adoption between two and four years of age. Many helpful publications and books are available to help with the specifics of how a parent can best present this information to the child. (See, for example, the on-line factsheet offered by the NAIC.) Most of these approaches emphasize the special nature of the situation and of the child. All are intended to assure children that they are no less important as a result of their adoptive status. Some approaches emphasize that the adopted child is special because he or she was chosen and not simply born into a family without choice. This is not the best communication, as it does not address why the special child was given up by the biological parents. Adoption professionals now discourage this approach.

One point that almost everyone involved in adoption agrees upon is that children will need more than one occasion to discuss and process their adoption and what it means. If you begin telling the adoption story in the preschool stage, you will likely need to update, enhance, and add detail in subsequent discussions, which mirror your child's increased cognitive abilities and questions they will formulate. Allowing the child to take the lead on this topic is a good approach. If you feel the need to start the conversation, watch for your child's reaction. If you see body language or other signs that your child is not ready or willing to discuss the matter, defer to another time. If you believe the time will never come, going to see a therapist who specializes in work with adopted children is the best alternative.

Probably the most important message for a child/teen to know is simply this—being adopted does not change your value as a human being; you matter as much as everyone else. Concerns that a child will replay abandonment issues or will be confused when told that a birth parent "gave them up because they loved the child" are a reality. The best answer to the question of why a child was placed is that the birth parents knew or became convinced that they could not properly care for the child. Without getting into the specific whys or why nots, this explanation covers almost all reasons (other than death) for why children are placed.

What if an adopted child is unaware of his true status? This is a truly complicated and delicate issue that cannot be adequately addressed in one small part of a parenting book. Again, factsheets available from the NAIC Web site can be helpful. There is a well-written piece on the history of adoption disclosure as well as a summary of the two prevailing points of view about when to disclose adoption to a child (ages 2–4 [David Brodzinsky] versus 8–11 [Herbert Weider]).

Suffice it to say on my part that the truth almost always surfaces. I fully believe it is a necessary parental obligation to inform an adopted child of their legal status, if just for any future medical/genetics issues that could arise. A child's right to the truth of his or her origins, however, is the basic argument. "Family secrets," often actually big lies, are almost 100 percent harmful to all family members to some degree. If you are a parent wondering what harm could be done by not telling, it is the self-esteem bombshell of feelings of betrayal by the adoptive parents coupled with a renewed sense of abandonment by the biological parents. When discovery is made abruptly, a person may believe that his or her life is and has been a lie and wonder about what else has been hidden or what other bad news is waiting to be delivered.

In my own clinical work, I once saw a teenage girl who had not been told about her adoption, soon after she learned the news. Her perceived mother and father were actually her biological grandparents; her big sister was truly her biological mother. This was the big family secret. When a mean-spirited neighbor told her the truth, the girl had a nervous breakdown requiring months of hospitalization. This family had many other problems that contributed to her situation as well. But my and my team's efforts to help this teen were unsuccessful. One year later she was still in a post-psychotic state and unable to function in the world as she had been able to 12 months earlier. Yes, this is one example, with other complicating factors, but my point is made about the devastation that *can* arise. Why risk it?

One final note before we change topics is in order. In most information about adoption, you will run across data that show that adopted children have higher incidences of mental health problems and learning disabilities. In the case of learning disabilities, it is possible that some prenatal factors may be the cause, and no one could have known at the time of adoption unless the child adopted was already in school. As to increased levels of depression and other psychological disorders, the data are also true. Why adopted children are at higher risk is the result of many factors, only some of which their parents have control over. In any event, family therapy is usually the best treatment route to prevent or minimize psychological problems.

Adoptive families face special issues related to belonging, loyalty, entitlement, and attachment. Family therapists choose to work with every member of the family. In some sessions, they may work only with parents; in others, with siblings. Recall the information in chapter 4, and remember that a prime focus is the system and its subsets, and all family members are considered to be part of the solution.

CHRONIC AND LIFE-THREATENING ILLNESS IN CHILDREN

We next turn our attention to another area of parental concern and anxiety—the scenario of raising a child with a serious chronic or life-threatening illness. Serious chronic illnesses would include uncontrolled asthma, juvenile diabetes, and any other ailment requiring years of ongoing medical attention. There is always the possibility of serious harm to the child if the condition is not properly treated and followed up. Life-threatening illnesses would include diagnoses of childhood cancers and some genetic disorders with short life expectancies.

These medical issues are clearly among any parent's worst nightmare. Some limited research has been conducted to examine what the best parenting responses can be in order to make the child's and family's lives the most functional and mentally sound. Each situation is somewhat personalized and unique, so relevant and practical research is difficult to conduct. In this section, allow me to share some personal insights and experiences, and some selected research findings.

Much of the family impact research data is related to work in support groups for patients, their parents, and siblings. Support groups are excellent resources for additional information and emotional assistance to deal with the stresses of loss and potential loss. Just about every urban area in the United States has a set of support groups of some sort; most can be found through contacts with a local hospital or medical facility. For siblings, support groups are usually organized by developmental level, so teens would be with teens and preteens with other preteens. Groups should be optional and not forced upon anyone.

In my three years of working with pediatric cancer patients and their families, I was always aware of one life lesson that permeated the clinic and hospital milieu—the importance of living each day to the fullest. Of the many children I encountered, I took great comfort in observing, in most cases, their acceptance of their situation. Part of this acceptance was a seemingly precocious attainment of many of life's usually hard-earned philosophical lessons. Among these was the desire to live as normal a life as possible—to the fullest, in the present, and with little regret for the past and a restrained hope for the future. I watched young children looking out for and protecting their wounded, worried parents. I observed some families become stronger in their shared love and support for one another, and other families broken apart by the many stresses and strains that were encountered.

I was fortunate to work with support groups for parents and for siblings of young cancer patients. I had the privilege of being directly involved in medically supervised residential summer camp activities that allowed the children a chance for a real "kid experience" with little of the overprotective restraints that parents would impose. At the same time, when the children were at camp, families could take a one week respite from their 24/7 caretaking responsibilities knowing that their child was surrounded by caring and qualified nurses, doctors, and patient-friends. I also spent some time in the chemotherapy clinics doing work now described as "child life" activities—entertaining on treatment days and helping to make painful and anxiety-producing situations a little more tolerable.

Parental Responses to Ill Children

Once you have heard that your child has been diagnosed with an illness of chronic or life-threatening eventuality, your world as you knew it comes to an abrupt halt. All things once certain are suddenly unknown. You were sure your child would outlive you; now you don't know. The list of big worries and concerns you had the day before are now trivial annoyances. Your world becomes reduced to a single focus—medical treatment regimens and the search for some possible cure or intervention to get your child's life back to normal.

Once you endure and pass the initial stages of shock and denial, you as the parent have to get down to business. Big, life-changing judgments need to be made—about treatment choices and other medical decisions for a start. Financial issues will need to be addressed. Schedule changes and job-related allowances will need to be arranged or fought for. Your family's quality of life will be questioned and tried.

Kenneth Doka has reported that it is often typical for parents to have guilt reactions from the way they thought or behaved during what he terms the prediagnostic phase. This is the time period between initial symptoms or problems and the eventual diagnosis. Some parents may feel guilt about not having reacted more quickly, for failing to have been as attentive as they should have, for the child to be ill rather than the parent, or even for some perceived punishment for previous wrongdoing. In some families, one parent may become angry at another for dismissing or ignoring early symptoms or warning signs. This leads to blaming. The actual case of the matter is that, even if you were a physician, the prediagnostic period would probably not have been handled much differently. In fact, the vast majority of children get medical care as soon as was reasonable or at a point where any earlier discovery would have made little difference.

A stable marriage will be tested; an unstable one will be tested severely. Through all of the worries about financial issues, insurance hassles, and general family business/caretaking, you still have to find the strength and energy to be an effective parent. Now more than ever, you will be challenged to be a nurturer, comforter, and guide for your child who is diagnosed and his or her siblings.

Much of what we have discussed in the previous chapters will apply here as well. One of the most important things that can be done to make the unimaginable manageable is to turn to your spouse. A loving supportive couple can use each other's strengths to get through each day, week, and month. You will need someone to cry with, to yell at, to encourage you, and to cheer and push you further. And you will need to be there for your spouse in the same ways.

If your relationship is strained or less close than you hoped, now is a time to make it better. I have seen couples become stronger and closer when faced with the challenge of raising a child with immediate health needs. This did not come about on its own—marital counseling helped to make the difference. Don't hesitate to get professional assistance for your marital survival and well-being.

This is my point—it is very difficult to manage all of the competing needs and resource drains as a parent, as well as the emotional roller coaster effects, alone or as separate members of a couple. To best help your child and your family, help yourself as a marital couple first. Although this may seem like a second priority, I assure you that if you don't pay attention to the marital situation immediately, more troubles will emerge at a time when you don't need them. A strong marital system can carry the entire family through one of life's most challenging situations. Relying on a good spouse can serve as your personal life recharger.

Once your emotional base and personal recharger arrangements are in place, you will be in a better position to help your child. Your child's psychosocial needs will be dependent upon his age, developmental level, and severity of the medical needs and interventions. A child who requires surgery will be different from one who requires multiple treatments, especially treatments that cause sickness and weakening responses. Reliance on advice from your medical group will be important.

Getting to the right specialist in your area (or going out of your area) will be essential to help you keep a hopeful and positive frame of mind. It is most important that you and your child have confidence in the training and abilities of your medical team. Including or allowing your older child/teen to have a say in treatment options is another issue to be decided. Data suggest that teenagers be fully apprised of their situation and choices. They should be allowed a role in the discussions, but not necessarily a full vote or veto power. In the majority of cases a teen will defer to the parental and medical advice.

Once all of the initial phase has been lived through, your parenting is now tested by seeing whether you can try to maintain some family normalcy. Aside from keeping the perspective of fully living one day at a time, the next most important thing a parent can do is to reestablish routine and a sense of a return to control. Children will look for what you say and do a little more carefully. For both the child with the illness and his or her sibling(s), returning to a daily schedule of regular bedtimes and meals and homework best make the point that the immediate crisis has passed. By restoring this order, children will regain some sense of security, and there is tangible proof that things can get better. This is a major stress-reducer for children of all ages.

A total return to the "old way" cannot be fully achieved, as there will be the new medical routines to work in and there likely will be changes in family resources. However, a return to regular discipline and such expectations as homework completion and clean rooms, best make the point to children that the family is back on track. It becomes difficult for some parents to treat their ill child the same way as before, but this is important to try to do.

By allowing guilt, pity, or some other unneeded emotion get in your way, you send the wrong message to your ill child if you begin to spoil him or let him get away with things he knows not to do. If you want to convince your child that you believe he will experience a recovery or live on for a long time, you start by maintaining the same demands and expectations of his behavior. If you don't, no matter what you say, your child will see you doing things differently and will figure out that something very bad is about to happen.

Let me clarify this further. Am I saying to not make any allowances for the ill child or his siblings? No. I am saying keep such changes to a minimum. If your child wants to crawl in bed with you to sleep at night, you need to decide if the trade-off in comfort gained by your child is worth the possible establishment of a new undesirable habit. If your child wants dessert before or instead of a meal, would this moment of happiness be a good trade-off for a poor nutritional choice? These potential problems will only become real problems if they are allowed to continue or gain in momentum. Obviously allowing some "cheating" or rule-breaking is a fun treat. All children need a little of that. The key is to keep it a little.

How much information do you reveal to a child or teen? Again, the answer depends upon age, developmental level, and psychosocial needs. The best general advice is to tell the truth and answer all questions at a level that can be understood. If your child asks if he or she will die, the truthful answer is no one knows when. If your child asks about the side effects of treatment, he should be told the best-case scenario as well as the likely response. He should also be told why that treatment is needed, how it will help, and how you and the medical team will keep discomfort and pain to a minimum. Great progress in the medical field has been made in training all involved to be child-centered and child-sensitive. Almost every child I worked with appreciated the truth and handled hearing the reality very well.

You also need to ask questions of your child. Many sick children have been known to go out of their way to withhold important symptoms or pain responses from their parents in order to spare them. Such nondisclosure can cause big problems, as the symptom changes may be indicative of a need to make medical changes. You need to be proactive and ask your child specific questions about how he is feeling or other questions related to specific side effects.

In the case where treatment compliance becomes an issue, allow the professionals to help your child. If the opposition of your child is a reflection of your own uncertainty, then you need to go off and decide whether you believe in the treatment regimen or not. A sensitive child can pick up cues about parental reluctance or doubt—don't let your problems become your child's problems. In other situations, especially prescient or intelligent older children or teens may challenge the treatment or the value of continuing after a long period of involvement. Again allow professional intervention to help guide your child; discussions with a social worker or other professional can often get to the underlying issues related to treatment persistence. As a parent, you need to remain supportive of your child and his feelings. It is best if you don't get in a position of having to argue or fight over medical matters.

Doka has presented a task-based model for families coping with life-threatening illnesses. He argues that as a child progresses through diagnosis and treatment, he or she passes through different phases with different tasks. These tasks include learning about the disease and its treatment, and then coping with symptom management, medical matters, and side effects. Time- and stress-management strategies must be implemented to deal with the increased demands in different life phases. And on the emotional level, there is an ongoing need "to vent feelings and fears." A more reflective task involves the search for meaning of the illness in the lives of both parents and children. Existential and spiritual issues will emerge. Why are innocent children allowed to suffer and die? Where is God? Questions about life and its meaning all come into play as time moves on. As each task is confronted, parents are urged to seek professional help if needed to deal with the issues at hand.

Should the situation progress to an end-stage, it is unlikely that your child will ask if he is near death. Most medical experts will tell you that such children know the answer already and often won't discuss the issue in order to protect their parents. It is certainly okay to follow your child's lead if he wants to discuss the afterlife or even the details of an eventual funeral. These are gut-wrenching discussions but help to bring closure to all involved.

Sibling Responses

When a child has a chronic or life-threatening illness, the whole family is deeply affected. How does a sibling react to having a brother or sister with a chronic or life-threatening illness? In every way imaginable. Depending upon the age, gender, spacing, and number of siblings, any individual child could be accepting, considerate, or helpful. Or a sibling could become resentful, jealous, and angry. Whatever the child's response, it was his or hers, not to be judged but to be dealt with. In some cases, the angry, acting-out child is the only family member to fully grasp and emote the system's grief and hurt and fear. In such a case, the child is doing the whole family system a service in acting as a conduit to help the others to be more emotionally expressive and accepting. The comments about family therapy previously reviewed also apply here.

Some siblings do resort to attention-getting behavior as a result of being put on the family back burner. One of the immediate changes to any sibling or sibling group is the experience of losing parental attention and focus, which naturally is shifted on to the child with the illness. When siblings act out, it is important for parents to be reminded that they maintain a responsibility to all of their children. Parents can continue to be mutually supportive of each other in such a way that they can share their encouragement even at times when they are physically separated. The expectation that the other siblings "will understand" that they must settle for less parental time does not always come naturally, if ever. The need for attention by other children in the family will vary and has many causes. Younger siblings are particularly vulnerable if they were used to having more parental and adult attention prediagnosis. An abrupt change is difficult to cope with.

The key to helping children in need of more attention is to give it to them. In a two-parent family situation, one parent can be freed from the ill child to spend time with their other children. As a parent, you are going to have to continue on with life's routine tasks. A way to get your work done and spend time with a child is to combine the tasks. You can, for example, make a rule that you will always take Sibling One grocery shopping every week. This will be private, one-on-one time. Even while sorting through produce or picking out cereal, you can engage in personal conversations and make your child feel important to you. Sibling Two may be your buddy for other household duties. Again, you can get two needs satisfied at the same time. You and your child may work together cooking meals and cleaning up afterward, sharing time and being available to discuss matters that otherwise might have been deferred.

One expert suggests that parents work hard at finding times and places, no matter how brief, to allow the child to communicate his or her feelings and thoughts with you in an exclusive interaction. Going to a park, walking around the block, or sitting in an ice cream parlor over a giant sundae are three places and ways to get one-on-one time. Be sure to encourage sharing of all sorts of topics, not just conversation about the child with the illness.

If it is not possible for a parent's time to be freed up, having another family adult spend more time with the affected child can be a short-term substitute. However, some children will only settle for their parents, so even at this crazy and chaotic time in the family life, parents must make at least some time for all of their children.

Some children may take the opposite response and act as if they do not need parental attention. They may be compliant and understanding, yet secretly harmed and affected. Over time, I came to be more worried about the child who "was handling everything" than the one who was "having problems dealing with" the family stress caused by the illness. The child who tries to be "extra good" is actually at-risk if left alone or allowed to go his or her own way with little family support. According to the physician Charlotte Thompson, "the goody-goodies who hide their distress wind up with long-term problems" (Thompson, 2000, p. 59). In Thompson's experience, the two major problems with siblings are acting out or acting so good that they miss their childhood in exchange for taking on a mature response to the family situation.

In sibling support groups, Thompson had many of the same experiences I had. Thompson's group work was with siblings of children with progressive motor/muscular disabilities. The issues between sibling groups for chronically ill versus life-threatening patient outcomes are both similar and different. With a disabled brother or sister, the severity of the disability similarly changes family life and adds stress as does the situation with life-threatening illness. Parents' focus and attention have to be on the special needs of the disabled child. One major difference is that the disabled child in most cases will not be in immediate danger of death. With siblings in a support group for life-threatening illness, death was always in the shadows and added another layer of anxiety and uncertainty. The anxiety and uncertainty were sources of heightened stress that permeated their new life situations.

Both in Thompson's report and my experience is the encountering of strong feelings of responsibility quickly taken on by the siblings. These include desires and responsibilities to take care of their parents. Children can sense that their parents are hurting and are not in a position of complete control as they were previously perceived to be. This affects children on two levels. Their own personal security is now threatened by the parental instability, and these children are unsure of how to support and emotionally care for a parent in need. Both of these situations are tough for children, who are then affected and changed in ways that could be considered to be unfair. Yet the family situation is the child's reality. Such a fate will be a force in shaping how the child will develop from that point forward, for better or worse.

A second danger parents must be aware of is that if the other children see the child with an illness being treated differently, that is seen as unfairness. Continue to try to treat and interact with each child equally, or nearly the same, to the extent that is possible. Children can handle and endure many things, but being treated unfairly in their family is not one of them. If the ill child gets away with behavior not tolerated when the siblings do it, there will be resentment and other problems. As reviewed earlier, keeping a sense of "normalcy" in the face of the unknown can help restore security and reduce stress at the child level.

If there is more than one sibling, a stronger in-family sibling bond can develop as they begin to count on each other more. There is the ultimate in bonding experiences—shared problems to be coped with—which the sibling group can freely discuss without having to explain themselves. Depending upon the ages and developmental levels of the siblings, this can be an important source of strength and support.

It may also be the case that a sibling will bond with a close peer. Such a good friend is another important asset. Often such a peer and his or her family will take the sibling more into their family as a way to show support. This can be by way of baby-sitting when needed or providing meals or social outlets. Such family friendships can be made strong and enduring as a result. Having a person outside the family to talk with is also important for a child. With that outside person, a sibling may feel more free to discuss his or her personal resentments and problems without the guilt feelings that could easily arise within the family unit.

Research reviewed by Kenneth Doka is applicable here. He reports that in some families, siblings' lives are "characterized by constant sadness and depression" and that the healthy siblings' needs are trivialized or "made contingent upon the health of the ill child" (Doka, 1996, p.103). Those siblings can fall into a world of isolation and disrupted development if not properly attended to. As mentioned earlier, the need for both parents to stay involved with the entire children subsystem is essential for everyone's sake.

Doka believes that other caregivers involved with the siblings can help parents. His two primary suggestions for caregivers working to help parents are to be available for communication and validation of the children, and assistance with the coping needs of the siblings. He also believes such caregivers can be of great help in keeping parents aware of, and "sensitized" to, the sibling needs as they are learned by the involved caregivers. If parents are unavailable to help, then caregivers can help make a difference in the siblings' lives and experiences.

DEATH AND LOSS ISSUES

All children need to know about life's full cycle, and this includes learning about death and what it is. Fortunately, most young children will not be in a position to have to confront death directly through losses of a parent, sibling, or peer. However, in the lives of extended family, friends of the family, and family pets, a death experience will transpire at some point in a child's life. Allow me in this section to first address the more common scenario of the death or loss of a pet.

Loss of a Beloved Pet

I often encouraged families in my practice to include pets in their child's lives. I strongly recommend the practice each semester as I teach my child psychology course. Pets can become attachment objects and serve as a daily model for the importance of caring about and for other living beings. Pets enrich children's lives on many levels. Yet another advantage having a pet can provide is that of a teachable moment about death and loss.

Different pets will be attached to by children at different levels. Very strong attachments can form when children are closely involved in direct care, as in the case of a 4-H club participant. Just about any animal can be a significant source of attachment, affection, and caring responses. The proverbial goldfish in a bowl is often a first opportunity to teach children about death in a way with minimal emotional impact. However, even a goldfish that was watched, named, and cared for for five days can be a catalyst for a serious emotional response depending upon the characteristics of the child-owner.

Carolyn Butler and Laurel Lagoni have written on the topic of helping children to grieve the loss of a beloved pet. They describe up front the close bonds that can be formed. They describe the level of a child's grief upon loss as sometimes being "intense and even overwhelming." Butler and Lagoni's research review led them to categorize pet loss as either *expected* as in the case of old age and euthanasia, or *unexpected,* defined as any sudden loss. In either event, they suggest that a child be fully involved in the final process.

Butler and Lagoni have debunked a number of myths about children and pet loss, among them: children's resiliency about loss allows a pet to be replaced easily and quickly by adults; children's grief is less intense than adults'; and the notion of pet loss as a mere dress rehearsal for the real test of death, with pet loss "a trivial" experience. Pet loss was once considered to be an opportunity for "unemotional discussions" about death and loss in general. This is wrong.

Pet loss is actually a chance for concerned adults to "ensure that children are informed, educated, included, comforted, and reassured about death." In this context, the very real and emotional response by children can be made into a learning event that teaches about grief, coping, and loss. These life lessons are no less true because they were in connection with a pet rather than a person. The experience is no dress rehearsal; it is the real thing concerning loss.

Coping Issues

Certain key factors can help a parent to assess how much support a child may need as a result of pet loss. Among these are: the age and cognitive/emotional maturity level of the child; the closeness of the relationship between the child and pet; other life stressors also being dealt with; any role the child may have played surrounding the pet loss; and a parent's confidence level in helping his or her children to process the loss and grief. If a parent believes that he or she cannot provide the right amount of help, or if some of these factors have exaggerated the situation, it would be appropriate to get help from professionals who work with children (e.g., counselors, teachers, or clergy).

Butler and Lagoni also believe that three steps should be followed by concerned parents in order to best help their children. The first of these is to be and remain honest about the pet's situation. When a pet is very ill, has serious injuries, or other outcomes such as accidental death occur, it is best to tell your child what has happened. The telling must be adapted to their level of understanding, but can and should be an honest accounting of the situation. All too often, to spare a child, adults have chosen to lie about the reality. Some will tell the child that the pet "ran away" or was "given to another family" in the event of unexpected loss.

As kind and considerate as this option may seem, it actually can create other concerns for the child. Now instead of dealing with death, the child has to cope with feelings of rejection or abandonment. The truth is the best option. What can (and does) happen when adults lie about the situation is that years later the parent or another person will reveal the truth (when the child is older and "can handle the news better"). This leads to distrust of the person who originally lied. Butler and Lagoni believe that if a person approaches you to help lie about a pet loss situation to a child, that that request be viewed as a plea for help. Such a parent or adult is really saying that they do not know how to handle the situation properly. Rather than go along with the lie, the fair thing for the child would be to get professional advice, tell the truth, and use the opportunity for a "normal, healthy coping" lesson.

A second important step recommended by Butler and Lagoni is to allow full involvement in the activities surrounding an expected pet death, and to allow for full participation in the events that are the result of unexpected loss. If a pet is to be euthanized, they recommend that the child be given the option of attending the procedure. There would need to be complete preparation of the child for such an event. One would also need a cooperative veterinarian in such a case. Many vets prefer to conduct such procedures without family involvement. However, others fully understand and appreciate the desires of loving family members to be present with their pet as they breathe their last.

At what age could one expect a child to have the level of understanding needed to attend a euthanasia procedure? That is very child specific, but most five-year-olds would be projected to handle this event. Some four-year-olds might be able as well; some six-year-olds might struggle. Check back to the list of key factors mentioned above to help guide your assessment of a child's ability to participate. Please note that even adults often prefer to not be present for this final act of respect and kindness.

They also recommend that children be given a full voice in "how to say good-byes, how to honor their pets' memories, and whether or not to view their pets' bodies after death" (Butler & Lagoni, 1996, p. 186). Again all of this very emotional material can appear scary and overwhelming for the adult, let alone the child. However, death is an emotional reality and children attached to their pets deserve the right to take full part in the painful, sad ending as they had been involved in the joyful, happy lifetime.

Family-run ceremonies or rituals to help with closure can also be held. Butler and Lagoni have a number of basic suggestions. You can hold a backyard funeral, plant memorial trees or flowers, make scrapbooks, or decide to make a donation to animal service groups. Allowing your child to help plan whatever ritual you choose can also be important. Some children may want to give a eulogy. Family members may want to each tell a favorite story about the lost pet. Do whatever makes sense for your child and family, but do something. Of course, lots of crying should be expected. That's a normal human response—for both children and adults touched by loss.

On the issue of viewing a pet's body after death, Butler and Lagoni cite the grief literature on this important piece of the closure process. A commonly held belief is that "seeing dead bodies can help both children and adults accept the fact that death has occurred" (Butler & Lagoni, 1996, p.

196). Again, great care must be given to the preparation of a child before having access to the dead pet. This choice should be the child's to make. It is not a required step in the grieving process. Specific descriptions must be used. These may seem gory or morbid. If a pet had to be shaved for a procedure, or if stitches or other changes have been made, the child needs to know this before viewing.

When allowed in the room with the pet's body, a parent may want to take the lead in modeling appropriate behavior. Touching or holding the body, or talking to the body are several initial behaviors one might do. Being open to your child's questions is essential. In the immediate aftermath of the pet's death, one must be careful about how the body will be placed or positioned. Butler and Lagoni recommend a sleeplike position denoting peaceful rest be used. They also suggest that a child be given a few minutes of alone time with the body if requested. Again, you, as the parents, need to carefully assess your child's ability to handle these events as you decide what will or will not be allowed.

Why would any parent put their child through such a seemingly painful ordeal as viewing a dead pet's body? It has been argued that the seeing allows for acceptance and closure. Further, what a child might imagine or concoct in his head can be equally frightening. The reality allays those imagined fears. On this issue, I would urge caution, but do think through these points and the needs of your child before deciding how to proceed.

The final step Butler and Lagoni teach is to avoid euphemisms. They offer several powerful examples. Parents should avoid phrases like "put to sleep" or the pet "got sick and died." In the first case, small children especially could be confused as they go to sleep every night and may now wonder if death is a possibility. In the second case, one must be careful about connecting being sick with death. Even though that may be a shorthand, accurate description, to a small child the regularity of sickness in his or her life could lead to unneeded worries about death. Instead, fuller explanations, using words like "died" or "helped to die" again bring home the reality of the situation to a child.

Similarly, in the case of euthanasia, veterinarians should not be made out to be pet killers or bad guys. The role of the vet in assisting the pet over the course of its life should be reviewed as should the vet's role in ending pain and suffering. There is a value-laden message here that can open the door to additional discussions about the value of life and questions about pain and suffering, and humane responses. If the question about a pet's afterlife comes up, there is another opening to more general discussions about life and spirituality. As a parent, you can be a great source of comfort and guidance at such moments.

To further assist you, I have added an appendix to this chapter of a list of books on the topic of death and pet loss as recommended by Butler and Lagoni. Close to 20 books are on this list. I would suggest a trip to a library or bookstore to check several out. You can choose the book that best fits your family situation and your child's developmental level.

TEACHING ABOUT DEATH AND LOSS

Most discussions about teaching children about death begin with a review of a child's cognitive development and his or her ability to understand death and its finality and irreversibility. Many good books and Web sites are available for your further review. As with other topics we have discussed, teaching your child about death and loss issues is a very individualized matter.

You are encouraged to pursue these additional resources as a couple, and decide, within the framework of your family values and your religious/spiritual principles, when and what you will say to your child. You may wish to begin discussion without a precipitating event, or you may prefer to be prepared with your response in the event of a loss. In the first case, book or movie themes to which your child will be exposed are great ways to introduce a discussion about your child's thoughts about death and loss. You may then follow up as needed.

Finally, remember that all thinking and feeling human beings—adults and children alike—need to grieve and mourn losses. A child's immature developmental level does not remove him or her from this need, but rather alters the way in which it is best handled.

Appendix
Suggested Readings about Pet Loss

Brackenridge, S. (1994). *Because of flowers and dancers*. Santa Barbara, CA: Veterinary Practice.

Brown, M. W. (1990). *The dead bird*. New York: Harper & Row.

Buscaglia, L. (1982). *The fall of Freddie the leaf: A story for all ages*. Thorofare, NJ: Slack.

Carrick, C. (1981). *The accident*. New York: Clarion Books.

Cazet, D. (1987). *A fish in his pocket*. New York: Orchard Books.

Gipson, F. (1989). *Old Yeller*. New York: Harper & Row.

Grollman, E. A. (1990). *Talking about death: A dialogue between parents and children* (3rd ed.). Boston: Beacon.

Hamley, D. (1989). *Tigger and friends*. New York: Lothrop, Lee & Shepard.

Heegaard, M. (1988). *When someone very special dies: Children learn to cope with grief.* Minneapolis: Woodland.

Hewett, J. (1987). *Rosalie.* New York: Lothrop, Lee & Shepard.

Jewett, C. L. (1982). *Helping children cope with separation and loss.* Cambridge, MA: The Harvard Common Press.

Rogers, F. (1988). *When a pet dies.* New York: Putnam.

Sanford, D. (1987). *It must hurt a lot.* Portland, OR: Multnomah.

Stein, S. B. (1984). *About dying: An open family book for parents and children together.* New York: Walker & Co.

Varley, S. (1984). *Badger's parting gifts.* New York: Lothrop, Lee & Shepard.

Viorst, J. (1971). *The tenth good thing about Barney.* New York: Atheneum.

White, E. B. (1952). *Charlotte's web.* New York: Harper & Row.

Wilhelm, H. (1985). *I'll always love you.* New York: Crown.

Wright, B. R. (1991). *The cat next door.* New York: Holiday House Books.

BIBLIOGRAPHY

These resource materials are listed in alphabetical order by author. I have listed the primary reference for information presented. Any college library will have most of the following; some public libraries may have these as well. All Web sites were accurate and accessible as of March 2004.

Adams, D. (1998). *The parent maze: Searching for childcare in the United States.* On-line at: *parenthood.library.wisc.edu/Adams/Adams.html.*

Affonso, R. (1999). *Is the Internet affecting the social skills of our children?* On-line at: *sierrasource.com/cep612/internet.html.*

Ainsworth, M.D.S. (1979). Infant-mother attachment. *American Psychologist, 34,* 932–937.

Amato, P. R. (1998). More than money? Men's contributions to their children's lives. In A. Booth & A. C. Crouter (Eds.), *Men in families: When do they get involved? What difference does it make?* Mahwah, NJ: Erlbaum.

Ambert, A.-M. (2001). *The effect of children on parents (2nd ed.).* Binghamton, NY: The Haworth Press.

Aponte, H. J., & VanDeusen, J. M. (1981). Structural family therapy. In A. S. Gurman & D. P. Kniskern (Eds.), *Handbook of family therapy.* New York: Bruner/Mazel.

Aurelli, T., & Colecchia, N. (1996). Day care experience and free play behavior in preschool children. *Journal of Applied Developmental Psychology, 17,* 1–17.

Ball, T., Holberg, C. J., Aldous, M. B., Martinez, F. D., & Wright, A. L. (2002). Influence of attendance at day care on the common cold from birth through

13 years of age. *Archives of Pediatrics and Adolescent Medicine, 156,* 121–126.

Barkley, R. A., Edwards, G. H., & Robin, A. L. (1999). *Defiant teens: A clinician's manual for assessment and family intervention.* New York: Guilford Press.

Barrios, B. A., & Hartmann, D. P. (1997). Fears and anxieties. In E. J. Mash & L. G. Terdal (Eds.), *Assessment of childhood disorders* (3rd ed.). New York: Guilford Press.

Baumrind, D. (1971). Current patterns of parental authority. *Developmental Psychology Monographs, 4,* (1, part 2).

Bayley, N. (1970). Development of mental abilities. In P. H. Mussen (Ed.), *Carmichael's manual of child psychology, Vol. 1.* New York: Wiley.

Belsky, J. (1981). Early human experience: A family perspective. *Developmental Psychology, 17,* 3–23.

Belsky, J. (1986). Infant day care: A cause for concern? *Zero to Three, 6,* 1–7.

Belsky, J. (1996). Parent, infant, and social-contextual antecedents of father-son attachment security. *Developmental Psychology, 32,* 905–913.

Belsky, J. (2001). Emanuel Miller Lecture: Developmental risks (still) associated with early child care. *Journal of Child Psychology & Psychiatry & Allied Disciplines, 42(7),* 845–859.

Benson, B. (1998). *The child, the parent and the school.* On-line at: *parenthood.library. wisc.edu/Benson/Benson.html.*

Biller, H. B. (1993). *Fathers and families: Paternal factors in child development.* Westport, CT: Greenwood Publishing.

Booth, P. B., & Koller T. J. (1998). Training parents of failure-to-attach children. In J. M. Briesmeister & C. E. Schaefer (Eds.), *Handbook of parent training: Parents as co-therapists for children's behavior problems* (2nd ed.). New York: Wiley & Sons.

Bornstein, M. (1998). *Refocusing on parenting.* On-line at: *parenthood. library.wisc.edu/Bornstein/Bornstein.html.*

Bowlby, J. (1969). *Attachment and loss.* (Vol. 1) London: Hogarth.

Bradt, J. (1989). Becoming parents: Families with young children. In B. Carter & M. McGoldrick (Eds.), *The changing family lifecycle: A framework for family therapy* (2nd ed.). Needham Heights, MA: Allyn & Bacon.

Bremer, J., & Rauch, P. K. (1998). Children and computers: Risks and benefits. *Journal of the American Academy of Child & Adolescent Psychiatry, 37,* 559–560.

Brenner, V., & Fox, R. A. (1998). Parental discipline and behavior problems in young children. *The Journal of Genetic Psychology, 159,* 251–257.

Bretherton, I., Page, T., Golby, B., & Walsh, R. (1998). *Fathers in post-divorce families seen through the eyes of mothers and children.* On-line at: *parent hood.library.wisc.edu/Bretherton/Bretherton.html.*

Briesmeister, J. M., & Schaefer, C. E. (1998). *Handbook of parent training: Parents as co-therapists for children's behavior problems* (2nd ed.). New York: Wiley & Sons.

Brodzinsky, D. M. (1984). New perspectives on adoption revelation. *Early Child Development & Care,* (18, 1–2), 105–118.

Brown, F. H. (1989). The impact of death and serious illness on the family life cycle. In B. Carter & M. McGoldrick (Eds.), *The changing family lifecycle: A framework for family therapy (2nd ed.).* Needham Heights, MA: Allyn & Bacon.

Bushman, B. J., & Cantor, J. (2003). Media ratings for violence and sex: Implications for policymakers and parents. *American Psychologist, 58,* 130–141.

Bushong, S. (2002). Resources for parents and children: Parenting the internet. *Teacher Librarian, 29(5),* 12–16.

Buss, A. H., & Plomin, R. (1984). *Temperament: Early developing personality traits.* Hillsdale, NJ: Erlbaum.

Butler, C. L., & Lagoni, L. S. (1996). Children and pet loss. In C. A. Corr & D. A. Corr (Eds.), *Handbook of childhood death and bereavement.* New York: Springer Publishing.

Cantor, J. (1998). *Media and parents: Protecting children from harm.* On-line at: *parenthood.library.wisc.edu/Cantor/Cantor.html.*

Cantor, J. (1998). *Mommy, I'm scared! How TV and movies frighten children and what we can do to protect them.* San Diego: Harcourt Brace.

Carter, B., & McGoldrick, M. (Eds.) (1989). *The changing family lifecycle: A framework for family therapy (2nd ed.).* Needham Heights, MA: Allyn & Bacon.

Carter, B., & McGoldrick, M. (1989). Overview: The changing family life cycle. In B. Carter & M. McGoldrick (Eds.), *The changing family lifecycle: A framework for family therapy (2nd ed.).* Needham Heights, MA: Allyn & Bacon.

Caspi, A., Henry, B., McGee, R. O., Moffitt, T. E., & Silva, P. A. (1995). Temperamental origins of child and adolescent behavior problems: From age three to fifteen. *Child Development, 66,* 55–68.

Cavell, T. A. (2000). *Working with parents of aggressive children: A practitioner's guide.* Washington, DC: American Psychological Association.

Children's Defense Fund (1997). *The state of America's children: Yearbook 1997.* Washington, DC: Children's Defense Fund.

Christophersen, E. R., & Mortweet, S. L. (2001). *Treatments that work with children: Empirically supported strategies for managing childhood problems.* Washington, DC: American Psychological Association.

Clarke-Stewart, K. A. (1989). Infant day care: Maligned or malignant? *American Psychologist, 44,* 266–273.

Coley, R. L. (2001). (In)visible men: Emerging research on low-income, unmarried, and minority fathers. *American Psychologist, 56,* 743–753.

Cummings, E. M., Davies, P. T., & Campbell, S. B. (2000). *Developmental psychopathology and family process: theory, research, and clinical implications.* New York: Guilford Press.

Cummings, M., & O'Reilly, A. (1997). Fathers in family context: Effects of marital quality on child adjustment. In M. E. Lamb (Ed.), *The role of the father in child development*. New York: Wiley & Sons.

Daly, K. J. (1995). Reshaping fatherhood: Finding the models. In W. Marsiglio (Ed.), *Fatherhood: Contemporary theory, research, and social policy*. Thousand Oaks, CA: Sage.

Deutsch, F. (1999). *Halving it all: How equally shared parenting works*. Cambridge, MA: Harvard University Press.

DeWolff, M. S., & van IJzendoorn, M. H. (1997). Sensitivity and attachment: A meta-analysis on parental antecedents of infant attachment. *Child Development, 66,* 571–591.

Dienhart, A. (1998). *Reshaping fatherhood: The social construction of shared parenting*. Thousand Oaks, CA: Sage.

Doherty, W. J., Kouneski, E. F., & Erickson, M. F. (1996). *Responsible fathering: An overview and conceptual framework*. Washington, DC: U.S. Department of Health and Human Services. On-line at: *fatherhood.hhs.gov/concept.htm*.

Doka, K. J. (1996). The cruel paradox: Children who are living with life-threatening illnesses. In C. A. Corr & D. A. Corr (Eds.), *Handbook of childhood death and bereavement*. New York: Springer Publishing.

Dowd, N. (2000). *Redefining fatherhood*. New York: New York University Press.

Dreskin, W., & Dreskin, W. (1983). *The day care decision: What's best for you and your child*. New York: M. Evans & Co.

Elkind, D. (1979). *The child's reality: Three developmental themes*. Hillsdale, NJ: Erlbaum.

Elkind, D. (1981). *The hurried child syndrome*. Reading, MA: Addison-Wesley.

Erikson, E. H. (1963). *Childhood and society* (2nd ed.). New York: Norton.

Fallows, D. (1985). *A mother's work*. Boston: Houghton Mifflin Co.

Garbarino, J. (1998). *Supporting parents in a socially toxic environment*. On-line at: *parenthood.library.wisc.edu/Garbarino/Garbarino.html*.

Gardner, R. A. (1989). *Family evaluation in child custody mediation, arbitration, and litigation*. Cresskill, NJ: Creative Therapeutics.

Garmezy, N., & Masten, A. (1990). *The adaptation of children to a stressful world: Mastery of fear*. In L. E. Arnold (Ed.), *Childhood stress*. New York: Wiley & Sons.

Garrity, C. B., & Baris, M. A. (1994). *Caught in the middle: Protecting the children of high conflict divorce*. New York: Lexington Books.

Goddard, H. W., & White, C. P. (1996). *Helping your child succeed at learning*. On-line at: *humsci.auburn.edu/parent/learning/index.html*.

Halfon, N., McLearn, K. T., & Schuster, M. A. (2002). *Child rearing in America: Challenges facing parents with young childen*. Cambridge: Cambridge University Press.

Hammond, B. (2002). *The parent-teacher trap.* On-line at: *parentsoup. com/edcentral.*

Harris, J. R. (1998). *The nurture assumption: Why children turn out the way they do.* New York: Free Press.

Hawkins, A. J., Christiansen, S. L., Sargent, K. P., & Hill, E. J. (1995). Rethinking fathers' involvement in child care: A developmental perspective. In W. Marsiglio (Ed.), *Fatherhood: Contemporary theory, research, and social policy.* Thousand Oaks, CA: Sage.

Hetherington, E. M. (1991). The role of individual differences and family relationships in children's coping with divorce and remarriage. In P. A. Cowan & E. M. Hetherington (Eds.), *Family transitions.* Hillsdale, NJ: Erlbaum.

Hetherington, E. M., & Kelly, J. (2001). *For better or for worse: Divorce reconsidered.* New York: Norton.

Hetherington, E. M., & Parke, R. D. (1999). *Child psychology: A contemporary viewpoint.* Boston: McGraw-Hill.

Hoffman, M. (1970). Moral development. In P. H. Mussen (Ed.), *Carmichael's manual of child psychology* (Vol. 2), New York: Wiley.

Horatio Alger Association (2003). The 2003 State of Our Nation's Youth Report. On-line at: *http://www.horatioalger.com/pubmat/surpro.cfm* (*http://www. horatioalger.com/pubmat/surpro.cfm*).

Howes, C., Matheson, C. C., & Hamilton, C. E. (1994). Maternal, teacher, and child care history correlates of children's relationships with peers. *Child Development, 65,* 264–273.

Huston, A. C., Watkins, B. A., & Kunkel, D. (1989). Public policy and children's television. *American Psychologist, 44,* 424–433.

Kagan, J. (1989). *Unstable ideas: Temperament, cognition, and self.* Cambridge: Cambridge University Press.

Kimichi, J., & Schaffner, B. (1990). Childhood protective factors and stress risk. In L. E. Arnold (Ed.), *Childhood stress.* New York: Wiley & Sons.

Koren-Karie, N. (2000). Attachment representations in adulthood: Relations with parental behaviors. *The Israel Journal of Psychiatry and Related Sciences, 37,* 178–189.

Koren-Karie, N. (2001). Mothers' attachment representations and choice of infant care: Center care vs. home. *Infant & Child Development, 10,* 117–127.

Lamb, M. E. (1997) *The role of the father in child development* (3rd ed.). New York: Wiley.

Lamb, M. E. (2000). The history of research on father involvement: An overview. In H. E. Peters, G. W. Peterson, S. K. Steinmetz, & R. D. Day (Eds.), *Fatherhood: Research, interventions and policies.* Binghamton, NY: Haworth Press.

Larzelere, R. E. (1996). A review of the outcomes of parental use of nonabusive or customary physical punishment. *Pediatrics, 98(4),* 824–828.

Levine, J. A., & Pitt, E. W. (1995). *New expectations: Community strategies for responsible fatherhood.* New York: Families & Work Institute.

Levy, S. (2002). Don't dumb them down. *Newsweek,* April 22, 2002, p. 56.

Lines, P. (1999). *Homeschoolers: Estimating numbers and growth.* Washington, DC: National Institute on Student Achievement, Curriculum, and Assessment data. On-line at: *http://nces.ed.gov/pubsearch/pubsinfo.asp?pubid =2001033 (http://nces.ed.gov/pubsearch/pubsinfo.asp?pubid=2001033).*

Main, M., & Weston, D. R. (1981). The quality of the toddler's relationship to the mother and to the father: Related to conflict and the readiness to establish new relationships. *Child Development, 52,* 932–940.

Marsiglio, W. (1995). Fatherhood scholarship: An overview and agenda for the future. In W. Marsiglio (Ed.), *Fatherhood: Contemporary theory, research, and social policy.* Thousand Oaks, CA: Sage.

McCrae, R. R., Costa, P. T., deLima, M. P., Simoes, A., Ostendorf, F., Angleitner, A., Marusic, I., Bratko, D., Caprara, G. V., Barbaranelli, C., Chae, J., & Piedmont, R. L. (1999). Age differences in personality across the adult life span: Parallels in five cultures. *Developmental Psychology, 35,* 466–477.

McKay, M., Rogers, P. D., Blades, J., & Gosse, R. (1984). *The divorce book.* Oakland, CA: New Harbinger Publications.

McLanahan, S., & Teitler J. (1999). The consequences of father absence. In M .E. Lamb (Ed.), *Parenting and child development in "nontraditional" families.* Mahwah, NJ: Erlbaum.

Metcalf, K., & Gaier, E. L. (1987). Patterns of middle class parent and adolescent underachievement. *Adolescence, 23,* 919–928.

Minuchin, S. (1974). *Families and family therapy.* Cambridge, MA: Harvard University Press.

Minuchin, S., & Fishman, H. S. (1981). *Family therapy techniques.* Cambridge, MA: Harvard University Press.

National Adoption Information Clearinghouse (2002). Factsheets. On-line at: *calib.com/naic.*

National Association for the Education of Young Children (1986). Position statement on developmentally appropriate practice in programs for 4- and 5-year-olds. *Young Children, 41,* 20–29.

National Coalition for Parent Involvement in Education (2002). Home page and links. On-line at: *www.ncpie.org.*

National Institute of Child Health and Development, Early Child Care Research Network (1997). The effects of infant child care on infant-mother attachment security: Results of the NICHD study of early child care. *Child Development, 68,* 860–879.

National Institute of Child Health and Development, Early Child Care Research Network (2001). Child care and children's peer interaction at 24 and 36 months: The NICHD study of early child care. *Child Development, 72,* 1478–1500.

National School Boards Foundation (2000). *Safe & smart: A guide to using the Internet.* On-line at: *www.nsbf.org.*

Naylor, C. (1995). *Do year-round schools improve student learning? An annotated bibliography and synthesis of the research.* On-line at: *www.bctf.bc. ca/Research Reports/95ei03.*

Nunberg, G. (2001). The Internet filter farce: Why blocking software doesn't, and can't, work as promised. *American Prospect, 12(1),* 28–33.

O'Connor, T. G., & Croft, C. M. (2001). A twin study of attachment in preschool children. *Child Development, 72,* 1501–1511.

Palmer, E. A., & Bemis, A. E. (1999). *Year-round education.* University of Minnesota Extension Service Report, # BU-07286.

Parke, R. D. (1996). *Fatherhood.* Cambridge, MA: Harvard University Press.

Parke, R. D. (2000). Father involvement: A developmental psychology perspective. *Marriage & Family Review, 29,* 43–58.

Phares, V. (1996). *Fathers and developmental psychopathology.* New York: Wiley & Sons.

Pleck, J. (1997). Paternal involvement: Levels, sources and consequences. In M. E. Lamb (Ed.), *The role of the father in child development.* New York: Wiley & Sons.

Roland, J. (1989). Chronic illness and the family life cycle. In B. Carter & M. McGoldrick (Eds.), *The changing family lifecycle: A framework for family therapy (2ⁿᵈ ed.).* Needham Heights, MA: Allyn & Bacon.

Rosenthal, R., & Jacobsen, L. (1968). *Pygmalion in the classroom.* New York: Holt.

Rothbart, M. K., & Jones, L. B. (1998). Temperament, self-regulation, and education. *School Psychology Review, 27(4),* 479–484.

Rudisill, T. L., Rudisill, J. R., Johnston, I. B., & Eddy, M. F. (1999). A parent's guide for responding to a child's disclosure of sexual abuse. In L. VandeCreek & T. L. Jackson (Eds.), *Innovations in Clinical Practice: A Sourcebook* (Vol. 17), Sarasota, FL: Professional Resource Press.

Rutter, M. (1997). Clinical implications of attachment concepts: Retrospect and prospect. In L. Atkinson & K. J. Zucker (Eds.), *Attachment and psychopathology.* New York: Guilford Press.

Ryan-Wenger, N. M. (1990). Children's psychosomatic responses to stress. In L. E. Arnold (Ed.), *Childhood stress.* New York: Wiley & Sons.

Sameroff, A. J., & Chandler, M. J. (1975). Reproductive risk and the continuum of caretaking casualty. In F. Horowitz (Ed.), *Review of child development research* (Vol. 4). Chicago: University of Chicago Press.

Sanson A., & Rothbart, M. K. (1995). Child temperament and parenting. In M. H. Bornstein (Ed.), *Handbook of parenting* (Vol. 4). Hillsdale, NJ: Erlbaum.

Scarr, S. (1998). American child care today. *American Psychologist, 53,* 95–108.

Schaefer, C. (1997). Defining verbal abuse of children: A survey. *Psychological Reports, 80,* 626.

Schaffer, H. R., & Emerson, P. E. (1964). The development of social attachments in infancy. *Monographs of the Society for Research in Child Development, 29* (3, Serial #94).

Scharff, L. (1999). Assessment and treatment of recurrent abdominal pain in children. In L. VandeCreek & T. L. Jackson (Eds.), *Innovations in Clinical Practice: A Sourcebook (Vol. 17),* Sarasota, FL: Professional Resource Press.

Schneider, B. H., Atkinson, L., & Tardif, C. (2001). Child-parent attachment and children's peer relations: A quantitative review. *Developmental Psychology, 37,* 86–100.

Sclafani, J. D. (1995). Children, changes and challenges: A co-parenting workbook for parents of divorce. Unpublished manuscript.

Sclafani, J. D. (2000). Parental & teen attitudes and beliefs about the Internet. *Perspectives, The Journal of the American Association of Behavioral & Social Sciences, Vol. 3.* On-line at: *aabss.org/journal2000.*

Sheeber, L. B., & McDevitt, S. C. (1998). Temperament-focused parent training. In J. M. Briesmeister & C. E. Schaefer (Eds.), *Handbook of parent training: Parents as co-therapists for children's behavior problems (2nd ed.).* New York: Wiley & Sons.

Siegal, M., & Cowen, J. (1984). Appraisals of intervention: The mother's vs. the culprit's behavior as determinants of children's evaluation of discipline techniques. *Child Development, 55,* 1760–1766.

Slaby, R. J., & Eron, L. D. (1994). Afterword. In L. D. Eron, J. H. Gentry, & P. Schlegel (Eds.), *Reason to hope: A psychological perspective on violence and youth.* Washington, DC: American Psychological Association.

Snyder, J. J. & Patterson, G. R. (1995). Individual differences in social aggression as a test of a reinforcement model of socialization in the natural environment. *Behavior Therapy, 26,* 371–391.

Sroufe, A. (1996). *Emotional development: The organization of emotional life in the early years.* New York: Cambridge University Press.

Stahlman, S. D. (1996). Children and the death of a sibling. In C. A. Corr & D. A. Corr (Eds.), *Handbook of childhood death and bereavement.* New York: Springer Publishing.

Straus, M. A. (1996). Spanking and the making of a violent society. *Pediatrics, 98(4),* 837–842.

Thomas, A., & Chess, S. (1986). The New York longitudinal study: From infancy to early adult life. In R. Plomin & J. Dunn (Eds.), *The study of temperament: Changes, continuities, and challenges.* Hillsdale, NJ: Erlbaum.

Thompson, C. (2000). *Raising a handicapped child: A helpful guide for parents of the physically disabled.* New York: Oxford University Press.

Tofler, I. R., Knapp, P. K., & Drell, M. J. (1999). The "achievement by proxy" spectrum: Recognition and clinical response to pressured and high-achieving children and adolescents. *Journal of the American Academy of Child and Adolescent Psychiatry, 38,* 213–216.

Visher, E. B., & Visher, J. S. (1991). *How to win as a stepfamily* (2nd ed.). New York: Brunner/Mazel, Inc.

Wallerstein, J. S., & Blakeslee, S. (1990). *Second chances: Men, women and children a decade after divorce.* London: Grant McIntyre.

Walsh, W. (2002). Spankers and nonspankers: Where do they get information on spanking. *Family Relations, 51,* 81–88.

Weiss, L., & Wolchik, S. (1998). New beginnings: An empirically-based intervention program for divorced mothers to help their children adjust to divorce. In L. E. Arnold (Ed.), *Childhood stress.* New York: Wiley & Sons.

Werner, E. E., & Smith, R. S. (2001). *Journeys from childhood to midlife: Risk, resilience and recovery.* Ithaca, NY: Cornell University Press.

Wieder, H. (1977). On being told of adoption. *The Psychoanalytic Quarterly, 46(1),* 1–22.

Wills, T. A., Sandy, J. M., Yaeger, A., & Shinar, O. (2001). Family risk factors and adolescent substance abuse: Moderation effects for temperament dimensions. *Developmental Psychology, 37,* 283–297.

Yarrow, M. R., Campbell, J. D., & Burton, R. (1968). *Child rearing: An inquiry into research and methods.* San Francisco: Jossey-Bass.

Zinsmeister, K. (1988). Brave new world: How day care harms children. *Policy Review, 44,* 40–48.

Zinsmeister, K. (1998). The problem with day care. *The American Enterprise, 9,* 44–53.

Zinsmeister, K. (1999). Fatherhood is not for wimps. *The American Enterprise, 10,* 41–45.

INDEX

About the Author

JOSEPH D. SCLAFANI is Associate Professor of Psychology and Associate Dean of the College of Liberal Arts and Sciences at the University of Tampa.